REFORMATION IN FOREIGN MISSIONS

A call for change in the way foreign missionary work
is carried on by evangelical Christians

Bob Finley

TABLE OF CONTENTS

CHAPTER ONE

A CALL FOR CHANGE

Contemporary foreign missionary operations as carried on by churches and para-church organizations of the USA, Canada, Korea and other industrialized countries are in dire need of reformation. Generally, with a few notable exceptions, those who go from one country to another as missionaries end up hindering rather than helping the cause of Christ.

It's not that their motives are wrong. In most cases involving evangelicals, our intentions are good and objectives are noble. But the very thing we seek to accomplish is discredited by the way we operate. Like European crusaders a millennium ago, we march off to "the field" with dreams of glory, confident that we are following "the call" of God. But many times our actions bring dishonor to His Name and prove to be a denial of the very message we are there to proclaim.

You will note that I have put "the field" and "the call" in quotes. These are specialized terms for which unique meanings have been developed by evangelical Christians. In traditional missionary circles these specialized meanings are usually taken for granted. Those who use them assume that all within their circle will assign the specialized meaning in their conscious minds whenever one of the terms is used. To further clarify how certain words mean specific things, or may be used to denote unique concepts within the Christian community, I have prepared a glossary of specialized terms (chapter 23). So if you wish further comment on a word or phrase in quotes, please check chapter 23 to see if more has been added about its meaning to evangelical Christians involved in foreign missionary activities.

Half a century ago I was a young idealist eager to go out and save the world. It is understandable, then, that I was deeply disturbed at that time to read in Dr. Eugene Nida's book, *Customs and Cultures*, that in African countries when a person wished to slander an enemy he would call him a "son of a missionary." During the years I lived in Asia I found a similar attitude wherever I went. The typical foreign missionary from an industrialized country was looked upon as the ultimate hypocrite. The exact opposite of Jesus of Nazareth.

I found Christ to be held in high esteem by Hindus, Muslims, Buddhists and, yes, even by many atheistic Communists. But His self appointed representatives from "western" countries were often looked upon as being a travesty of what Christianity was presumed to represent.

When I arrived in China in 1948 I was confident that I had received a "divine call" to spend the rest of my life there as a "missionary to the heathen." I followed in the train of a great host of foreign missionaries who had gone before, holding in reverence such names as Robert Morrison (who arrived in China in 1807), Hudson Taylor (1853) and Jonathan Goforth (1888).

But something went terribly wrong. The Communists took over in 1949 and 6000 foreign missionaries were forced to leave, never to return. How could God allow such a thing?

Or was the hand of God involved in it, as He was in the Babylonian captivity of the ancient Hebrews? The prophet Jeremiah declared that the king of Babylon was God's servant (Jeremiah 43:10). Could it be that God was trying to tell us something when He allowed the largest "mission field" on earth to become permanently closed off to thousands of professional missionaries who said we had been "called" to work there?

Likewise India, the second largest. After His resurrection our Lord declared His eternal purpose to take out a people for His name from among every tribe and nation on this earth. So why should He permit 1600 "nations" in the subcontinent of India to be permanently cut off from thousands of idealistic young people in other countries who said they had received a "call" to go there?

Obviously there are some things amiss in our thinking about the whole concept of "foreign missions," and the purpose of this book is to reveal what they are.

Also, it is to present how things ought to be, in view of the fact that the multi-billion dollar missionary enterprise has largely missed out on what we should be doing. That's why a reformation is necessary.

I intend to show how the foreign missionary movement of the past 100 years is simply a church tradition that has no basis or precedent in the New Testament. That the ways in which we conduct it are often a denial of the most basic principles of Biblical Christianity. And it should be phased out and replaced with an entirely new approach that more closely conforms to the will of God. There are other alternatives which are much more sensible and far more effective than those being followed today by mission organizations based in America, Canada, Korea and other industrialized countries.

But before I discuss the faults of the system and the ways to change it, I want to express my appreciation for the deeds of the early pioneers who went out beginning over 200 years ago. Whenever I have mentioned the need for reform someone usually retorts, "Are you suggesting that great men of God like William Carey, Adoniram Judson and David Livingstone were outside the will of God?"

Definitely not. But there is no point in dwelling on the heroes of the past, except to learn what we need to know for today. Of course there were great accomplishments, just as there were great mistakes and hopeless failures. While respecting the past, and learning from it, our purpose must be to deal with the present and prepare for the future. If we are going to honor God and discern His will, we must be prepared for change. We must have a reformation that will cause us to replace the antiquated, unscriptural, counter-productive methods by which we seek to carry out the great commission of our Saviour, which is to plant His church in every nation.

A key to the problem may be found in the way we use the word, MISSION. Generally it denotes the expansionist objectives of our respective organizations and denominations, just as "crusade" did a thousand years ago. Like colonial era military conquerors, we are bent on ruthlessly expanding our territory to include foreign countries. We want maps on the wall and graphics in our yearbooks showing places all over the globe where we have affiliated branches. The tragedy today is that we so often accomplish our objective by running roughshod over our fellow believers who are already there. The whole situation is completely different from the way it was 200 years ago.

When William Carey went to India in 1792 he found no indigenous evangelical churches or missionary teams. So he did not appear on the scene as a competitive threat to fellow believers. But when I first went to India in 1948 (on my way to China) I found many thousands of churches from which tens of thousands of native missionaries were going forth to spread the gospel. Also on hand were representatives of dozens of American organizations and denominations eager to employ Indian citizens to establish branches of their respective empires. Is it any wonder, then, that God allowed the Hindus to put us out of the country? His kingdom was being labeled "cultural imperialism" and "institutional colonialism."

One of our great mistakes is our failure to recognize that our Sovereign Lord is the Head of His whole church. If He were truly leading us, He would cause us to respect the fellow members of His body (meaning all true believers) in every nation, and to strengthen their hands rather than competing with them and causing divisions among them. Instead, we go all over the world hiring away the workers of indigenous missions and devastating their ministries. We send comparatively rich "missionaries" to live in large houses and drive around in expensive cars among the poorest people of this world. Their presence brings discredit and suspicion upon local believers who are generally poor.

If we believe God wants us to do something for His kingdom in poorer countries, we should send financial help to our fellow believers who bear witness for Him in their respective locations. Sending a rich foreigner to live among them tends to misrepresent our Saviour. It also breeds covetousness among local Christians who may envy the foreigners' wealth and thus be tempted to want some of it. And in many cases our presence identifies God's kingdom with foreign governments and destroys its credibility in the eyes of local citizens.

The present system of sending out Americans (and Canadians and Australians and Koreans and others from industrialized countries) is a tradition left over from the 19th Century that should have been phased out 50 years ago. And, as I will discuss later, it has no precedent in the Word of God. Here is a sampling of some problems related to its continuation.

1. Economic Disparity. When we send Americans, Canadians or others from affluent countries abroad as resident missionaries in poorer countries, they appear fabulously rich in comparison to the people they hope to reach. How then can they represent our Saviour "who though He was rich yet for our sakes became poor?" They misrepresent Him, and their presence is generally a hindrance to His cause.

2. Political Implications. When comparatively affluent foreign missionaries move into countries like Pakistan, Cuba, China or Vietnam they are often thought to be spies sent by the CIA or its equivalent. Otherwise, where would they get all that money they appear to have? By thus identifying the Christian faith with foreign governments we stigmatize it and bring irreparable harm to our fellow believers who are citizens of the countries to which we go.

3. Cultural Offenses. When a missionary from an industrialized country invades a people group of diverse culture, he identifies the gospel of Christ with aliens who appear weird to those people. By so doing he erects artificial barriers of prejudice against the gospel and hinders its acceptance. Often it takes one or two whole generations before those artificial barriers can be overcome and the Christian faith can become acceptable to an unreached people group which has been so invaded. Among native Americans the barriers have persisted in many tribes for more than 300 years.

4. Sending the Wrong Message. Colonial-type mission boards generally assume an attitude of superiority toward our fellow believers in poorer countries, taking the position: "We are superior, they are inferior; therefore we have to go over there and train them." But the American missionary usually goes with a personal support package greater than the entire budget of the school where he is teaching, or the local ministry with which he works. No way, then, can he teach "Love your neighbor as yourself" when he is rich and they are poor. It would be laughable for him to say, "Deny yourself, take up your cross and be crucified with Christ." The foreigner's presence is likely to breed covetousness and destroy any sense of self-sacrifice which may already exist among Bible school students or native workers in poorer countries.

5. Misuse of Resources. It makes no sense to spend $60,000 of God's money annually sending an American with his family to live as a missionary in a poor country where hundreds of local citizens have been called of God to reach their own people, and have no personal support. Any one of them, already knowing the local languages, would be ten times more effective than the foreigner. And is likely to be eager to serve with support of $600 or less annually, because he lives on the same economic level as those being reached with the gospel. In many countries the support package of one American could supply the support and ministry needs of 50 native missionaries. By what unreasonable stretching of our imaginations have we come to the point of arrogant pride by which we conclude that one American not knowing the language is more valuable to the cause of Christ in a poor country than 50 resident citizens of that country who learned the local language(s) in childhood?

6. Carnal, Sectarian, Denominational Mission Board Expansionism. Every foreign missionary agency is doing its own thing, often ruthlessly competing with indigenous Christian witness in poorer countries. Ambitious to expand their territory, mission executives go overseas and hire away the workers of indigenous ministries. Excellent works of God are virtually wiped out by this carnal practice. Hundreds of indigenous Bible institutes and other schools operated by native missions have been damaged or destroyed by "rich foreigners" coming along and setting up competing schools nearby, then hiring away teachers and luring away students from schools operated by local Christians. Small indigenous churches in pioneer areas are often split and demoral-ized by zealous foreigners who move into their neighborhoods and start competing ministries, usually with a peculiarity of doctrine or the use of material bait to attract members from the struggling churches that were already there.

As I will explain later, many other aspects of foreign missions need reformation, in addition to these few samples briefly mentioned here. Change must come if we expect to know God's will and receive His blessings. But as a student of history I am well aware that church people tend to resist change because we are more comfortable with our past traditions. Opposition is sure to be strong, but I believe that those who are willing to pay the price and speak out for reform will be the ones who contribute the most toward the fulfillment of our Lord's eternal purpose.

CHAPTER TWO

CROSS CULTURAL MISSIONS HAVE NO BASIS IN SCRIPTURE

C hange the way we do missionary work? Many Christians say, "No way."

Among those who resist change are the true believers. The evangelicals. The fundamentalists. The Pentecostals. With good reason. Evangelistic soldiers of the cross have taken the message of salvation to almost every part of the planet, translated portions of the Bible into every written language, and reduced hundreds more languages to written form.

They have healed the sick. Fed the hungry. Housed the homeless. Clothed the poor. Educated the illiterate. Saved the lost. Transformed individual lives, whole families, entire communities.

In spite of competitive practices, ambitious colonialism, frequent materialistic indulgence, financial abuses and racial prejudice the evangelical missionary movement of the past 200 years has been the most redemptive force in all of human history. Nothing can be compared to it except possibly the original spread of Christianity throughout the Roman empire in the first and second centuries.

"So why change it? Can't we simply mend the flaws? Why throw out the baby with the bath water?"

That's the usual response I have received after speaking in church missionary conferences. In Bible institutes and Christian colleges the thought of change often provokes fear among school administrators. Much of their contribution income is generated by convincing donors that they are "training and sending out missionaries." After I had addressed the student body at Houghton (NY) College many years ago, the President, Dr. Stephen Paine (a long time personal friend who earlier had given me an honorary doctors degree when I was his commencement speaker) begged me, "Please don't scuttle our foreign missions program." At the C & MA college in Nyack, NY some faculty members suggested that I should not be permitted to speak to the students at all, even after they had invited me. I went ahead, nevertheless, and the entire student body stayed on for three hours after I had finished, asking questions and responding with both agreement and disagreement.

Around 1960 I shared the pulpit at a missionary conference in Minnesota with L. E. Maxwell of Prairie Bible Institute in the Canadian province of Alberta. Apparently he was blessed by my messages because he invited me to visit his school and preach to the students. My coming was listed ahead of time in *Prairie Overcomer* (publication of PBI) and by the time I arrived Dr. Maxwell had received an avalanche of warnings about the dangers of having me speak there. So he sat me down and requested that I not say one word contrary to their teaching. I obediently complied, and later had to ask God to forgive me for my failure to speak the whole truth.

The same thing happened at Ontario Bible College in Toronto a few years later. The president invited me to speak there as a result of a personal friendship we developed during our joint participation as Board members of another ministry. But when the word was out that I was coming he also was bombarded with warnings from leaders of other missions. He wrote me a nice letter in which he said, "I am learning that you are regarded as Public Enemy Number One by leaders of some of the mission boards here in Toronto." So at his request I modified my message to the students, and again had to pray for God's forgiveness.

The wall of resistance I have run into has been that our concept of foreign missions is divinely ordained, set in stone, established forever, and cannot be changed. Let me deal with this presupposition, then I can tell you more about why change is needed and how to do it. Discussion will be limited to the historically evangelical perspective. Activities of the Jesuits and other Roman Catholics since Francis Xaviar went to Asia in the 16th Century is another subject. Likewise the activities of Eastern Orthodox churches. And the liberal wing among Protestants (those who do not believe in the divine inspiration and authority of the Bible). Their concern is more likely to be socio-political than evangelistic and redemptive. I speak to Bible believers. Those who are concerned with evangelism, soul winning and church planting.

In obedience to our Lord's command, we "go into all the world and preach the gospel to every creature." That cannot be changed, we say.

All right. So be it.

Dare we talk about changing the *way* we do it?

I will dare, and accept the consequences.

To my brothers and sisters who object, let me say this word, "I know where you are coming from." I have been there. And am there still in faith, if not in methodology.

But I believe you have missed something. A revelation which I had never seen until I had been a born again believer for ten years and had lived in Asia for three years. I hope you will see it too, without having to give up the beliefs you cherish. Or denying the faith you staunchly defend.

As an evangelical (or fundamentalist, if you prefer) it is to be expected that you should resist change. Perhaps you came into the faith out of a liberal background with no absolutes. Or have seen people in your original church, school or organization drift into liberalism and lose out spiritually (as my good friend and former co-worker Chuck Templeton of Canada did 40 years ago).

So I would expect you to "contend earnestly for the faith that was once (for all) delivered to the saints." As I do. Never again will we defer to those who deny the inspiration of the Scriptures or the deity of Christ. We will steadfastly affirm His virgin birth, sinless life, sacrificial death, bodily resurrection, ascension, exaltation and second coming. Having been redeemed by His blood, saved by His grace and transformed by His power we are ready to die rather than change our position. Amen and amen.

We will not change our basic beliefs. But, of course, most of us would give up a church tradition if we could be convinced that it actually is tradition rather than eternal truth. Especially if we see that a particular tradition is a hindrance to the cause of Christ. That's what the original Reformation was all about.

Fine. We are agreed. God's truth as revealed in His Word we will protect, defend, expound, preach, practice and proclaim. Church traditions, like Christmas trees and clerical collars, we can say take it or leave it.

Then what about the present day foreign missionary programs of our churches? Truth, or church tradition? Ask my fellow Southern Baptists about the annual Lottie Moon offering for overseas missionaries, and some will equate it with the Ten Commandments.

Can we distinguish? What is the truth? And what is tradition?

Those who say we can't phase out the traditional way we do foreign missionary work stake their claim on one major premise. "The command is to go," they say. So we must perpetuate a system that has been obsolete for 50 years.

"Obsolete? Never!"

So goes the argument. "The command to go is once for all. Fixed forever. Binding today. And go we must."

Even if "going" sometimes does more harm than good?

We won't admit to such a possibility. We just keep on going. Leave it to God to judge the results. That's the orthodox position.

So what have we missed?

Just this, for a starter. There is no record anywhere in the New Testament that God ever sent a missionary to where he did not know the major language of the area or would be looked upon as an invader from another culture.

The whole multi-billion dollar missionary enterprise of our day has its roots in the belief that God commands "cross cultural" sending. But the "sending" concept is a church tradition which developed during colonial days of the 19th Century. It has no basis in the New Testament.

There is no mention of the "send out your missionaries" philosophy in the Word of God. No mission boards. Or candidates. Or missiologists. Or missions conferences. All these developments are unique to our times.

When I mention these facts to my fellow fundamentalists or evangelistic evangelicals, a frequent response is, "But what about Paul?"

Yes, what about him?

Saul of Tarsus was a native of Cilicia, which was part of greater Greece (the Hellenistic world) at that time. Greek was his mother tongue. He went as a foreign student to "the feet of Gamaliel" in Jerusalem, and while away from home God called him to be a missionary.

Here let me define the word "missionary." It is from the Latin *missio* which was transliterated directly into English. *Missio* is equivalent to *apostello* from which comes *apostolos* (apostle) in the Greek New Testament. Thus the word "missionary" is the same as the word "apostle" and vice versa. Every apostle is a missionary and every missionary is an apostle. The two words are interchangeable, and correct usage doesn't limit the missionaries of the early church to twelve only. Barnabas is called an apostle, as are Silas and Timothy. And others.

Apostles had unique and specific responsibilities in the early churches. They were the pioneers who planted assemblies of believers in places where there had previously been no witness for our Saviour. That's why Paul said he had "received grace and apostleship for obedience to the faith among all nations" (Romans 1:5). And then added, "So have I strived to preach the gospel, not where Christ was named" (Romans 15:20). After the apostle had gotten an assembly started, God would raise up prophets within each one to purify it (by revealing secret sins of believers), evangelists to bring in more sheep, pastors (yes, several pastors in each small assembly) to mentor and shepherd them, and teachers to build up the whole local body in the knowledge of God's Word.

Having said that, let's go back to Paul, whom God called and anointed while he was away from home.

While Paul was in Damascus and Jerusalem there was no hint or suggestion that he should go to India or Egypt or any other place where he wouldn't know the language. God sent him back to his own (Greek speaking) people as a pioneer apostle to the Hellenists

(Greeks), and that's where his life's work was fulfilled.

True, near the end of his career he went to *visit* the churches in Rome. But not as a pioneer to plant new churches. Believers there were so numerous that their faith was spoken of throughout the whole (Christian) world (Romans 1:8).

Paul also hoped to visit his fellow Hebrews in Spain, but we don't know that he actually did. All we know is that one of the largest contingents of Hebrews outside of Palestine at that time was in Spain, and Paul had a great burden to share the gospel with his fellow Israelites. But there is no record in the New Testament of God sending Paul as a pioneer apostle to a culturally diverse people whose language he did not know and who would look upon him as a foreign invader.

So much for Paul.

Now what about the rest of those original apostles? The ones who received what we call "the great commission."

They were Palestinians, or Judaeans, if you prefer. The term "Judaean" (shortened to "Jew" in English about 400 years ago) at that time, in contrast to the situation 800 years earlier, included Hebrew residents of Galilee and Samaria in the north as well as those in the southern province of Judaea.

Anyway, none of those original disciples could speak a foreign language. They knew only the language of Palestine, which was colloquial Aramaic (from which came Arabic), and some knew Hebrew, which was closely related. There is no record anywhere in the New Testament that God ever sent any one of them to a foreign country as what we would call a "foreign missionary." In His divine wisdom our Lord never sent any missionary into a situation where he would not be able to understand or speak the language of that area.

True, there are church traditions that claim Peter went to Rome and Thomas went to India. But no mention of it in the Word of God.

With good reason.

Implicit in the New Testament record is a specific strategy which God has revealed for the spread of His witness among all nations. And it's just the opposite of 19th Century missionary colonialism. Once we comprehend this strategy it will revolutionize our ideas about missions and missionary work.

And make it difficult for us to live in harmony with those who are committed to the tradition of sending out missionaries from their home country to a strange land of diverse culture and language.

But didn't our Lord say, "Go ye into all the world and preach the gospel to every creature?" Yes He did. And so we should. But we need to understand His meaning. The term "world" is a translation of the Greek word "cosmos." It refers to the world around us. In I John 2:15 we are told, "Love not the cosmos, neither the things that are in the cosmos. If a man love the cosmos, the love of the Father is not in him." So Mark 16:15 is a command to evangelize our communities. To reach the cosmos around us. In the Book of Acts we are told how the early believers "went everywhere preaching the word." House to house. Door to door. Village to village. Living churches still spread rapidly through such fervent evangelism in many parts of the world today. But in the USA it's usually the Jehovah's Witnesses and Mormons who practice what missiologists preach (I'm speaking of their methods, not their message).

I saw true Christians carrying out this responsibility among the people of Korea in 1950. Multiplied thousands of Korean believers were preaching Christ to their neighbors. But suppose I or other Americans had joined a team of Koreans going house to house? It would have been a disaster. The gospel would have been identified with weird looking foreigners in strange clothing who sounded so funny when they talked that they made people laugh. There were valid reasons why Europeans and American missionaries in China were called "foreign devils." And why parents did not want their children to be seduced by aliens whom they believed to be devils. But more about that later.

My point thus far has been to show that no "cross cultural" sending out of missionaries is mentioned in the New Testament. Next let me help you see how the gospel spread to every area of the Roman empire in one generation, by an entirely different method.

CHAPTER THREE

THE BIBLICAL PATTERN

After His resurrection, our Lord met with His disciples only a few times in Jerusalem. He, as well as some angels which appeared, told them to go to a mountain which He had appointed in Galilee. There He came and met with them, "speaking of things pertaining to the kingdom of God." His words are summarized in what we call the great commission, "All authority is given unto me in the heavens and on earth. Go ye, therefore, and teach all nations..."

But where did He say they should go?

Back to Jerusalem. That's where they would find "all nations." In fact, He led them back there Himself for His final meeting with them at the time of His ascension. And told them to stay there until He baptized them with His Holy Spirit.

In Acts 2:5 we are told how "devout men from every nation" were visiting in Jerusalem. From this fact it is obvious what our Lord meant when He said they should go tell all nations of His death and resurrection. "All nations" had come to them.

The great Hebrew historian Josephus wrote that during the first century nearly a million pilgrims would gather in Jerusalem for the festivities from Passover to Pentecost.

So Jerusalem was the place where the apostles would find men from all the nations of the Roman empire: Parthians, Medes, Elamites, dwellers of Mesopotamia, Cappadocia, Pontus, Asia, Phrygia, Pamphylia, Egypt, Libya, Rome, Crete, Arabia, etc. (Acts 2:9-11).

It seems implied in the New Testament record that all of the converts on the Day of Pentecost were foreign visitors. They were convinced by hearing the Galilean apostles miraculously speak to them in their native languages (Acts 2:6-8), which was a reversal of the Tower of Babel where God originally created the nations (Genesis 11:7-9). That's why Paul would later write: "Tongues are for a sign, not to them that believe but to them that believe not" (I Corinthians 14:22). The nations of mankind began from Babel when God scattered them all over the world by languages. He gave them up temporarily and limited His witness on earth to one nation, the descendents of Abraham, Isaac and Jacob. But the one nation was temporary. All the while it was God's purpose to regather the nations through His only Son, as is explained in Isaiah 54 and quoted in Galations 4:27. That's why when God called Abraham He told him how he would be the spiritual father of many nations because through one of his descendents "all nations" would be blessed.

Following the outpouring of the Holy Spirit and the ingathering of new disciples at Pentecost, those 3000 converts entered immediately into a fellowship of believers where they shared in teaching, breaking of bread and prayers (Acts 2:42).

How long this lasted we are not told, but my guess is that it was only for a few months. After Stephen was stoned there was a great persecution against the church which was at Jerusalem, and they were all scattered abroad *except the apostles* (Acts 8:1).

This is crucial to the strategy. Many traditionalists quote Acts 1:8 as evidence that we should go "to the uttermost part of the earth." But if we compare Acts 8:1 we discover that the original apostles themselves stayed in Jerusalem. They did not go to foreign countries. Rather, the foreign visitors went back to their homelands as ambassadors for Christ. That's how the witness of the Apostles extended to the "uttermost parts." And thus was fulfilled our Lord's prayer in John 17:20: "Neither pray I for these alone, but for them also who shall believe on me through their word."

Most of the 11 original apostles (missionaries) apparently stayed on in Jerusalem for many years. In later chapters of Acts, at least 20 years afterwards, they were still there.

Some traditional missionaries of our day have tried to impose

19th century colonial traditions onto the New Testament record by saying that the original apostles were disobedient. That's pure nonsense. Our concept of going to work in foreign countries is simply not to be found anywhere in the New Testament.

When God would have a witness for Himself in Ethiopia, He did not send Philip there as a resident missionary. He sent Philip (Acts 8:26) to reach a prominent Ethiopian who was away from home, and then sent that Ethiopian back to his own people with the gospel message.

Only twice in the New Testament is there any reference to one of the 11 original apostles going outside of Palestine.

One is in Galatians where Paul tells about Peter visiting the church in Antioch several years after it was established. But what happened? He brought along his Old Testament Hebrew custom of segregation and split the church. You can bet those dear brothers sent old Peter back to Jerusalem on the next available chariot (or merchant ship, perhaps).

Some say Peter also went to Babylon because in his first epistle he sent greetings from others in "Babylon." But I disagree with the idea that he went to Mesopotamia. "Babylon" was a code word for Jerusalem, the center from which most of the persecution and terrorism against Hebrew believers was being directed at that time. Jerusalem is also called, in a spiritual sense, "Sodom and Egypt" in Revelation 11:8. True Hebrew believers in the New Testament are collectively called "the Israel of God" (Galatians 6:16). Hebrews still outside of Christ, and thus not reconciled to God, had been "broken off the olive tree" of God's family and were in bondage under the control of legalistic, hypocritical Pharisees, twice referred to as "the synagogue of Satan" (Revelation 2:9, 3:9). Their bondage was equated with the 70 years of Babylonian captivity in the Old Testament. So it was only natural that believers in the Messiah would refer to "Jerusalem which . . . is in bondage with her children" (Galatians 4:25) as "Babylon."

The other mention of an original apostle being outside of Palestine is in Revelation where John was on the island of Patmos. From what he wrote we can deduce that rather than doing apostolic work he was probably visiting numerous churches in that area, especially the seven that are named in chapters 2 and 3. He did not go as a pioneer missionary to plant new churches in unevangelized areas. He went as a brother to visit his fellow (native) believers who had been there for several years. There are also references about other Judaeans going abroad to visit churches already established. But only Agabus went to bless them. Others that are mentioned went to cause sectarian divisions.

So how did the gospel spread to every area of the Roman empire in one generation? It seems impossible to us if there were no mission boards. No Bible schools. And no "cross cultural missionaries" being sent out in the colonial sense of the 19th century.

We tend to overlook the strategy because of its simplicity. It leaves no room for what I heard my friend Ralph Winter of the U. S. Center for World Mission in Pasadena call "the missionary industry." In other words, "big business."

In Acts 11:19 we are told that those who were scattered abroad (Acts 8:1-4) traveled as far as Phenice, a possible reference to the chief port city on the island Crete. Acts 2:11 mentions Cretes being in Jerusalem on the Day of Pentecost. They went home and started churches.

The record continues: they traveled to Cyprus (from whence came Barnabas and his nephew, John Mark) and presumably started churches. As others did in Antioch.

In his epistle to the believers in Rome, Paul sends greetings to the church in this house and the church in that house and the churches in other houses. Who started these churches? No "professional missionary" had ever been to Rome.

The key is in Acts 2:10. Strangers (pilgrims) from Rome were in Jerusalem on the day of Pentecost. Paul mentions two of them in Romans 16:7. He says Andronicus and Junius were in Christ before he was, which means they turned to Christ at Pentecost and were driven out of Jerusalem in the wave of persecution that followed the stoning of Stephen. With no Bible school or seminary training, no mission board or sending agency, they went home and started churches. Paul says they "are of note among the apostles" (missionaries). I believe he meant that these two pioneers were noteworthy missionaries. But by 19th Century colonial standards they wouldn't qualify as missionaries because they didn't work "cross culturally." They went home to Rome and worked among their own people.

Now let's go back to Antioch. Apparently that was the first place where non-Hebrews were taken into the fellowship of believers. The 3000 who turned to Christ at Pentecost included both "Judaeans and proselytes." When some of these new believers returned to Antioch they preached the Word at first to none but Judaeans only. But Greek speaking men of Cyprus and Cyrene (on their way home), when they came to Antioch, began to speak to the Greeks (probably their own relatives), preaching the Lord Jesus. And the hand of the Lord was with them and a great number of Greeks believed and turned to Christ (Acts 11:21). But they had not become Hebrew proselytes, so a new title was needed. Hence the first use of the word "Christian." This probably happened before Peter went to the house of Cornelius (Acts 10) because chapter 11 beginning at verse 19 is a continuation of chapter 8:1-4.

When tidings of these things came to the original apostles at Jerusalem (Acts 11:22) they decided to send someone to evaluate the situation. But who could they send? None of the Galileans knew Greek. Answer: send Barnabas, a native of Cyprus. Although a foreigner in Palestine, he had escaped being driven out of Jerusalem during the earlier persecution because he owned property and had roots there (Acts 4:36-37). His sister, Mary, mother of John Mark, owned a house in Jerusalem (Acts 12:12). Greek was his mother tongue, so he could communicate well in Antioch.

It's interesting that the Jerusalem apostles told Barnabas to go "as far as Antioch." There was no thought of sending him out as a pioneer missionary in the colonial sense. His commission was to go visit an established church and bring a report back to the apostles in Jerusalem.

But when Barnabas came to Antioch his life turned around. He discovered what the Christian experience was all about. Instead of going back to Jerusalem he went on to Tarsus to find Saul and brought him back to Antioch. Three years (Galatians 1:18) after God had called Saul, the Jerusalem church sent him home to Tarsus in Cilicia (Acts 9:30). He and Barnabas had been close friends in Jerusalem, so it was natural for them to get together again in Antioch.

Traditionalists like to speak of the church at Antioch as a "sending" church. But they fail to see what actually happened. Antioch was a crossroads gathering place of Greek speaking people from many areas. The church there was a diverse Greek congregation. The five Antioch leaders mentioned in Acts 13:1 all came from other places. There must have been dozens more.

When the Holy Spirit spoke, it was not to send out missionaries "cross culturally." Rather, He sent His servants back to their own people.

The time had come for Barnabas to go home to his native Cyprus where Greek was the local language. And Saul (Paul) went with him. Later they would travel up into the environs of Cilicia, homeland of Paul. Paul and Barnabas would be right at home in all these Greek speaking cultures.

Eventually, Barnabas settled permanently in Cyprus. Paul's life work was within the area where his native Greek tongue was the principal language. Once when he thought of going to Asia and Bithinia (Acts 16:6-7) he was restrained by the Holy Spirit. Instead, the Lord called him to go over into the Greek language areas of Macedonia and Achaia. But one of the first souls he won after he landed at Philippi was Lydia, a business woman from Thyratira in Asia. It is quite likely that she planted the first church there after her return. God's way for Paul to plant churches in Asia was to reach Asians who were away from home. While in Corinth he won Aquila, who was born in Pontus, then took him and his wife Priscilla back to Asia and left them there to plant new churches (Acts 18:18-19).

Never did Paul exhort his disciples to go work in foreign countries where they would not know the languages. Nor did he encourage any church he fathered to "send out missionaries." That whole 19th Century concept is totally foreign to the New Testament.

I do not say these things to put down our modern way of doing things. As I said at the beginning, the evangelical missionary movement of past 200 years has been the most redemptive force in human history. God has used and blessed colonial mission boards just as He has used other present day institutions that have no precedent in Scripture. Church buildings. Sunday schools. Bible colleges. Theological seminaries. Christian day schools. Radio broadcasts.

The servants of our Saviour have found many unique and ingenious ways to serve Him on this earth, and we should pray for and support all that appear to be fruitful.

I have but one purpose for pointing out the Biblical pattern for Christian expansion and church growth. It is to defend my thesis against those who try to use the authority of Scripture to condemn this book, and to further perpetuate colonialism.

For the past 50 years I have preached the need for reform in the way we do missionary work. And inevitably I have met with opposition from leaders of traditional missions. Their chief weapon has been to accuse me of heresy. Not knowing what the Scriptures actually teach on this subject, they have used isolated verses to give divine sanction to the way they operate. Anyone who suggests an alternative to the colonial approach is likely to be charged with transgression of the Word of God. The organization with which I served Christ 40 years ago (International Students, Inc.) was called "a cult denying the great commission" by Dale Crowley, a radio preacher in Washington.

When our Lord was similarly accused, His reply was, "Laying aside the commandment of God, ye hold to the traditions of men. Thus have ye made the commandment of God of none effect by your traditions."

What prompted Dr. Crowley's opposition was an article I wrote about the need to phase out colonialism in foreign missions. I recommended withdrawing all American missionaries from poorer countries and using our financial resources instead to help indigenous missions which are usually ten times more effective than we are within the context of their own cultures. What we spend sending an American family overseas to go to language school for three years (then come home on furlough and forget most of it) would support 50 to 100 native missionaries who already know the local languages. Apparently, Dr. Crowley looked upon this teaching as a threat to traditional missions. As have many others. But I have continued to repeat it over and over again.

Granted, indigenous missions weren't there when pioneer European missionaries first went out 200 years ago, or even 100 years ago in some countries. But today (2004) no less than 6000 indigenous missions have more than 300,000 missionaries on the fields of the world, many with no regular financial support. Tens of thousands more would go out if financial support were available to provide for their families while they are gone. The best thing we can do for the cause of Christ in "mission field" countries is to get behind these indigenous ministries by providing the financial support they need, and then they will finish the job.

But our traditions hold us back. Tradition dictates that we keep on sending out "our missionaries." We published the article that upset Dr. Crowley in 1960. Vehement responses also came to us from several other evangelical leaders in the U.S. and Canada. Clyde Taylor, head of the Evangelical Foreign Missions Association at that time, told me quite frankly that EFMA leaders had "gone through it with a fine tooth comb" looking for statements they could condemn as contrary to the traditional approach. A former missionary to China, Dr. Nelson Bell (father of Billy Graham's wife Ruth), wrote me a very strong letter saying, in summary, "Christian works on the field can't possibly get along without us being there to guide them."

However, let it be said that the number of favorable responses we received to that editorial far outnumbered those who disagreed. The opponents were all involved with traditional colonial missions. Most of the ones who approved were citizens of "mission field" countries whose work had been made difficult by competition from "the rich foreigners." As the word spread around the world that an American mission leader had dared to speak out boldly to present their point of view, a chorus of encouragement swelled among the ranks of indigenous ministries, and my heart was cheered. Even some traditional American missionaries expressed agreement, like one with the Africa Inland Mission who said he had come to exactly the same conclusions soon after he arrived in Africa.

The traditional way of doing missionary work is not only without Biblical precedent but is also out of focus for our time. Having established that it has no basis in Scripture, I want to tell you why we need to phase out the old and find new, more Biblical ways to work in the future. But first let me tell you a bit about where I am coming from.

CHAPTER FOUR

WAKE-UP CALL IN CHINA

S o, then, who am I to call for change in Christian missions? Many times I have felt unworthy to wipe the dust from the feet of traditional missionaries whom I have known. I have not suffered or sacrificed nearly as much for the cause of Christ as have some of them. Generally, foreign missionaries have been the most committed Christians that American churches have produced. Most of us, therefore, feel hopelessly inadequate to say one word that might be considered as criticism of those who are in so many ways more zealous for the faith than we are.

But almost every reformer has come from within the system he seeks to change, even though he himself may be unworthy. So I call for reform out of my own experience as a traditional missionary.

As a child in a Presbyterian home 75 years ago I was taught to say my prayers before going to bed. The same thing every night. Then we had a missionary visit our Sunday school and a new petition was added: "Bless the missionaries and help them in their hardships."

That missionary told us what a terrible time he was having in China, and no doubt he was. Compared to us, he was making unbelievable sacrifices. Then he frightened us with some long needles he pulled out of his packet of curios. He told how ignorant Chinese medicine men had no better sense than to stick those needles into people to drive out their sickness. Among other things, his mission was to save the victims of "this heathen practice." As children, we could well agree. We had no knowledge of the science of acupuncture, and that missionary had obviously dismissed it as primitive ignorance. Years later, I would learn that it was he who was ignorant and the Chinese who were smart. And not only he but hundreds of others who have foolishly looked upon the natives of Asia and Africa as being ignorant and inferior.

My home church was so dead that it was unlikely I would ever find salvation there. So when at the age of 16 I began to secretly read the Bible day and night, the Holy Spirit led me to go seek employment a thousand miles away where He had numerous people prepared (some of them Presbyterians) to explain the gospel and lead me on in spiritual growth. Perhaps that's one reason why I am so convinced that it's best to reach people while they are away from home. My inhibitions were so great that I could not bear to tell anyone in my family or home community that I was seeking God through frequent prayer and daily reading of His Word. But once away from those constraints I could talk freely to anyone about my personal faith.

Simultaneously with my born again experience came a call to apostleship. While my friends urged me to go to a Bible institute or Christian college, God led me to return to my home state and enroll in the University of Virginia as a missionary to unbelievers. It was a wonderful experience and I had the joy of seeing many of my classmates come to Christ out of agnosticism.

Two new movements were taking off about the time I graduated: Youth for Christ and InterVarsity Christian Fellowship. I went to work with both of them simultaneously as an evangelist among high school and university students. Billy Graham and I worked together as the first two field evangelists for YFC. We traveled all over the U.S. and Canada speaking in super rallies in big stadiums, and in many of the largest churches in each city. I had the privilege of attending classes at many different Bible institutes, Christian colleges and seminaries as well as meeting outstanding pastors and teachers. Some whom I got to know and whose ministry blessed me especially were Torrey Johnson, Harry Ironside, A. W. Tozer and Wilbur Smith of Chicago; Donald Grey Barnhouse and Carl McIntyre in Philadelphia; Jack Wyrtzen in New York; Harold Ockenga in Boston;

Oswald Smith in Toronto; W. B. Riley in Minneapolis; Bob Jones in South Carolina; Lewis Sperry Chafer in Dallas; R. G. Lee in Memphis; and Charles E. Fuller of Los Angeles.

Everywhere I went I sought out men of God so I could sit at their feet and ask them questions, seeking to learn as much as I could of what God had given them. But the chief burden of my heart was foreign missions. I was greatly influenced by personal association with Robert McQuilkin of Columbia Bible College. By David Adeney, recently returned from China. Margaret Haines from India. Samuel Zwemer from Iraq. And Hubert Mitchell, back from Indonesia. They planted within my heart a burning zeal to carry the gospel to those who had never heard it. At almost every meeting where I was the principal speaker I would urge young people to volunteer to go out as foreign missionaries. Hundreds, possibly thousands, did volunteer. I have no idea how many actually went overseas. But I did go myself.

The overseas arm of InterVarsity was the International Fellowship of Evangelical Students. In 1948 the head man, C. Stacey Woods, commissioned me to go out as "InterVarsity's Ambassador to the Orient." My job was to find Christian fellowship groups in universities and line them up with IVCF. But things didn't turn out as I had expected.

In China I spoke in evangelistic meetings among university students arranged by David Adeney, who had by then returned to China. He was one of the dearest and most precious Christian brothers I had ever known. As an undergraduate in Cambridge University he had been involved in one of the first of all university Christian fellowships. Inspired by Hudson Taylor he had left England and gone to serve with the China Inland Mission. I idealized him as the model missionary.

By the time I arrived in China, Christian student fellowship groups were coming together in almost every university. The driving force behind this movement was a Chinese apostle who invited me to participate in a student conference in Canton.

After all the meetings were over one night, this leader asked me to go for a walk with him. He told me how God was greatly blessing the student fellowship groups. Then he shared with me one of his greatest problems. He said it was David Adeney.

I was dumbfounded. To me, my precious brother David was a man who could do no wrong. Never had I known a more consecrated Christian. One more zealous for the kingdom of God. I spoke up quickly in his defense, but that was not necessary. My Chinese brother also spoke highly of David as a person. The problem was something different.

It had nothing to do with dear David personally or his walk with the Lord. He tried so hard to be like the Chinese, as Hudson Taylor had before him. The problem was simply his being there. He had a passionate concern to see the InterVarsity movement established in China, so he eagerly attended student meetings everywhere he could to lend his encouragement. Little did he realize that the students preferred he not be there. And in keeping with Chinese manners, they were too polite to tell him.

His presence as a European at student gatherings in China cast a shadow which could be exploited by the Communists and used against the Christians. The same could be said concerning nearly all of the other 6000 foreign missionaries then in China, including me.

Communists were everywhere. They operated as Marxist missionaries. All were Chinese. No foreigners. Most of their leaders had been converted to the movement as foreign students in Europe and America. While living abroad, hundreds of these Chinese scholars were challenged by the camaraderie they found in Communist cells. The idealism of utopian socialism gave them something to live for, and a cause for which many were willing to die.

In fact, Lenin is said to have defined a true Communist as "a dead man on furlough." Those who joined the movement considered themselves to have died. Then they were granted a furlough from death to serve the Party. Possibly only for a few weeks. A few months. A few years. It didn't matter. The individual sacrificed himself for the whole of humanity (or so they believed at that time). Men and women with graduate degrees from foreign universities went back to China willing to live as simply as the poorest peasant. Any income they earned above the national average (about $20 a month at that time) they contributed to the Party for the furtherance of their cause.

Before I went to Asia it was impossible for me to imagine how the average person had to live there at that time. In small towns and villages, the whole family including relatives would likely be living in one or two rooms. Usually they had no furniture, but would all sleep on the floor in one or both rooms. There would be no running water, hence no bathrooms or separate kitchens. No electricity or telephones. In cities the buildings were larger, but still most families were crowded together into one or two rooms. Of course there would be no clothes closets or even a change of clothing for many. They wore the same thing all the time. At night they would lie down on the floor and sleep in what they had worn all day.

Although many Communist leaders had lived abroad as students, they understood the psychology of their people. They knew that the way to win followers was to live on the same economic level as the average person whom they wished to reach (as Gandhi did in India) even though with their higher education they could easily have found employment earning income well above the national average. But as zealous missionaries for their newly found political religion, they would live without running water or bathrooms and sleep on the floor in their single outfit of clothing. And they took China.

Such dedication sounds remarkably similar to the New Testament. "I am crucified with Christ, nevertheless I live; yet not I but Christ liveth in me." Our Lord sent forth His apostles without money, or two coats, or extra shoes. The Apostle Paul spoke of being poor yet making many rich, as having nothing yet possessing all things. Believers in the early church were of one heart and one soul, neither said any of them that any of the things he possessed was his own, but they had all things in common (Acts 4:32). The Chinese Communists developed (temporarily) a counterfeit copy of the original Christian community (although it quickly vanished once they seized power).

But what of foreign missionaries in China?

We had always slept in beds, so we took our beds and bedding with us. Together with kerosene stoves, washing machines, refrigerators, movie cameras, sewing machines, typewriters, tape recorders, even automobiles. And several steel drums packed with canned food, dry cereal, summer and winter clothing, toothpaste, soap, shampoo, paper products, toys for the kids, everything.

To protect it all from thieves we would construct a two story, six room brick house with cheap labor. Then put a high stone wall around the area with iron spikes or broken glass bottles sticking out the top to stop intruders from climbing over. A small hut by the gate housed the security guard, on duty 24 hours a day in exchange for food and lodging, plus an occasional ten cent tip. The adjoining garage housed the missionary's car and provided padlocked storage for barrels not yet empty.

The whole complex was fondly called the "mission compound," and there were hundreds of them all over China, as well as in Korea, India and elsewhere.

In larger cities missionaries could buy private homes in more upscale suburban communities. In Shanghai I was invited to visit the new home of my dear friend David Morken who was there as a missionary for Youth for Christ. I had shared meetings with him in the USA two years earlier. His house might well have been transplanted from a neighborhood in suburban Chicago.

It was located in an exclusive section of the city reserved for ambassadors, news correspondents and foreign business men. I still remember the "Williamsburg blue" walls of the long living room, the nice carpeting and the fireplace at the end where I'm sure his kids would hang their stockings at Christmas time. There was a modern kitchen and spacious, separate dining room. Upstairs there were ample bedrooms and bath for his large family. The house was beautifully decorated with hand crafted (in China) cherry wood furniture which the Morkens would later ship to their new station in Japan when they had to leave China.

So why shouldn't the Morkens live as well in Shanghai as they did in California? Think of the great sacrifice they had made, leaving home and family to go work among people who couldn't even speak English. Unless they maintained minimum comforts their children might end up being maladjusted, as had the children of many other American missionaries. That was my thinking at the time, because I didn't fully realize the dynamic revolutionary forces of the new Marxist religion that was soon to force all foreign missionaries out of China.

Now let me say that not all foreign missionaries had modern houses like the Morkens did. Some single workers lived quite simply. But nine out of ten married missionaries with children tended to have the finest homes in the towns or villages where their mission station was located.

I thought for sure I would find one that was different when I was invited to visit a family who had gone to work among the boat people in Hong Kong harbor. I knew that thousands of Chinese families lived in tiny boats with no rooms, just an arched covering about four feet high and six feet in length, open on both ends. The whole family would sleep on the floor of the boat under the arched covering at night, then paddle around during the day trying to find sources of food. Were the foreign missionaries any different? Their motor driven boat was many times larger than any other, with private rooms and most of the comforts of home. It even had a separate kitchen, and a bathroom with running water coming from a large storage tank mounted above the kitchen. They refilled it on shore daily. How generous of their supporting churches back in America to provide them with these basic necessities so they could live among the people to whom they wanted to preach the gospel. But how could these poor boat people possibly receive the gospel message from foreigners who appeared to be millionaires living in their midst?

As Christian missionaries we appeared fabulously rich in comparison with the average Chinese. No way could we honestly represent our Lord, "who though He was rich yet for our sakes became poor?" We could only misrepresent Him. No way could we teach, "Love your neighbor as yourself," when we were rich foreigners living among the poor natives.

Never could we challenge a Chinese, "Deny yourself, take up your cross, and follow our Lord to the top of Calvary to be crucified with Him." But the Communists could make comparable challenges. So it was easy to see why foreign missionaries were often looked upon as hypocrites, while the Communist missionaries (at that time) were seen as heroes.

To say I was shocked is to put it mildly. All my life I had

considered foreign missionaries to be the best Christians in the world. Their sacrifices inspired many in our churches to follow their example. Now we were being castigated as hypocrites.

Gradually I came to realize that as traditional missionaries we had blind spots in our thinking. While operating "cross culturally" we had adopted ways of doing things which hindered more than helped the cause of Christ. Foreign missionaries from wealthy countries have found it necessary to take their standard of living with them when they have gone to live in poorer countries. In most cases that I have observed these comparatively wealthy missionaries appear oblivious to the fact that their affluence is a stumbling block to people who are forced to live in poverty.

A former missionary to Korea, Dr. T. Stanley Soltau, had me speak in the church of which he was pastor in Memphis soon after I returned from service overseas. He gave me a copy of a book he wrote in 1954 titled *Missions at the Crossroads*. In Chapter 12, Page 88 I found this paragraph: "In most mission fields the homes of missionaries are much more comfortable and their scale of living is far higher than that of the common people among whom they work. This is not said in any spirit of criticism of the missionaries, for their health and the effectiveness of their work depends in a large measure upon the maintenance of those standards of living. Often when I was in Korea, people would come in and ask to look over our house, and as they saw the rugs and the pictures and the books, they would say, 'Will heaven be any nicer than this?'"

In 1937 Rosalind Goforth published a biography of her husband Jonathan in which she tells how when they first arrived in China they rented "a small native house" owned by a Dr. Williamson who was away at that time. "It consisted of a row of rooms, all with doors and windows facing an open court." Included was "a study, dining room, bedroom, and two rooms filled with Dr. Williamson's things." To a foreign missionary this seemed like a small house, even though at that time 90% of the families in China were living in two rooms or less. The Goforth's second house was more spacious: "a two-story semi-detached foreign built house within a minute's walk of the seashore."

I have been told that one of the questions most frequently

asked by natives regarding foreign missionaries is what do they do with all those rooms. And probably a billion people have never seen stairsteps, only ladders. So they can't imagine what use there would be for two story houses. Why would anyone want to climb a ladder up to a higher floor? Was it the place where they stored all their money?

Missionaries' houses served to assist the Communist cause in China. Zealous young Marxists would point out the mission compounds and ask, "Where do these rich foreigners get all their wealth? They don't work at any job or profession. They are not engaged in business. There is only one answer. They are spies sent here by the CIA." And most people would believe these allegations. To follow the Communists (at that time) was considered patriotic because they were exposing these foreigners as enemies of China.

In countries that are not industrialized, what limited wealth that exists is to a large extent held by the government, or by "blood-sucker" landlords. Individuals who have above average property and power are assumed to be working with the government (even more so after World War II when so much foreign aid was doled out to socialistic government bureaucrats by industrialized countries) unless they are land-owners who rent to sharecroppers. They are universally envied and despised by the poor. So when foreign missionaries build spacious houses, drive around in cars, and seem to have abundant money for food, clothing, special schools for their children, medical care and plane tickets, it is assumed that they have been sent there by their governments or are absentee land-lords. This assumption hurts the cause of Christ in many nations because it identifies the Christian faith with the wealthy class of people who are usually hated.

For these and other reasons I believe that our Sovereign Lord Himself wanted all foreign missionaries out of China. Just as surely as there appears to have been a time when He wanted us to be working there, the time came when He wanted all of us to leave. Had we stayed, I believe, the multiplication of churches and individual Christians would have been greatly retarded. We were in China building our respective denominational churches. By moving us out of the way our Lord could begin building *His* church, and all the gates of hell have not been able to stop Him.

After we left, most foreign missionaries I knew assumed that Christianity would gradually disappear in China until we returned. It was generally agreed that the presence of the foreign missionary was essential to the preservation of the faith. But God proved that the opposite was true. The presence of the foreign missionaries was the primary hindrance to church growth. Why? Because the foreigners identified Christianity with personal wealth and foreign governments. Their denominational branches were looked upon as "institutional colonialism."

When I asked one Chinese man about his faith he replied, "I am a Lutheran of the Missouri synod." Why should Missouri be transplanted into China? Another told me he was "Chinese American Dutch Reformed." There were also Canadian Presbyterians, Australian Presbyterians and (at that time) Presbyterians U.S. as well as their competitors, Presbyterians U.S.A. The United Presbyterians were a separate body then, as were the Bible Presbyterians and several others. There were United Methodists and Free Methodists and Wesleyan Methodists and other Methodists. Every independent non-denominational mission became a denomination as soon as their agents were able to win a few followers in China. And at least a dozen different kinds of Baptists each had their separate followers. I facetiously asked my good friend and fellow Baptist, Baker James Cauthen, if the reason he worked in southern China was so his followers could be called "Southern Baptists," after our parent body in America.

Altogether there must have been about 300 different (often competing) foreign denominations (or otherwise distinctive foreign groupings) of Christians in China when I arrived there in 1948. It was the "free enterprise" business model applied to religion. The laissez-faire economy is more successful than socialism because it gives business firms freedom to compete. Human beings are competitive by nature, and are spurred on by an incentive for profit. Communist economies failed because collectivism destroys the profit motive. It does not exploit personal ambition. Socialists have mistakenly tried to apply altruistic principles to men and women who by nature are prone to be selfishly ambitious. In its early revolutionary stages the

Communist movement copied the New Testament concept of the "body of Christ," which is that all true believers are "one body in Christ and every one members one of another." I remember reading one writer, a former Communist, who said 50 years ago that there was something diabolically supernatural about "the tie that binds Communists together in comradeship."

Of course it didn't take long for history to reveal that such a concept can never last among sinful men (and all are sinners by nature) unless they have first been to the cross of Christ, reconciled to God, and regenerated by His Holy Spirit. Free enterprise works well among sinners because every man is trying to advance his own business. Socialism will never work unless all are saints, which they never are.

So a major offense of the contemporary foreign missionary enterprise is that it operates on the same principles of ambition and expansionism that businesses do. The motivation is not profit but power. And the self satisfaction derived from expansion into new territories. It is of the flesh rather than of the Spirit. Independent and denominational missions in China were all setting up branches and extending their territory, just like Ford and GM or Coke and Pepsi have done all over the world. So when the Communists came on the scene with their altruistic message of "love your neighbor as yourself" (at that time – once they gained control they became just as selfish as any before them) it exposed the colonial, carnal aspects of foreign missionary operations.

Is it any wonder then that God allowed the Communists to wield a big political broom and sweep out all the foreign missionaries and our 300 denominations. He cleaned house and started over. True to free enterprise methodology, we had all gone to China to plant branches of our respective businesses (although we called them churches). Our Lord must have wanted us all out of the way so He could build HIS church in China. About which I have much to say later.

CHAPTER FIVE

CARNAL COMPETITION

Competition among denominations and Christian organizations is so common in America that we take it for granted. And it doesn't really bother most of us. We accept it as part of our culture. I remember seeing a brochure sent out by the Home Mission Board of my own denomination, the Southern Baptist Convention, around 1950. It showed a map of the then 48 states with 18 white (where Southern Baptists were) and 30 black (where they weren't). A big headline at the top said PIONEER MISSIONS IN 30 STATES. Southern Baptist "pioneer" missionaries were being sent out to plant "Southern" Baptist churches in those 30 darkened states where the light was not yet shining.

In the free enterprise economy of America, most of us take this sectarian expansionism in good humor. "Sure," we say, "come ahead. We already have a dozen different kinds of Baptists in North Dakota; perhaps a little southern flavor will add spice to the mix." In other words, the more choices the better. A basic principle of the free enterprise system is that competition usually brings improvement. So why not have Southern Baptist churches in North Dakota?

But when we export our different brands to other countries and cultures we are not received so freely. At first we are looked upon as spies sent by the U.S. government. Then when people begin to comprehend how the free enterprise economy works, they realize that our church denominations are competitive businesses like

Honda and Toyota.

The tendency toward colonization is so strong that it eventually affects every organization and denomination. I know several that started out helping other ministries in poorer countries without taking them over or insisting on affiliation, but then gradually moved toward making them their overseas branches. I think of one that sent financial assistance to several indigenous ministries based in India, including Sharon Bible Institute headed by Dr. P.J. Thomas (who earned an M.A. degree at Wheaton College, near Chicago). Then this U.S. group went colonial and demanded that Sharon become a part of its newly formed denomination. When Dr. Thomas declined, they demanded that he repay $4000 which they had contributed for one of his Bible school buildings. Having no such cash reserves, Thomas approached me for assistance, and eventually Christian Aid sent $4000 to that U. S. organization to repay its original "gift" to an indigenous mission in India.

One that I originally thought would never go colonial was an excellent ministry called the Navigators. It was started by Dawson Trotman, with whom I had many precious hours of fellowship. During the last 12 years of his life on this earth he served on our Board of Directors and was always faithful in attending board meetings. Daws was different. He would assign his disciples to work with other ministries for the purpose of building them up. In the late 1940s he assigned several key men from his staff to work with Billy Graham in his evangelistic meetings. When I came back from overseas to launch International Students, Inc. (in 1953) he assigned Warren Myers to help start the work in Berkeley and Bill Michel to set up operations in Washington. He loaned many other men and women whom he had trained to serve with various ministries, and it was always to build them up as viable works of God, never to make them part of the Navigators.

But then God called Daws to his reward (at the age of 50) and I soon began to see changes in the work he left behind. It's not for me to say that his successors weren't being led of the Lord. Lorne Sanny carried on as Elisha did after Elijah. Seldom have I ever seen a more terrific gang of Christians that those who were part of the Navigators.

But I noticed an interesting thing. When ISI staff would introduce a newly won foreign student to Navigators personnel to be discipled, there was often heard a comment like, "This is great! Maybe we can train him to be our Nav representative in Nepal." Or in Japan, or Sri Lanka, or Thailand, or whatever country the student came from. The first thought seemed to be how the U.S. organization could be extended to yet another country. The tendency toward colonialism takes us away from thoughts of how the kingdom of God can best be initiated within a non-Christian society. Instead, we are more likely to think in terms of how we might establish a beachhead for our enterprise in some new territory.

Recently I was invited to join a farewell party for a missionary being sent out by a major U.S. denomination to a country where he did not know the language. His support base was $80,000 annually – more than 40 times the average family income in that country. I knew of numerous evangelical churches there, and many native missionaries who had virtually no support. I casually mentioned that what his mission board was spending to send him to that country would provide support for 40 native missionaries who already knew the local language. But I found that such a suggestion was not appreciated in those circles. After all, if God had "called" him to go, how could anyone dare to question the wisdom of what he was doing?

I further inquired about what his purpose was and learned that he had just one objective: to start the first branch church of his denomination in that country. And I knew that in order to succeed in doing it, he would have to take away members from existing churches.

Ruthless competition has been the hallmark of U.S. and Canadian foreign missions for nearly a century. In the early years of my ministry I became good friends with an energetic religious entrepreneur whose interdenominational ministry now spans the globe. I saw him at a convention about 20 years ago, and the first thing he said was, "We are in 90 countries now; how many are you in?" His swagger sounded just as I would imagine a British army commander might have boasted during the reign of Queen Victoria.

I knew exactly how he had expanded his empire. He sent his emissaries all over the world to hire away the workers of indigenous ministries. Chosen apostles who had labored long and sacrificially to win souls and train disciples saw their ministries devastated as the rich foreigners came along and lured away their staff with offers of higher pay, better facilities and other material advantages. If this ambitious American were truly zealous for the cause of Christ, he would have used some of his wealth to strengthen Christian witness that was already in place in poorer countries. Instead he virtually wipes it out, and leaves in its place the operations of his foreign organization which local anti-Christian forces can condemn as "agents of the capitalistic imperialists." And thus bring discredit on the cause of Christ.

If this were an isolated example it might be excused, but hundreds of organizations and denominations from industrialized countries are doing the same sort of thing in poorer countries all over the world. While preaching in Korea 55 years ago I was asked by a group of church leaders, "Isn't there something you can do to get all these foreigners to go home and leave us alone? For 80 years we have had churches here, yet these foreigners keep coming to interfere with us. They bring their denominational quarrels with them and divide our churches. Could you please ask them to all go back where they came from?"

Today, however, the situation is reversed. The head of an indigenous mission in Paraguay was asked what his biggest problem was. "Oh, it's the Koreans," he said. "Their missionaries hire away our workers and divide our churches. They try to convince our members to join them on the basis of some peculiarity of doctrine or unusual practice. Churches in Paraguay would be much better off if all foreign missionaries left our country, especially the Koreans."

In one poorer country after another I have seen missionaries from industrialized countries set up Bible schools almost across the street from indigenous ones. Then they hire away the teachers with offers of increased compensation, and lure away the students with offers of scholarships. Hundreds of excellent missionary training bases have been decimated by this carnal practice. If we claim God has called or sent us to serve Him in a particular place, why not strengthen the work that is already there? Why go out and compete with it, and weaken it with selfish use of our greater resources?

Granted, indigenous ministries did not exist in most "mission field" countries when European and American missionaries first started sending out emissaries 200 years ago. But now they are active in every country where we Americans are allowed to work. Any foreign mission that enters those countries is likely to become a competitor by so doing.

The root of the problem is that we are still controlled by 19th century traditions. When William Carey went to India there were no Indian mission boards in that vast country. Now over 3000 of them, with more than 100,000 missionaries, are doing the work many times more effectively than the foreigners ever could. But what mission board in an industrialized country will ever give them a dime? Each one is bent on the furtherance of its own work, and none will share their vast resources with our fellow believers on the basis of us being one body in Christ. We want maps on our walls with pins stuck in every country to show the extent of our empires. We want to display all of our overseas branches in publications of our missions to graphically portray the locations of our denominational or organizational presence.

Since the Hindu majority barred foreign missionaries from further activity in their country, many ambitious colonial missions have tried to find ways to place India on their corporate maps. Two or three decades ago the head of the foreign mission board of a certain Baptist denomination visited Delhi as a tourist and approached Dr. P.N. Kurien, head of All India Prayer Fellowship, to learn about that ministry. In addition to a Bible Institute with 60 students and five faculty members, AIPF had over 100 missionaries serving in pioneer areas of several states. Most had hardly any support, and to carry on their work was a constant financial struggle.

"Why don't you become our Baptist work in India?" the American asked. "We could give you everything you need."

"No, thank you," Dr. Kurien replied. "We prefer to go hungry."

He well knew that if AIPF became a subsidiary of a foreign denomination it would destroy the ministry's credibility in the eyes of his fellow Indians. But the U.S. visitor could not offer help on any other basis, because his Baptist denomination (at that time) was locked in to a combination of 19th century colonialism and the free enterprise business cycle. Funds within their missionary program were pretty much restricted to projects that were affiliated with the denomination.

What will it take for our churches (especially my own denomination) to recognize the Biblical principle that all true believers are one body in Christ, and that we should minister to the needs of our Lord's body where He lives within His people? To go into foreign countries bent on the ruthless expansion of our denominational domain is a deed of the flesh rather than a fruit of the Spirit. And let us not forget that independent missions and para-church organizations are no different from denominations in the eyes of the citizens of poorer countries. All are regarded as forms of economic colonialism or cultural imperialism. As each independent group sets up a branch operation it becomes the equivalent of yet another foreign denomination.

This carnal aspect of foreign missions has disgraced the Christian faith in the eyes of millions of people in "mission field" countries all over the world. It is especially repulsive in the eyes of those who become mature Christians through reading the Word of God. I have heard hundreds of my fellow believers express their revulsion to it in Asia, Africa, Latin America and Eastern Europe. One who set it forth in writing was (Watchman) Nee To-Sheng of China about 66 years ago. While he was visiting some churches in England in 1938 he was asked by Norman Baker of the China Inland Mission if he (Nee) could agree with the policies of CIM to an extent that some of his assemblies in China might work cooperatively with the CIM. This is Nee's response, (edited for brevity, but no words added except those in brackets).

Dear Brother,

I have read the Principles and Practices which you gave me. May I, with all love to you and to those whom I have come to love during my recent visit, say that I do not agree with what is said under "Church Government," to which you draw my attention especially.

After being in this country [England] twice, I have found that your way of child education is to let your children think for themselves. They could decide for themselves whether they wanted grapefruit or porridge for breakfast! You honour others' individuality and personal free will, but I am sorry to say that what you have shown to your children you have not shown to the Chinese

Christians. No mention is made of their opinion. In such an important matter as church government, they are totally ignored. One missionary is given the authority to decide what form the church should take, and the whole church has nothing to say as to it. Do you think this is right?

From the Chinese Christian's point of view, they are just a kind of little toy terrier, to be taken up and set down without their opinion being consulted. Should the missionary be given the power to decide the form of church government for them?

You may argue that the Chinese churches are so young and they do not know much; therefore missionaries have to decide for them; but do you mean to say that because of the immediate babyhood of the Chinese churches you try to make a regulation for their permanent immaturity? Brother, in the Principles and Practices there was no provision made for the Chinese churches in case they do get into maturity. It is taken for granted that they will always continue to be babes, and hence the form of church government instituted by the first missionary is to be the permanent form. There is not even a suggestion that some day they would be otherwise, and that they could decide for themselves. Do you never expect the Chinese churches to grow out of their infancy? If missionaries will try to live less within "missionary circles" and get into the sphere of the works of the Holy Spirit today they will find with me that, although the Chinese churches are not what they ought to be, they are more that what we think they are. Times and things have changed, Brother.

One deplores the sectarian divisions of churches in Christendom. I know your opinion as to these divisions, that they are inevitable. If the enlightened servants of the Lord find that they are helpless as to the present state of things in the so-called Christian countries, there is no reason why, when they are working in heathen countries, they should import these forces into them. It is bad enough not to be exercised by these divisions. It is really worse trying to perpetuate them instead of stopping them.

I am sorry to find that the Principles and Practices should license such a continuation of the evils of Christendom. They may be inevitable in this country [England], but to make this the ground for propagating them in China is really going too far.

You told me that divisions are inevitable, but, Brother, that is no adequate reason for the missionaries to make divisions for the Chinese churches beforehand. Before they know it they are already being divided according to the particular divisions their missionaries are in. Converts in different missions only know that they are converted to Christ to be Christians, but without their knowing it they are converted to be at the same time Baptists, Methodists, Presbyterians, Congregationalists, Anglicans and what-not. They have no conscious reason for being a different Christian from their fellow men, but divisions were made for them by the different missions with which they come into contact. Your Mission is not a denominational mission. You ought to be able to avoid these evils, but the difference in result between your Mission -— for which I have the highest esteem – and other denominational missions is immaterial, because your Principles and Practices make provision for the missionaries to divide the Chinese Christians according to the respective denominations from which they come.

Besides this you have started a new denomination by the name of China Inland Church! The probability and possibility of Chinese Christians in the future making their own divisions will never justify the missionaries introducing Western divisions beforehand. The attitude of, "we might just as well introduce our denomination" is not of the Lord. The Lord fully knew what was going to happen to His Church. But that did not stop Him from speaking through His servant Paul that "ye are yet carnal, whereas there is among you divisions . . ." Others' failure did not justify ours. It will be good for China if the true, self-sacrificing missionaries when they leave all and come to China, leave also their denominations behind. China needs their Gospel but China does not need their denominationalism. The testimony of the one Body has been spoiled in this country [England]. Why do you try to spoil it also in China; a piece of more or less virgin soil? In my younger days I could never understand why Christians should be so divided and yet all profess to be Christians. I have since been meeting hundreds who have the same question.

My plea for the Chinese churches is, let them have a chance to <u>start</u> right without being schismatic in the Body from the beginning. If the Chinese churches should be divided, may I plead with you, let *them make their own divisions and do not bring divisions ready-made to them.*

Judging by what I read it seems that the China Inland Mission does not know what a New Testament Church is. We all know the difference between "the Church" and "the churches" in Scripture. As to the Church, we differ very little. It is too spiritual to be quarreled over by men. The difference is, and difficulties are, always connected with "the churches," because they have an earthly aspect. But I wonder how many have really seen the basis upon which the Church is divided (in the best sense of the word) in the churches. On the basis of geography alone. This is most important. The church is divided into churches on the ground of the difference of localities of the people of God. In the Word of God we can only find localities connected with the churches of God and nothing else — the church in Ephesus; the church in Rome; the church in Thessalonica, etc. etc. Any other ground of dividing the people of God and forming them into a separate people is sectarian and condemned by the Word. The basis for forming a church in distinction from other churches is not doctrine (i.e. holiness), sacrament (i.e. baptism), form of government (i.e. congregational), order (i.e. Presbyterian), nation (i.e. Anglican), experience (i.e. Pentecostal), leaders (i.e. Wesleyan). These are not good enough reasons for making a separate church. The only reason advocated by the Word is the difference of locations by the people of God. If you want to change your church you have to change your residence. If you leave one place and go to another, you leave one church and join another. There is only one church in one place. You cannot change your church without changing your home.

So you see "the Church" and "the churches" are essentially the same. They are both composed of the children of God. The only difference is that the former is composed of all the children of God, irrespective of time and space, the latter is composed of all the children of God in a given locality. These two – being the children of God and in the same locality – are the conditions for forming a church. No matter who they are, what they are, whence they are, what they hold (in addition to the faith), how they practice, whom they follow; if they possess the same life in the Son of God, and live in the same city, they belong to the same church. The New Testament knows of no other kind of church. Every other division threatens the very life of the church, but this "Scriptural division" is the only one which does not touch the life.

The church which the China Inland Mission sets out to establish is not a New Testament local church at all. The "church" mentioned in that paragraph is, at its best, just a mere mission station. It is formed according to the denominational affiliation of the missionary at the outset, and it is a church under the charge of a missionary in its continuation. When one missionary in charge goes you will get a succeeding missionary of the same inclination. The Apostolic pattern of appointing local elders to govern local churches is not followed.

Dear Brother, I believe that when those who have the charge of mission work know the difference between apostles (missionaries) and elders, it will be a great day for missions. Missionaries are for the Gospel work they are called to, but elders are local men appointed to take the oversight of local churches. It is when the missionary leaves this position as a missionary to assume the role of an elder that the troubles begin. I believe that the Word is abundantly clear as regards a missionary's vocation. He is (1) to save the lost, and (2) to form them into local churches; churches of the localities where they live and not branches of the church of the missionary. What we are finding today is that missionaries do preach the Gospel and win souls, for which we thank God, but they do not establish churches of the localities where the converts are; instead they either establish denominational branch churches or mission churches, the China Inland Church in your particular case. You know, some have gone so far as to make China's converts members of the Anglican Church in China!

Peter belonged to the church in Jerusalem. You find him founding churches in other cities, not establishing branches of the Jerusalem Church. Paul came from the church in Antioch. When he was in Ephesus he founded the church in Ephesus; so also in Corinth; so also in Thessalonica, etc., but he did not form the Antiochian Church in those places. The apostolic pattern which reveals the mind of the Lord is that a missionary should establish the church in the place where he has gone, and not make branches *of the church from which he has come out.*

Now imagine these two apostles coming to the same city, say Rome, to work. How could they, and how did they co-operate? It was not that Peter was a little self-centered trying to establish a Jerusalemic Church in Rome, and Paul tried to be a little more liberal, forgetting his own Antiochian Church and helping Peter to edify his church; or Paul was a little selfish trying to form an Antiochian Church in Rome, and Peter tried to be a little broader forgetting his own Jerusalemic Church and helping Paul to build his church. Nothing of that sort. Peter came to Rome to establish the church in Rome. Paul came to Rome to establish the church in Rome. They established the same and one church. They did not extend the churches in the place to which they both have gone. If they tried to extend and to make branches of their respective mother churches, then you will find two churches in the place they have gone to. But instead they established a totally new church in that place, not an extension or a branch of the churches they came from. So you have only one church in that place. It does not matter that they do not come from the same church, but it does matter that they do establish the same church. It is unthinkable that the apostles [could] have done otherwise. This is the basis for apostolic co-operation. They had different ministries. The ministry of Paul was quite different from that of Peter, but when they came to the same place they served the same church. The Lord has not ordered that we should have a unity of ministry, but the Lord did order that we should have the oneness of church. Apostles were out to form local churches, and nothing else. It was on this basis they co-operated. It is to this end modern apostles should work, and it is on this basis modern apostles could co-operate.

In order that the Church should be local instead of missionary (denominational included) the missionary should appoint local men to be elders to govern and pastor the church in that locality. He himself bears no official local responsibility. On his first missionary journey, which did not last very long, Paul on his return "appointed for them elders in <u>every</u> church" (Acts xiv. 23). When he was in a hurry to come back he left Titus in Crete that he "should appoint elders in every city" (Titus 1:5). The apostolic pattern was that they *did not govern the churches they established, either directly or offi-cially. They left them to local men, men who were comparatively more spiritual than others in these churches.*

I have written this at length because you ask me to write out the basis upon which we can co-operate, which I believe will be much to the glory of God. The basis is simply this: establishing local churches, with local governments, and not denominational or mission churches. That is all. I myself and those with me will be willing to co-operate with any true servant of the Lord if he is out to establish local churches and not other kinds of churches. Other points should be settled by the churches themselves under the sovereignty and teaching of the Holy Spirit. If the C.I.M. will make no provision for its missionaries to extend their own particular "churches" in China, we could have the heartiest co-operation. Missionaries should establish local churches alone.

May I suggest the following which I believe is according to the mind of the Lord. When a missionary has preached and won some souls, teach them the fundamentals of the faith, lead them to read the Word and teach them how to trust the Holy Spirit for teaching, and commit them unto the Lord, but do not decide for them what "church" they are going to be and what form of government they are going to take. At least give them the liberty you gave to your children. They must get things out of the Word for themselves. If those with you are prepared to establish local churches according to the Word, if they are prepared to trust the Holy Spirit to lead their converts, through the study of the Word, to decide for themselves what they will do as to church government and order, I and those that are with me are prepared to co-operate with them.

Dear Brother, in the work of God we must not take convenience for our principle of guidance. We must do the will of God. The present Principles and Practices may be convenient and minimize trouble among missionaries, but when God works, when more life comes to the Chinese Christians, you find there may not be trouble among the missionaries but there will be trouble arising from the Chinese Christians. They will only be silent if they are dead. If there is life, and abundance of it, then you cannot expect them to keep quiet. Dare we deprive them of life so that we can keep them quiet?

The present trouble in different churches shows that unless you keep them in ignorance the Chinese Christians will decide for themselves how to do the will of God. You cannot have both life for Chinese Christians and convenience for the mission and missionaries. You must be awakened to what God is doing in China. There are spiritual men, and men much taught of God. They come under the Lordship of Jesus Christ, and they cannot take orders from men to defy the will of the Lord. Many of the Chinese Christians have gone forward and they do know the will of God. Trust them, and trust the Holy Spirit in them, Brother. Don't be afraid. You must recognize that the spiritual state of the churches under the permanent charge of the missionary is a definite lack of life. Some day life will reach them from other sources and you cannot help it. When life comes that kind of un-Scriptural management will be challenged. God is doing a new thing in China [in 1938, no less].

Brother, do not measure the work of God in China with what there is in this country [England]. Do you or do you not believe that God can do a new thing? Some may be baptized by immersion, but this does not make them Baptists. Some may have miraculous gifts, but this does not make them Pentecostals. A church of God is composed of all the people possessing the same life of the Son and living in the same locality. These are the churches that every servant of God should establish.

I hope I have made myself clear as to our basis of co-operation, and what I think of the Principles and Practice of church government. The Lord knows how much I desire co-operation for His glory, and I hope that they know it too. I hope I have spoken the truth in love and not in any other spirit.

Dear Brother, this question not only concerns China. It concerns all the missionary work in the world. I pray that God will lead the C.I.M. to take a lead in the right direction, so that other lands may be blessed. With much love, yours in the Lord, [signed] Watchman Nee.

By rejecting the carnal competition of traditional foreign missionary organizations and denominations, Watchman Nee opened his mind and heart to receive the Biblical revelation of a church congregation being the body of Christ in that locality. This dynamic aspect of New Testament Christianity has been largely overlooked by evangelicals since the Reformation, due in large part, I believe, to the fact that our traditions of denominational competition have blinded us to things that are clearly presented in the Word of God.

We should note how Watchman Nee was repulsed by the way foreign missionaries seemed always to want complete domination and control over their overseas branches, relegating them permanently to the status of children, always to be under the watchcare of their missionary parents. I have found this to be the pattern wherever I have gone in "mission field" countries.

I could cite hundreds of examples, but will mention just one. While in Japan in 1949 I worked with a dear British/Irish lady named Irene Webster-Smith. She had gone out in the 1920s with a ministry called Japan Evangelistic Band, started by Barclay Buxton of England in the late 19th century. Through her introduction I was invited to minister years later at the annual conference of JEB in London where I met Barclay Buxton's son, Godfrey. He gave me an autographed copy of his father's biography which he had written. No doubt Barclay was a great man of God, but I wasn't surprised to see the way he treated Japanese believers.

When he returned to England for his second furlough in 1899, Barclay left written instructions behind for all of his disciples in Japan. Here are excerpts: ". . . *about the conduct of the work in my absence . . . I believe that as you have obeyed me whilst I have been with you, much more in my absence will you follow my convictions . . . I wish Mr. Wilkes [fellow British missionary] to have absolute control of everything. I ask the [Japanese] brothers to consider themselves wholly under him and to obey him . . . he will have control of the dismissal or acceptance of evangelists [native missionaries], of their removal from one place to another, of all money matters, and of all else. I ask [Japanese workers] not to administer baptism without his consent . . . to submit journeyings and work to his approval . . . to follow his wishes as to who should preach, and that you all loyally work under him. This may require that you often give up your own judgement and work under his . . . he alone will be responsible for final decisions . . . if there is anyone*

who cannot loyally and gladly work under him it will be better for
such a one to leave this field and work [elsewhere]."

I have inserted the words in brackets for clarity and brevity;
they do not change the meaning.

Is it any wonder that foreign missionary work in Japan brought
forth so little fruit? Like Buxton, almost all other European and
American missionaries treated Japanese believers like children. In
contrast, consider how churches grew and multiplied in Korea. The
main reason is, I believe, that the first churches there were started by
Korean traders who met Christians in China and brought the gospel
back to their homeland. Thousands of believers were meeting in
hundreds of house churches in Korea for many years before the first
foreigners were admitted to that (then) closed land in the 1880s.

When I was in Korea for evangelistic meetings in 1950 I asked
Harold Voelkel, a Presbyterian (USA), "What are you doing here?
There is no need for foreign missionaries in Korea today." His
reply: "We are trying to hang on to the coattails of the Korean
churches for the blessing it will bring to our own souls."

Which illustrates what I have often said: rather than being inferior, as traditional missionaries have often regarded our brothers in
"mission field" countries, many leaders of indigenous ministries are
far superior to us in their zeal for the kingdom of God and in their
understanding of certain areas of Biblical knowledge. Those who
have come from non-Christian backgrounds did not have to first
unlearn a lot of medieval and Reformation-era tradition in order to
comprehend what God revealed for His church, especially those
truths found in the Epistles of Paul.

I intend to say more about this later because it has a strong bearing on my conviction that God wanted all foreign missionaries to be
removed from China and India so He could make a new beginning
there. I am likewise convinced that it would be better for the cause
of Christ if foreign missionaries were withdrawn from all other
areas of the world as well, and believe that our Lord would have us
withdraw voluntarily so that He doesn't have to use unfriendly
forces to accomplish His purpose, as He did in China.

CHAPTER SIX

THE RICH FOREIGNERS

When God allowed all foreign missionaries to be put out of China (and also India) 55 years ago, churches and mission boards in America should have realized that He was showing us how the time had come to phase out the colonial approach to world evangelization. But few of us did. The evangelical establishment went full speed ahead, not realizing that our presence was a hindrance to church growth in most "mission field" countries.

Of course we had no way of knowing what God was going to do (in our absence) among His people in China and India. And as I will explain later, I see no way it could have happened if the foreigners had been allowed to stay on. The whole colonial apparatus had to be moved out of the way. Likewise I sincerely believe that if we would clear out of many other areas and redirect our financial resources toward helping indigenous missions instead, the cause of Christ would be advanced a hundred fold.

In further chapters I also want to say more about the unbelievable growth of evangelical assemblies that has taken place since foreign missionary activities were phased out in China and India. I use the word "foreign" to mean anyone who goes to live as a missionary in a diverse culture where he is looked upon as an alien. Or as the representative of a foreign government, religion or way of life, and who is likely to appear somewhat weird in the eyes of native inhabitants. To a large extent, I believe, the explosive advances that have occurred in China and India are due to the fact that Christian faith is no longer associated with colonialism in those countries. But it took many years to remove the stigma. European and American missionaries who went out to the colonies from 1800 to 1950 were, I believe, generally unaware that their presence identified the Christian faith with foreign invaders and colonial rule, thus creating a prejudice against it.

It would not be fair to say that colonization was all bad. Quite the contrary. By putting in roads, railways and irrigation the British enabled the Indians to produce and transport enough food to end the horrible famines that had previously wiped out millions of people. By putting down tribal warfare in certain parts of Africa, European rulers brought a measure of stability to numerous tribes which had never known peace. But, of course, there was the downside also. During the first winter after Captain John Smith settled at Jamestown in 1607, he and his company were probably saved from extinction by benevolent assistance from the friendly Powhatan nation. But within two generations the Powhatan population had been reduced from 100,000 to less than 2000 by British guns and diseases.

There is no need for me to go into a lengthy discussion of the pros and cons of colonial rule during the centuries leading up to 1950, except as it relates to the evangelical foreign missionary enterprise. And the major implication of that relationship is that by 1900 the foreign missionary presence was generally looked upon by native peoples as part and parcel of the colonial establishment. Even where the missionaries were opposed or restricted in some ways by colonial authorities.

As might be expected, the European rulers assumed an attitude of superiority toward the peoples they had conquered. Some early missionary pioneers tried to avoid such appearances, but after two or three generations of missionary colonization, the distinction would gradually disappear. Foreign missionaries tended to live and operate on a par with the rest of the foreign community.

For example, during the century and a half before 1950 virtually every foreign missionary ministry operating in Africa practiced racial segregation. The homes of the missionaries were usually palatial mansions compared to the huts around them. No African was allowed to enter a missionary's home except as a servant. Children of the missionaries were sent to strictly segregated private schools. Intermarriage between Africans and foreign missionaries was unthinkable. In the eyes of the average African, there was little or no distinction between a missionary family and the family of someone serving with the colonial government.

In fact, it was very important to the missionaries to maintain favorable relations with the ruling authorities. Their social intercourse was carried on primarily within the foreign colony. They did not relate socially to Africans any more than an officer in the German military (prior to 1946) might socialize with an enlisted man. Of course there were notable exceptions, but it was a rare missionary who could live apart from the foreign establishment and still see his family survive. Either his children would become basket cases or his wife would have a nervous breakdown.

In 1954 I was visited in Washington by one of my "disciples" from Inter-Varsity days who had just come home "on furlough" after four years in Africa. Inspired by my rhetoric he had gone "to the mission field" determined to "identify with the people." But upon arrival the oldtime heads of his affiliated mission sat him down and laid out the code of conduct which he was to follow. He was there to become identified with the foreign community that made up the spiritual family of his mission, not with the "nationals" who were to be kept "in their place."

"And don't you come out here with any of those nonsensical ideas about Africans being equal to us," the director told him. "These people ARE inferior, and the sooner you recognize it the better."

On numerous occasions I have discussed these issues with a good friend whose parents were missionaries to Ethiopia with the Sudan Interior Mission. He said that even as a child he would relate to adult Ethiopians as though they were slaves. He would order them around and tell them what to do as though he were the adult and they were children. We should not be surprised, then, that after education in America when he himself returned to Ethiopia as a traditional missionary he was put out of the country within two years. Although when back in Africa he tried to take upon himself the form of a humble servant, remembrance of the past was still there.

My first culture shock came when I passed through India in 1948 on my way to China. While in Delhi I was invited to speak at the North India conference of The Methodist Church. Millions of Hindu refugees who had fled from the Muslims in newly partitioned Pakistan were sleeping on the sidewalks of India's major cities at that time. Garbage trucks would often pick up the dead bodies of those who died of starvation and diseases. As I approached (riding in a rickshaw) the high brick walls that surrounded the compound of the First Methodist Church, I saw hundreds of homeless, starving people living along the walls in crude lean-to shacks made of rubbish. Outstretched hands begged for anything I might be able to share to relieve their hunger.

Guards were on duty to hold the mob at bay at the locked doorway entrance as well as the big iron gates that barred the driveway into the compound. Of course, only the foreign missionaries had cars, and the compound was large enough to park a dozen of them safely. The walls along the outside had sharpened iron spikes sticking up every few inches to keep out intruders.

To look at denominational church buildings in India you couldn't tell the difference between them and the Methodist (or Baptist or Presbyterian) churches back in my home town: each was a large brick building with slate (or tile) roof over the "sanctuary," stained glass windows showing European figures, and a bell tower rising over the entrance foyer. The inside was also typically American, with curved benches stationed in order before the podium, behind which was the choir loft and, of course, the pipes of the organ. This isolated atmosphere imported from rural American culture seemed a world apart from the turmoil of agony and suffering outside the compound.

As the Annual Conference began, the evening meeting at which I was the keynote speaker seemed strangely familiar: an organ prelude, invocation in song by the choir, opening prayer, two hymns by the congregation, Scripture reading, pastoral prayer, anthem by the choir, sermon, closing hymn, benediction and organ postlude. It was just like home, and English was the only language used throughout.

Although this was my first month in Asia, I could not help but ask, "How in the world do these missionaries ever expect this sort of thing to relate to the people of this land?" It was like a palm tree from Panama transplanted in Pennsylvania during the summer months. When winter comes, it will die. During colonial days of British rule, foreign denominations could transplant their religious practices into small communities of followers in places like India, but they would never take root, never grow and never spread. And when independence came they tended to disappear. Yet the same pattern is being repeated by traditional missions in many parts of the world today.

I am reminded of a Hindu temple planted by a swami from India in suburban Washington. It had oriental architecture and the statue of a prominent Hindu displayed inside a front picture window of the educational building. Since it was only two blocks from my house, I used to drop in occasionally (about 40 years ago) to observe, and listen to their sermons on "self realization." Most of those attending were Indians, and proceedings were in Hindi as well as English. It was easy to see that such an alien culture would never catch on in America. Quite naturally, there would always be a few cultural dissidents within the D.C. population who might want to pursue "eastern religions," but they would probably be regarded as an oddball minority by the general population. Because it represented an alien culture, this Hindu group was not likely to take root, grow and multiply in America.

So it has been with the colonial missionary operations of foreign missionaries. I couldn't help but notice that a large number of those attending the foreign denomination churches of India were Anglo-Indians, largely the progeny of some liaison between British military personnel and Indian women.

While in Calcutta, also in 1948, I was asked to preach at Thoburn Methodist Church on Dharamtalla Street one Sunday morning. The American pastor requested that I bring a message of comfort, because many in the congregation were Anglo-Indians who had enjoyed special privileges during British rule. Now that independence had come they feared that they might lose their status, and even become victims of discrimination. Which goes to show how foreign denominations transplanted into diverse cultures are likely to appeal more to the foreign community there than to the local population.

While at the conference in Delhi I had dinner in the home of the Methodist Bishop, an American who was head man of the Methodists in northern India at that time. His beautiful eight room, two story brick home was also located inside the spacious church compound. He had several personal servants in addition to those employed by the church: a gatekeeper for the entrance, a driver (chauffeur), a cook, a laundry man, a sweeper, and a nanny for the children. These were all in addition to the staff of the church, some of whom served similar functions. Is it any wonder that foreign missionaries were seen by the general population as being an integral part of the colonial occupation?

During our five course dinner served by the cook at the Bishop's home, we talked of the starving multitudes outside in crude shelters along the walls of the mission compound. Women would give birth to babies during 100 degree heat or monsoon rainstorms in those wretched hovels. I mentioned that I felt somewhat like the rich man in Luke 16, who feasted sumptuously while Lazarus lay helpless at the gate, begging for crumbs from the rich man's table.

The Bishop's wife advised me that I would never survive in India if I tried to pattern my life after that Scripture. She reminded me of the other incident where our Lord said, "Ye have the poor with you always, and whensoever ye will ye may do them good" (Mark 14:7). Every scrap of food in the Bishop's home would be consumed in seconds if the starving masses outside their gates were allowed inside. And the hunger would continue thereafter, unabated. Obviously, foreign missionaries could never feed even one percent of the starving millions in India at that time. But our presence there as being fabulously rich in the midst of such poverty gave the wrong image of Christ's ambassadors. And caused educated Hindus to say that we misrepresented the Christ which many of them had read about in the New Testament.

As a single man 26 years old at that time I had very little knowledge of the rest of the world outside North America, or what it was like to raise a family in a place like India. Foolishly, I went around trying to tell the foreign missionaries that they should live more like the Indians do. One day while riding with an American, we passed a British cemetery (Hindus don't have cemeteries: they cremate all dead bodies, which helps control diseases). My companion suddenly slowed the car and turned into the cemetery. He said he wanted to show me something. It was the grave of a young missionary from England who had come to India long ago with ideas just like mine. He lasted six months.

Nevertheless, as I traveled third class on the trains from city to city speaking in churches and evangelistic meetings, I ate what the Indians ate and drank the same water. And ended up flat on my back for six weeks with two kinds of dysentery. I learned the hard way that foreign missionaries from industrialized countries had no immunities to the microbes that killed so many Indian babies in their first year. Those who survived developed a tolerance for infections which would kill Europeans. We cannot likely survive in poorer countries unless we are segregated from the general population. But that segregation is in itself an offense against the gospel we preach.

At that time I had no idea what possible solution there could be to this dilemma. It took me three years of living in Asia to find the answer: *we should not be there in the first place.* Our presence hurts more than helps the cause of Christ. There are other, better ways to get the job done, as I will explain later.

Everywhere I went in Asia during four crucial years of my life, 1948-51, the picture was the same. Missionaries lived in some of the finest homes in the city wherever I went. I have already mentioned David Morken's house in Shanghai. Presbyterian missionary Harold Volkel had a big house with detached garage and a protective wall around it in Seoul. In other Chinese and Korean locations the same pattern was repeated. Foreign missionaries had huge homes in premier locations in almost every city.

The Presbyterian compound where I stayed in Taipei had two large brick homes that before 1950 were among the finest in the city. Missionaries James and Lillian Dickson graciously provided accommodations (at cost) for missionaries like me, Dawson Trotman of The Navigators and Dick Hillis of Orient Crusades. We were all there at the same time in 1951. The Dicksons were very apologetic that their big brick house which appeared so impressive on the outside offered no showers with hot and cold running water on the inside. Because there was no refrigerator their cook had to go to the market and buy fresh food for every meal. By American standards, the Dicksons made a real sacrifice to live in Taiwan. But in the eyes of impoverished masses living in their tiny huts in those days, we gave the outward impression of opulent wealth.

And the practice continues until this day. All over the world I have seen examples of foreign missionaries misrepresenting our Lord by their display of wealth in the midst of poverty. A man in an Arab country told me how he lived near a foreign mission compound in his youth. The family owned a large dog and he noticed that at a certain time each day they would feed meat to their dog. The boy's family barely had meat to eat even once a month. So he thought within himself, "How I wish I could be a missionary's dog. Then I would have meat to eat every day."

Another told me how as a child he never had even one toy to play with, but nearby on a mission compound lived a foreign boy who received many, many toys every Christmas (sent by well meaning supporters back in the USA). A bright spot in the Arab boy's life came once when his mother arranged to take him for a short visit inside the foreigner's home where he would have an opportunity to look at all the toys.

"But you are not allowed to touch even one of them," his mother warned.

It is understandable that our churches back home would be sympathetic with their faithful missionaries who make such great sacrifices to go live in countries where they wouldn't have hot and cold running water, couldn't get cable TV, and if they can get them at all, the hamburgers, Cokes and ice cream cones aren't nearly as good as the ones they have at home. To compensate, we often load our missionaries with gifts (including toys for their children at Christmas) which alienate them from the poor people among whom they have gone to work.

A good friend of mine from IVCF days 55 years ago married a girl whose father was a wealthy executive in a major steel company.

After much attempted persuasion to guide his daughter in other directions, the father finally resigned to the fact that she was determined to go with her husband as a missionary to Africa. Not content to see her deprived, he loaded the couple with every conceivable item of comfort and convenience, then paid for shipping the entire lot to Africa. He also provided round trip plane tickets for special occasions when it might be pleasant to have his daughter home for family activities. What sort of testimony could that kind of "missionary" have among Africans living in one room huts, most of whom were so poor they couldn't afford bus fare, much less plane tickets?

A certain denomination has the policy that their missionaries should be compensated at the same level as their U.S. church pastors, and that no one who serves overseas should be called upon to live without comforts, conveniences and items of personal satisfaction which they might enjoy at home. So one missionary couple gets shipped overseas with two cars and a pony for their son to ride and enjoy. Imagine how that is perceived in a land where many native missions don't have one car for their entire staff of 100 missionaries, and desperately need horses to provide transportation to unreached tribes in the mountains, but have no money to buy them. Other toys missionaries take along include golf clubs, tennis rackets, video tapes, TV sets, VCRs, CD players, plastic Christmas trees and even elaborate toy train sets.

I learned first hand how one American missionary who was being supported at $75,000 a year in a tropical country dunned his supporting churches back home for thousands more "to buy special attachments for his air conditioners." He was also able to solicit additional funds to buy membership in the nearby country club so he "could have a ministry among the rich." All this in a third world country where average per capita income is about $600 per year. What kind of message does this "missionary" convey to the people of that land? Most rich people whom I have seen come to Christ are won by seeing the sacrifice of others who have chosen to be poor for Christ's sake.

One was lumber tycoon Frederick E. Weyerhaeuser of Minnesota who told me when I was a guest in his home almost 60 years ago that it was unlikely that he would have ever been won to Christ by any of the affluent people at the fashionable Presbyterian church he attended. Rather, his heart was opened by observing the sacrifice and zeal of a worker in a rescue mission who was saving homeless people off the streets of St. Paul.

Tom Phillips, while President of the multi-billion dollar Raytheon Corporation in Boston, was turned toward Christ in part by the testimony of Prem Pradhan, a practically penniless native missionary from Nepal. He went forward to confess Christ at a Billy Graham crusade soon after he had Prem in his home. My net worth wasn't much more than Prem's when I had the opportunity to be the first person to share the gospel with Charles Pitts, owner of the largest construction company in Canada. Shortly thereafter he also publicly professed his new-found faith at a Billy Graham crusade in Toronto, and went on to become an ardent witness for Christ.

I am convinced that missionaries who feel they have to appear wealthy in order to influence the upper classes are deceiving themselves. The Apostle Paul, like Peter, could say "Silver and gold have I none," yet win converts among the Epicureans on Mars Hill in Athens with a simple presentation of the gospel together with "a demonstration of the Spirit, and of power."

A missionary I knew several years ago could move an audience to tears with stories of need and suffering out there "on the mission field." After each speaking engagement he would receive a special "missionary offering" during which purses and wallets were emptied into the gift basket. In addition to this tax-free cash, he was able to generate sympathy for his "needs" sufficient to motivate certain members of a given church to make a special project of buying him a new car and shipping it "to the field." Soon after arrival overseas he would sell the car for triple what it cost in the USA, then fly back to America and itinerate again in another part of the country. Within two or three months he would have another new car and the scenario would be repeated.

I don't want to imply that a high percentage of American missionaries are like this car dealer, but there are many more than most churches realize. Also, I want to emphasize that there are many exceptions to the types of missionaries being discussed here. But they are just that: *exceptions*. While there are some who live simply and sacrificially, the majority of Americans and Canadians who work in poorer countries exhibit an image of wealth and power which contradicts the image of Christ portrayed in the New Testament.

Part of the problem, as I have said, is that we are not likely to survive if we try to live as do most residents of poorer countries. I remember a couple that went to the Philippines determined to "live like the nationals, limiting themselves to $60 per month total income." They rented a small two-room house with a sheet metal roof that kept out the monsoon rains but turned it into an oven on sunny days. They had no electricity or running water, hence no bathroom. There was a small outhouse so close by that the smell went all through the house. One luxury they enjoyed, as did few natives in the town, was that there were screens on the windows to keep out flies and mosquitoes (although many came in when doors were opened). They tried to home school their three small children, but were not able to do it in any systematic manner. They seemed to continually have some kind of sickness in the family. Nearly all their time was spent trying to survive: walking to the market daily to buy food and fuel, cooking over an open fire, carrying water from a nearby well, boiling it for drinking, washing clothes in the little tub they also used for washing their bodies behind the house after dark, continually swatting insects, and trying to sleep in the sweltering heat. The poor wife and mother went around in tears most of the time, crying continually. It was obvious that she was on the verge of, if not in the midst of, a nervous breakdown. Her husband was reluctant to leave her in order to "go out there and do missionary work."

So here's the dilemma. By trying to live on the same economic level as the "nationals," this American couple had no time or opportunity for "missionary work." But if they lived as traditional missionaries do (large house with electricity and running water, servants, cars, etc.) in order to have some free time that can be devoted to ministry or evangelism, their apparent wealth would nullify their witness. There is only one solution: go home where you belong and send your support money to an indigenous ministry whose missionaries can cope with the environment in which they have lived since childhood. They can do the work ten times more effectively than any American who comes from a totally different background.

Even in more developed areas American missionaries are often looked upon as hypocrites. A few years ago I was invited to speak at the annual missionary conference of an indigenous Baptist church in Puerto Rico. Never have I seen a more spontaneous reception of and agreement with the things I was teaching about the need for reformation in foreign missions. They had all seen it first hand.

While there I stayed in the home of a physician who was a member of the church. After we returned to his home one evening, my host invited his neighbor, also a physician, to come in for refreshments. The neighbor knew nothing of what I was teaching there. He did not attend that Baptist church. All he knew was that I was some kind of missionary from the USA. He politely asked if I would be willing to hear his evaluation of missionaries who had gone to Puerto Rico from major U.S. denominations. I told him to please speak his mind.

For the next hour he shared one observation after another of American denominational missionaries. His main objection was that so many of them never learned Spanish, chose to live near and belong to the country club, played golf or tennis in the mornings and swam in the afternoons, and attended parties or theaters in the evenings. Of course they went to local churches on Sunday mornings, and occasionally to a midweek meeting, but other than that there was very little religious activity that could be observed. The fact that these people were paid out of tax-exempt contributions to live this kind of life, especially when there is so much real need in the world, was a stumbling block to this neutral observer in Puerto Rico. I promised him that I would work toward bringing about a reformation in the way missionary work is done.

CHAPTER SEVEN

THE DEPENDENCY DILEMMA

During my many years as a born again Christian, one of my all-time favorite denominations has been the Christian and Missionary Alliance. After finding Christ in Miami I returned to my home town of Charlottesville in 1941 to enroll at the University of Virginia. The pastor of the Presbyterian church of which I was a member gave me books by Harry Emerson Fosdick and tried to destroy my faith in the Bible. He told me that I wasn't qualified to teach in the Sunday school because of my fundamentalist beliefs. As a new Christian I felt alone and rejected until one night when I heard the joyful sound of "Jesus Saves" coming from a big old house on a downtown street. Even though there was no sign outside to identify it, I walked right in and joined the song, of which I knew every word from memory. The little band of believers received me warmly and I soon learned it was a newly formed Christian and Missionary Alliance church. That congregation became my spiritual home for the next two years. I became so active there that the pastor, Rev. Kenneth Richardson, made me his associate pastor.

My only reason for leaving was due to the fact that World War II was going on and many pastors of rural Baptist churches had gone off to be military chaplains. Dr. Cecil Cook, pastor of University Baptist Church, was a longtime friend of my father and had known me from childhood. He invited me to join his church, be licensed to preach, and go out to minister every Sunday in some of those country churches that had no pastors. So I did. And that's how I became a part of the Southern Baptist Convention. But my heart was with that little Alliance fellowship, and I went to every meeting I could there whenever I was free.

While traveling with IVCF and YFC, I had the joy of preaching in dozens of Alliance churches around the country. Frequently I was asked to speak at Alliance missionary conventions where I would almost always quote one of my true heroes, A. B. Simpson (founder of the C&MA). During my nine months of graduate study at the University of Chicago, my spiritual home was the nearby Alliance church pastored by A.W. Tozer. I say all of this to emphasize that I have the warmest possible feelings in my heart for the many precious saints and missionaries who are also part of the greater Alliance family.

You can imagine my delight, therefore, when attending one of those big interdenominational missionary "consultations" many years ago I discovered that my assigned double occupancy roommate was Louis L. King, one of the truly great missionary statesmen of the C&MA. In my heart I thanked God for the opportunity to draw information from the rich storehouse of missiology residing in the heart and mind of this seasoned veteran of missionary experience. So I asked him many questions.

Of primary interest to me was the Bangkok Conference of 1955 which he called as area secretary of the Alliance in Asia. The purpose of the conference was to determine how to make "their" overseas churches indigenous, meaning (mainly) self-supporting. I don't recall saying one confrontational word to my dear brother in Christ. I wanted to learn from him. So I didn't tell him that my definition of "indigenous" was "native to the land." I couldn't see how a church started by foreigners and affiliated with their denomination could ever be considered indigenous unless, perhaps, it became completely independent from the foreign body and had no further association with it for many years.

The Bangkok Conference was attended, as I recall, by 17 native pastors of Alliance branch churches and about 35 C&MA foreign missionaries. I believe it is considered to be somewhat of a watershed in the development of Alliance missionary policy. At that time, Alliance churches in ten countries of Asia had about 52,000 members, and most of these churches received subsidies from the parent mission. Result: dependency.

Missionaries had gone out from America and set up institutional-type churches patterned after those at home. Each one was centered in a building with a paid pastor who conducted church "services" every Sunday. The pastor would have been educated by the mission and therefore was entitled to a stipend greater than the income of the mostly uneducated members of his church. Since most church members were pitifully poor, living on a barter system which afforded little or no cash income, they could ill afford to finance foreign-style church budgets. Also, the nearby presence of the apparently affluent (by Asian standards) foreign missionary undoubtedly caused poor believers to feel that the "rich foreigners" should pay necessary expenses for the institutions they had established.

Nevertheless, according to Dr. King, the Bangkok Conference was a triumph of indigenization. It was agreed that foreign subsidies would be gradually discontinued. Each local church would be on its own financially within five years. And most of them were, even though the weaning process was extremely painful. An excellent article about the Conference was published in the April 2001 issue of *Alliance life*. It states that "the Bangkok Conference in 1955 was like the epicenter of an earthquake." It quotes Dr. King as having been "left with many disturbing memories." The article goes on to say, *"There were many problems, many aching hearts," he [Dr. King] recalled years later. "Among church people, pastors and missionaries, not a few spiritual crises occurred. Some thought and even propagated that compliance with the Council-mandated requirement was a terrible setback . . . a certain wrecking of the work that had been built up at such sacrifice of human life and costly endeavor."*

A few missionaries had to be called home or forced "to find service elsewhere" and in bitterness spread damaging accusations against the Alliance. A number of indigenous pastors deserted to other missions willing to pay them. Congregations were lured to well-funded denominations all too eager to gather them into their fold.

I do not mention these things to in any way pass judgement on how the C&MA handled a difficult situation. On the contrary, I would rather congratulate Dr. King and his associates for their courage in reversing the traditional policies of their mission board. My point is to illustrate the problems which have arisen when U.S. missions have gone overseas and set up branch churches patterned after those at home.

In talking with Dr. King about these things, I sensed that he had never realized how we have followed the free enterprise business model in going overseas to set up affiliated branches of our denominations. I did not tell him of my close friendship with two Alliance pastors in Arabic countries. With deep concern and anguish of heart they had shared with me what a shock it was to them when they were told in 1956 that the subsidy they had been receiving would be cut back proportionally each year until it was eliminated altogether. They were totally unprepared for such a jolting turn of events.

Both were well-educated men with families who had been placed in their respective positions as upper class professionals. Each had been provided with a house and a church building with office, clerical help and an auditorium. But most of their parishioners were illiterate (or semi-literate) lower class peasants who were pitifully poor. Hardly any had jobs that provided regular cash income. It was extremely embarrassing, therefore, for these pastors to suddenly require their impoverished church members to contribute enough to maintain a church budget which was far beyond their means, particularly when the major portion of it was to pay the salary of their educated pastor. Hardly anyone in the church earned as much income as the pastor, so why should they contribute toward his comparatively high salary?

At this point I would like to mention that it appears to me (although I could be off the mark) that the C&MA policy of local churches being self-sustaining has been carried over in its application to missionary ministries as well. The foreign missions arm of the C&MA in the USA receives support internationally, but its leaders have appeared to me to adhere to a policy that mission boards, Bible institutes and other para-church ministries of C&MA associates in poorer countries should try to find all their support within the confines of their own countries. Why should we expect mission boards based in lands of poverty to adhere to restrictions which are not imposed on the parent mission in an industrialized country? Now let me give another example.

At the first of the IVCF "Urbana" missionary conventions (held in Toronto in1946) I conducted a workshop in which the star participant was a bright young fellow named David Howard. He went on to become president of the Student Foreign Missions Fellowship about three years later, while I served as Vice President. Almost 50 years later Dave and I shared in a consultation of evangelical ministries said to be involved in "the support of nationals." Now he was speaking as a missionary veteran, having served for many years as President of the Latin America Mission. He shared with us how in LAM "support of nationals" had become a problem. His experience was just the opposite of what we had found in Christian Aid, where sending financial help to indigenous mission boards has been a tremendous blessing. What's the difference in the two approaches?

Actually, it's easy to understand once you grasp the difference between "colonial" missions and indigenous missions. At that consultation Dave Howard shared how his mission was dealing with the dilemma of dependency created by their colonial methods of missionary operations. I explained how the problem never arises when we redirect our missionary giving to indigenous, rather than colonial, missions.

Dave told us how his mission, based in the USA, had sent well-educated North Americans to Latin America where they won converts and established churches, along with other institutions. Major emphasis was given to setting up schools to train "pastors" for their branch churches. Most of their church members were uneducated and pitifully poor.

Based on their cultural background and limited knowledge of ecclesiology, LAM missionaries set up churches patterned more or less after those thy had attended back home in the USA. First there had to be a building, then a paid, educated pastor, then musical instruments, hymnals, benches, and other things needed for conducting church "services" on Sundays. Even though most churches were in semi-rural areas, attendance tended to grow steadily because (so it was said) people other than devout Roman

Catholics had nothing else interesting to do on Sunday mornings.

With growth came need for larger facilities, Sunday school materials, church bulletins, clerical help and additional ministerial staff. All of which required quite a bit of money, so each church had to have an operations budget. Tithes and offerings from the congregations were never adequate to cover all expenses during the early years of setting up these congregations, so the parent mission provided a subsidy. In some cases the entire cost of setting up one of these new churches was borne by the parent mission. Most congregations tended to like this arrangement, and protested any suggestion that the subsidy might be reduced. So Dave Howard shared with us how his mission faced a big problem trying to eliminate the dependency which had been created by the colonial way of doing things.

There is also a second type of dependency which he didn't mention. All foreign missionaries sent out from the USA are totally dependent upon contributions given to their parent missions for their support. And this is as it should be. It provides local congregations and individual Christians with an opportunity to participate in the ministries of those they support. For Christian workers to be dependent upon their prayer partners for personal support and ministry expenses is surely a good thing. But a tragic mistake has been made by traditional missions when they have set up branch churches in poorer countries and made them dependent upon their foreign parents for the supply of their local church budgets.

By their very nature, local churches should be self-supporting. The reason so many thousands of them became dependent upon foreign subsidies is because the colonial missions made the unfortunate mistake of transplanting their social institution type churches into cultures that were radically different from their own. In an industrialized country like the USA it is not difficult to form a local church with its own building, equipment, paid clergy and other staff. But this pattern won't work in a poorer country without a foreign subsidy. Thus has developed the serious dilemma faced by the C&MA, LAM and a hundred other colonial missions of "how to make their branch churches indigenous." In other words, self-supporting. But a far more significant factor is the reality that the foreign style churches should never have been set up in poorer countries in the first place.

Faced with the problem of "making their branch churches indigenous," many colonial missions have vowed to phase out their subsidies, as did the C&MA and LAM. But there has been a serious flaw in their pronouncements. They are saying that affluent Christians in the industrialized countries shouldn't send any money at all to our fellow believers in poorer countries.

I could hardly believe it when I read an article entitled *Stop Sending Money* by Robertson McQuilkin in the March 1, 1999 issue of *Christianity Today*. He rightly pointed out the problems of dependency caused by colonial missions subsidizing their branch churches. He quotes Jerry Rankin of the International Mission Board, Southern Baptist Convention, as saying, *"One thing inevitably occurs when North Americans subsidize the work of churches and pastors on the mission field: potential growth is stalled because of a mind-set that it can't be done unless an over-seas benefactor provides the funds . . . . Jealousy often develops among the pastors and churches who don't receive assistance toward those who develop a pipeline of support from the United States. . . . In the long-term, support breeds resentment, especially if the support is not sustained indefinitely, because it creates a patronizing dependency."*

Then he goes on to comment, *"In other words, churches and church leaders that secure a financial pipeline to the United States soon become mired in an ecclesiastical welfare state, because the send-money approach, rather than strengthening the souls of national churches, keeps congregations from becoming self-govern-ing and self-supporting."*

Dr. McQuilkin and Jerry Rankin are certainly right in their comments regarding how the subsidy of branch churches by colo-nial missions has created dependency and caused their disciples to be more interested in money than in ministering. But they make a tragic mistake when they fail to make a distinction between subsi-dizing local churches and sharing our largess through other chan-nels with our fellow believers in lands of poverty.

At least 90% of what the New Testament says about the stew-ardship of money has to do with believers in more prosperous areas sharing their bounty with fellow saints in areas of poverty and persecution. In Acts 11:17-30 we are told that when a famine struck Judaea, believers in Antioch took up an offering to send relief to their brothers in Christ. Chapters eight and nine of II Corinthians both deal with the same subject, as does Romans 15:25-29 and other passages.

To teach that affluent Christians should not send financial help to our fellow believers who suffer from poverty and persecution is a denial of one of the most basic tenets of the Christian faith. True, this teaching is related to weaning branch churches away from dependency. But I believe that possibly another reason why traditional mission leaders are saying such things is because they want all missionary money for themselves. They don't want to share it with missionary ministries based in poorer countries.

The basic flaw in Dr. McQuilken's article in Christianity Today is that he makes no distinction between a local church and a mission board. Most local churches in America are self-supporting, as they should be in other countries. But there is no such thing as a self-supporting mission board, or Bible institute, or Scripture translation ministry or home for destitute children. All such para-church ministries are dependent upon the gifts of God's people for the continuation of their work.

One really ridiculous teaching of some traditional mission leaders is that ministries based in poorer countries should get all their support within their own countries. They are saying that none of it should come from the USA. Yet those same mission executives are busy raising support in Canada, Britain, Australia and other countries. It's really hypocritical for American mission leaders to say that ministries based in India should find all of their support there while the rich Americans are busy raising support in a dozen countries. "Yes," the hypocrites say, "it's okay for us to raise funds internationally, but you poor mission leaders in Africa and India shouldn't do it. You might become dependent on it." As if the American missions weren't dependent. Their works and workers are totally dependent on the contributions they collect, and nine out of ten collect part of it outside of America.

It's time to put an end to this nonsense. Yes, local churches should be self-sufficient, but mission boards must look to God in faith for the supply of their needs through the gifts of His people. And our God is no respecter of persons. He would be pleased to see members of His body in America sharing their abundance with His servants who live on a dollar a day in the poorest places on earth; more so, I believe, than giving it to some colonial mission to be applied toward the $60,000 annual salaries of their comparatively affluent missionaries, or their even more highly paid executives and administrators.

At this point let me repeat again my conviction that all local churches should be self-sufficient. I have visited hundreds of indigenous local assemblies (and know of thousands more) in the poorest places on earth that carry on effectively with no financial subsidy from outside their fellowship. All of us need to learn why so many thousands of indigenous churches are self-sufficient, while thousands of branch churches of colonial missions have been dependent on their parent bodies for financial subsidies.

They key to understanding this dilemma is to properly understand the word "indigenous." It means, essentially, that a church has taken root within a given culture without being transplanted from somewhere else. Colonial missions inevitably set up branch churches patterned after those in their own culture. That's why they are financially dependent. Truly indigenous churches are formed when believers within a given culture come together on their own and form a fellowship of faith. The most lively ones have been started by natives of a community who found Christ while away from home and returned to win their friends and relatives to the faith, and then formed them into church congregations.

Such local assemblies require no buildings, clergy or budgets. They begin as spiritual infants and then grow together to "the measure of the stature of the fullness of Christ" as described in Ephesians 4:12-16. Frequent visits by native missionaries and teachers help these bodies to grow toward spiritual maturity in Christ, but intrusion by rich foreigners from abroad will more than likely have a detrimental effect rather than a positive benefit.

The whole gamut of mission board finances needs a complete reformation. No less than 90% of foreign missions money donated by

American Christians is consumed by the costly overhead expenses of colonial missions, which do less than 10% of the actual work in "mission field" countries. The biggest item of overhead expense is the costly, outdated practice of sending Americans overseas. It would make much more sense if only 10% of all missionary offerings were given to traditional missions, and the remaining 90% was distributed to indigenous missions based in "mission field" countries.

Why? Because they do 90% of the work, and spend less than 10% of their income on overhead costs. Some American mission overhead items they avoid are plane tickets, language study, income tax, social security tax, medical insurance, foreign style houses with electricity and plumbing, special foods and furnishings, household servants, separate clothing for each season, personal automobiles, satellite phones, English language private schools for the missionaries' children and dozens more items which are not generally needed by native missionaries.

Yes, leaders of traditional missions say we should not share our wealth with indigenous ministries because of the bugaboo which they call "dependency." But we must remember that it goes back to things mentioned earlier about colonial missions thinking of their overseas branches as dependent children which must be weaned and "made self sufficient" by their rich parents. They act as though it never occurred to them that their overseas children might someday grow up to be equals with their parents, developing their own mission boards and parachurch ministries. These in turn should be encouraged to collect support funds internationally on an equal footing with the U.S. missions which do so.

We must examine this unbalanced reasoning more carefully in later chapters.

CHAPTER EIGHT

THE BODY OF CHRIST

Before He allowed all the foreign missionaries to be swept out of China, our God had prepared more effective apostles to replace them. Some had their roots in the colonial missionary enterprise. Others developed completely apart from foreign denominations or nondenominational foreign missions. They were truly indigenous in that their works were not started by or otherwise involved with any foreign ministries. In fact, many of them developed in spite of the foreign agencies because they were often severely criticized and bitterly opposed by the foreign evangelical establishment.

One major influence upon the indigenous ministries movement in China was Sung Siong-ceh (Christian name: John) who returned to China in 1927 after seven years in the USA. He earned a B.S. degree at Ohio Wesleyan College, and then took M.Sc. and Ph.D. degrees at Ohio State University in the field of chemistry. He graduated with highest honors and was inducted into the Phi Beta Kappa honor society. While thus away from home, primarily through reading the Word of God, Dr. Sung was anointed and transformed by the Spirit of Christ. He returned to China, not as a physicist or chemist but as a flaming messenger of the cross of Christ. He was known as "the father of 10,000 churches." I met numerous outstanding Christians in China (including John's younger brother) whose hearts had been touched and set on fire by this man of God.

Many such native Chinese leaders were raised up by the Spirit of God in the 20th century. My point is that wherever I went in China I met mature, outstanding Christians who were leaders of indigenous works which were quite separate from the churches associated with foreign missionaries. These apostles were leading diverse evangelistic ministries that were bringing tens of thousands of new believers into the kingdom of God. There was Wang Ming-tao in Beijing, Nee To-sheng (English name, Watchman, quoted in previous chapter) in Shanghai, Andrew Gih, Leland Wang, Calvin Chao, Timothy Tsao and many others.

While in Shanghai in 1949 I stayed in the massive building that served as headquarters for field operations of the China Inland Mission, and a temporary residence for missionaries in transit. To this day I cannot forget the warmth of love and fellowship that pervaded those premises. One anonymous and unknown saint would slip into my room every night and put a hot water bottle beneath the blankets at the foot of my bed. Although the building was as adequate as any hotel, it had no central heating. So to return at midnight in February from some preaching engagement and climb into bed in that unheated room would have been a rather dreary experience were it not for the cozy heat of that bottle at my feet. I was indeed grateful for the privilege of staying in such a wonderful place. It was a little bit of England transplanted into the midst of a human ant hill swarming with millions of people, many of them refugees who had fled from advancing Communist armies further north. I didn't know whether to feel thankful or guilty for such comparatively comfortable accommodations when so many Chinese were sleeping in the cold on streets outside.

It did seem paradoxical that the Communists used the CIM complex for their regional headquarters after they took over the city of Shanghai a few months later. At least that's what I heard but it's not the reason why I mention this incident. Rather, it is to quote something that was said at a meeting of missionaries at CIM head-quarters while I was there.

One goal of CIM was to push ever inward toward the interior, seeking to carry a witness for Christ where none had gone before. Accordingly, they had sent a missionary couple to a far distant city where there was no record of any foreign missionary having worked. But upon arrival they found a thriving, growing, praying church of 300 believers.

"How is this possible?" they asked. "No missionary has ever worked here."

"Dr. Sung was here," an elder replied. "Is he not a missionary?"

Yes, Sung Siong-ceh had been there for two weeks with nothing but his Bible and little knapsack in which he carried his earthly possessions. During the first week he had preached on the streets, won souls and discipled them. Then he sent them door to door to win others. During the second week he was preaching to crowds of up to 10,000 every night. Then he moved on to his next stop, leaving behind a solid congregation of born again Christians. What a contrast to churches started by foreign mission boards. I could name one that insisted on keeping two foreign ladies on hand for 50 years to "look after" a tiny church their missionaries had finally gotten started "after many years of patient endeavor."

All of which goes to illustrate the distorted concept held by colonial missions as to what an apostle (missionary) is. They would never say that John Sung was a "missionary." Since he was Chinese he could only be referred to as an "evangelist." During all the years the China Inland Mission worked in China, the official policy of the mission was that no person of Chinese ancestry could be admitted to their number or be recognized as a CIM missionary. Numerous other traditional missions had similar policies. Many years later the successor organization to CIM, Overseas Missionary Fellowship, finally did accept an Asian into the mission, and did so with considerable fanfare. Eventually many other traditional missions also changed their policies and accepted Asians as missionaries on an equal footing with those of European ancestry.

The true apostles (missionaries) which were most greatly used of God in China during the 20th century were primarily native Chinese, not self appointed foreign invaders who said God had "called" them there to work "cross-culturally."

Now, again, I don't want to imply that God never used any of us who went there from foreign countries. I saw the fruit of David Adeney's ministry in the lives of individuals. Likewise of David

Morken and Baker James Cauthen. And I sincerely believe that some Chinese were brought from eternal death to eternal life through my ministry while I was there. But I think the Holy Spirit worked, and the Word of God quickened, oftentimes regardless of the offensive aspects of our presence.

I remember once when Dave Morken and I were in Shanghai on a portable temporary platform preaching at an open air meeting, I became convicted within my heart about the contrast between our appearance and those who were listening. We were wearing worsted wool suits, dress shirts and ties. Our warm overcoats were laid beside us on empty chairs. Our shoes were polished leather. I couldn't help but notice the sharp creases in the legs of Dave's finely tailored trousers. The throng of men before us were all wearing dull, tan colored, often ragged cotton that looked like it hadn't been washed in weeks. Some had on two or three layers of the flimsy material to keep them warm as they shivered from the cold. Their shoes were tattered canvas. How could men so poor receive the gospel message from us when we appeared so rich?

Yes, one great weakness of foreign missionary enterprise in China was the fact that we who were comparatively rich were trying to represent our self-sacrificing Saviour to people who were pitifully poor. Another barrier was that we were thought to be spies working for the CIA. Then there was the offense of denominational and mission board expansionism which made our churches appear to be competitive businesses. But there was one still greater problem which, in retrospect, I think may have been the primary reason why our Lord wanted to clean out the whole foreign apparatus and start over in building His church in China.

That weakness was the anemic nature of the Christian faith and practice which we presented. I heard an Asian brother say politely, "I fear you Americans have been vaccinated with a mild form of Christianity, and it has made you immune to the real thing." In China, and other parts of Asia, I met native Christians who had an experience with God which I knew nothing about. And I met Bible teachers who had a much more mature understanding of the grace of God and the nature of His church than any teachers I had known in America.

As I said earlier, it was my privilege to know and learn from some of the greatest Bible teachers, theologians, pastors, evangelists and Christian leaders in all of the U.S. and Canada. During four years of constant travel with Youth for Christ and InterVarsity there were opportunities to meet and be mentored by outstanding preachers and teachers, as well as to audit classes in Bible institutes, Christian colleges and theological seminaries all over the continent. But after I had been among the young churches of Asia for a while, I began to see that the form of Christianity and church life with which I had so long associated was largely medieval tradition rather than the supernatural body of Christ revealed in the New Testament.

So, can it be that, like the farmer who plows under the stubble of the previous year so he can plant a new crop, our God wanted to phase out the traditions and practices which foreign mission boards had transplanted into China so He could start over with New Testament Christianity?

In our tradition the local church is usually a social institution with an official membership centered around a building where the congregation meets on Sunday mornings, with partial attendance at other meetings, usually Sunday and Wednesday evenings. All is under the direction of a "pastor" employed by the church or his mission and paid a salary. He orchestrates the meetings, commonly called church "services." Most of these "services" include the singing of hymns, accompanied by piano or organ (and other instruments in recent years), prayers, Scripture reading, "special music" by a soloist or choir, and always a "sermon" by the pastor or some visiting church dignitary. This pattern has been followed almost universally by the churches in North America which send missionaries overseas.

So, quite naturally, whenever any of us were successful in pulling together a congregation in China (or anywhere else in the world), we would transplant our pattern into a culture where it would appear totally foreign. We would want them to have a building with chairs or benches to sit on, a podium for the pulpit (sometimes split into two parts to accommodate the lectern) and a special place for the choir close to the organ or piano. Such facilities would cost a lot of money and as I said in the previous chapter, a major point of contention between foreign missionaries and their branch churches was who would pay the bill. Should it be the "rich foreigners?" Or would they lay this burden on the impoverished believers who made up the congregation.

Insistence on chairs or benches has often seemed weird in Asian cultures where everyone sits cross-legged on the floor at public gatherings. And musical instruments of European origin were out of place, as was the European music which the people were expected to use. When songs and hymns of foreign origin are translated into other languages, the words can sometimes be offensive. For example, the otherwise beautiful hymn by Isaac Watts, **Jesus Shall Reign**, has this verse in it: "From north to south the princes meet to pay their homage at His feet; while western empires own their Lord and savage tribes attend His word." Those "princes" who were continually sending their armies to war and killing other people didn't convey a very good image to the "savage tribes" who were often the victims of colonial subjugation imposed by "western empires."

One good way to gauge how our transplanted church traditions are perceived in other cultures is to invite foreign visitors from non-Christian backgrounds to visit our churches in America, and then ask for their frank evaluation. Almost universally the response I have received has been that our churches seem like theaters to those who have never attended a church "service" before. There is an auditorium where ushers show us to our seats and the stage is before us with master of ceremonies, musicians, and a structured program called the "order of service." The complaint I have heard most frequently is having to sit through a boring "lecture" (although some are less boring than others). The show starts at 11 and stops at 12 unless the lecture goes beyond 30 minutes. And instead of buying a ticket before you go in you are rather expected to pay up when plates are passed midway through the proceedings.

We take all these things for granted in our culture. It's the way churches have been ever since John Calvin formalized the Protestant church service in Switzerland in the 16th century. It never occurs to most of us to examine our practices in light of the New Testament to see if we might find there some other form of church life that would be more acceptable in Asia. Instead, we have routinely transplanted our cultural pattern all over the world.

In China before 1949 the focal point of human relationships was the family. Not just a married couple with children, but the extended family covering three or four generations and including uncles, aunts and cousins, all living in little huts within walking distance of each other. Then why shouldn't a local church be like a home, and a church meeting be simply a family gathering at which the Head (the Lord Jesus) was recognized as being "present in the midst" as He had promised? An organized "service" with a formal program conducted during a scheduled hour on Sunday morning would be ridiculous at a family gathering.

This contrast prompted native Christian leaders to search the Scriptures seeking guidance regarding "worship services." They found no directives as such, simply the mention of there being a "church in the house" of Philemon, and of Aquila and Priscilla, and of Aristobulus, and of Narcissus and many others who apparently had gatherings of believers in their homes. In Romans 16 the Apostle Paul seems to recognize half a dozen family style churches that apparently were gathering if different parts of Rome. Encouraged by these examples, hundreds (if not thousands) of Christian communities began to gather in homes all over China during the first half of the 20th century. They didn't have "worship services" in the traditional sense. Rather, they sang gospel songs which they had composed with tunes of familiar Chinese folk songs. Then they shared their respective burdens and victories and prayed for one another as they rejoiced together in happy fellowship. The only formal procedure conducted regularly at these get-togethers was when they would prayerfully remember our Lord's death in the breaking of bread and sharing of the cup. They also had a limited amount of ceremony at baptisms and weddings.

I heard many traditional missionaries bitterly criticize these "house churches" for various reasons, one being they didn't conform to the accepted pattern of what it meant to "go to church on Sunday morning." A few times I made the mistake of telling about Asian house groups while speaking in churches after my return to the USA. One pastor in New Orleans rebuked me publicly and would not permit me to speak again at the convention which I was attending at his church. That particular congregation looked upon meetings in homes as a possible source of divisions. As well they might be in our culture.

In America we are pre-programmed to want our meetings structured, to conduct activities on a schedule like news broadcasts or TV programs, and to have professionally trained personnel responsible to carry out assigned functions on each occasion. I have seen many would-be "new beginners" try to start house church movements in the U.S. and Canada, but few have been successful except in isolated cases. Well organized social-institution-type churches are indigenous to our culture and in many cases highly successful. But transplant them to China, let them be tested by the fires of Communist cultural revolution, and they will be burned up as wood, hay and stubble.

After the Communists took over, they insisted that everyone should work. Social institution type church congregations that paid salaries to "pastors" were reeducated to understand that their "pastors" were parasites who did not work (so said the Communists). So most pastors were rounded up and sent off to labor camps for re-indoctrination and job training, after which they were assigned to work at menial tasks which (it was supposed) would contribute to the industrialization of the country. Any who refused to go along were imprisoned or eliminated.

Professing to be believers, Communist missionaries joined many churches in order to take them over. From within they could proclaim, "Love your neighbor as yourself. How selfish it is of us Christians to have this fine building all to ourselves and not share it with others. It should be used for the benefit of all the people." So church buildings were converted to warehouses or granaries or other uses "for the benefit of all, not just the church members." Churches established by foreign missionaries were left with no buildings and no clergy. Then what could they do on Sunday morning? Without buildings or pastors most Baptists, Methodists, Lutherans, Presbyterians and other denominations couldn't hold church "services."

But the indigenous churches went full speed ahead. In fact they soon doubled after the Communist crack down because so many believers from foreign branches flowed into indigenous house churches after the foreign buildings were closed.

But more important than structure or pattern were the inadequate teachings of foreign denominations in China. So much tradition was combined with the truth that major aspects of Christian life and experience were sadly missing from the foreign missionary agenda. In all my experience with prominent Bible teachers in America, I never once heard an exposition of "charisma," the dynamic aspect of God's grace. Our traditions had blinded our spiritual eyes. I had to go to China to find Bible teachers who, coming out of backgrounds uncluttered by tradition, perceived the Biblical revelation of charisma when they first read it. (I also discovered teachers who were likewise mature in understanding charisma among the indigenous churches of India.)

Fortunately, I had courses in Greek for three years at the University of Virginia so I was able to discern by reading the New Testament in Greek what my Chinese brothers were teaching. God's grace is of two kinds. First, there is judicial grace: God's kindness to sinners. We deserve His righteous judgement, but He bore our sins in His own body upon the cross. So we can be acquitted of all guilt by His grace and declared innocent on the basis of His atonement. On this aspect of God's grace my American teachers were very clear, for which I will ever be thankful.

But most of them missed the scope of the second aspect of grace, that mighty power which God gives by measure to every true Christian (Ephesians 4:7). And the measure of grace we receive determines our place and function in a local body of believers. In Romans 12, First Corinthians 12 and Ephesians 4 the Apostle Paul describes the different graces which God gives to born gain believers in Christ. One has grace for teaching, another grace to be an evangelist, another an apostle, another a shepherd (pastor) of new believers and so on. The Greek word for these graces is *charisma*, or *charismata*.

Tragically, most English translations, following the lead of the Authorized (King James) Version, translate this word as "gift." I think that's because the translators of 1611, steeped in medieval tradition, knew next to nothing about the graces which God gives to individual Christians in a local body of believers. And succeeding translators likewise. Leave it up to our brothers in China and India to discern what should have been simple to see from Paul's epistles, but was lost beginning in the Fourth Century after the churches merged with the pagan religion of ancient Rome.

Thayer's lexicon had it right in 1886, but apparently the evangelical teachers of that day didn't act upon it because they lacked the experience in their own lives. And I would say that the main reason was due to virtually all the churches being locked in to the medieval clergy tradition. Anyway, here's what Thayer had to say: "In the technical Pauline sense charismata denote extraordinary powers, distinguishing certain Christians and enabling them to serve the church of Christ, the reception of which is due to the power of divine grace operating in their souls by the Holy Spirit." *Charisma* should never have been translated *gift*, because it is rather the spiritual grace that is given. Two other Greek words are used in the New Testament to denote the giving of a gift, including the gift of grace (charisma) by measure.

To understand the full meaning of this essential truth we must realize that our Lord was "full of grace" (John 1:14). Therefore He had all the graces. He was an apostle. He was a prophet. He was an evangelist. He had grace for teaching and for healing the sick. He had all the graces within His one body. And that body was the temple of God wherever He went (John 2:19-21), because God was living on earth in it. Then after His resurrection, ascension and exaltation, He multiplied Himself ten thousand times. He returned as a quickening spirit to live on earth again, not just within the body of each individual believer but also within corporate bodies, or local churches. When he poured out His Holy Spirit on the day of Pentecost, He appeared first as a supernatural fire burning in the midst of the 120 disciples who were gathered in an upper room. He thus signified that those "living stones" gathered in His name now constituted the temple of God on earth. That incident was a parallel to the occasion when God came as a supernatural fire into the temple which King Solomon had built in Jerusalem a thousand years earlier.

When tongues of fire then reached out and touched individual believers, God signified that each of their bodies was also His temple. This second truth has been well understood by most evangelicals since the Reformation. What we have missed is the corporate body being His temple also: God living on earth in a (corporate) body of humans. Our Lord was born in Bethlehem as an infant, then began to grow as He "increased in wisdom and stature and in favor with God and man." So also He was born within a body of believers in Ephesus, where in Him "all the building fitly framed together [grew] unto an holy temple in the Lord [as the Ephesian believers were] builded together for an habitation of God by the Spirit" (Ephesians 2:21-22).

The term "body of Christ" is used two ways in the New Testament. In a universal sense, the Apostle Paul uses it in Colossians 1:24 to include all true believers who thus constitute the whole church of God from Pentecost to our Lord's return. But more often it is used to refer to a body of believers in a given locality. Thus the corporate body of believers meeting together in Corinth are told, "Now ye are the body of Christ, and members in particular" (I Corinthians 12:27). As such, they were the temple of God in that locality (I Corinthians 3:16-17).

Just as our Lord's body was the temple of God while He was on the earth, so the corporate body of the believers in Corinth, and those in Ephesus, were God's temple, or Christ's body multiplied. True, these bodies weren't fully grown yet. But the Apostle promised those in Ephesus that as they continued to grow to maturity as a corporate body they would reach "the measure of the stature of the fullness of Christ" (Ephesians 4:13). In I Corinthians 12:12 he goes even further, saying that the body of Christ *is* Christ in a given locality. It is God living on earth in a body of humans. To be *in* Christ is to be part of a corporate body of believers.

With our emphasis on individual salvation in America, and the segregation and privacy of individual families, it is difficult for us to comprehend the concept of a corporate body of believers as presented in Paul's epistles. I think that's why our churches have largely missed the meaning of charisma. Within a local body our Lord gives to one member grace for teaching, another grace for evangelism, another grace for shepherding new believers, another grace for healing the sick, and so on. As the body grows to maturity, all combined can become the equivalent of what our Lord was when He walked in Galilee and Judaea. Any miracle you read about in the Book of Acts, I have seen duplicated among the indigenous churches of Asia, including the raising of the dead. Our Lord walks this earth again in ten thousand replicas of His body.

In Romans 12 the Apostle explained how each of us has a different measure of grace, and that within the local body we should exercise the particular grace that we have received. In a congregation where all are doing this, there would be no place or purpose for an ordained minister. Could that be another reason why our Lord allowed all ordained ministers to be removed from the scene in China?

I am not recommending that we try to change the theater style churches which we have in our culture. In each country God's people tend to form the types of churches that fit their society. With our private homes and roads and automobiles and on-time work schedules we have developed churches that suit our manner of life. We can drive 30 miles to a Sunday morning service and know we'll be home for dinner by 1 p.m. What I am saying is that when we try to transplant our types of churches into other cultures they are not likely to take root, grow or spread. The Bible was written in Asia, and Asian culture has changed little since that time. That's one reason why churches which follow the Biblical pattern are much more likely to permeate Asian society.

In saying these things, I don't want to suggest or imply that our Lord doesn't give grace by measure to individual believers in America. He surely does. The problem is that in our structured churches we fail to merge together as a corporate body which can grow to the measure of the stature and fullness of Christ and become the equivalent of His earthly person within a given community. And the positions held by educated clergy suppress opportunity for the exercise of various graces which God has given to other members of the local body.

Also, two systems of doctrine held by various church groups hinder the growth of a given local body of believers to where they jointly become Christ in that locality. One system is Pentecostalism, and the other is the "not for today" heresy taught in so many Bible institutes and seminaries, widely held by both evangelicals and fundamentalists. Let me mention the latter system first.

Professing to "rightly divide the word of truth" many thousands of Bible teachers in our culture have worked out a system by which we accept or interpret God's Word within the framework of our own limited experience. We don't see instantaneous, miraculous healings of the sick such as we read about in Acts, so we say, "Those are not for today." We don't see God supernaturally revealing hidden, secret sins in the lives of our church members, so we say, "Prophets are not for today." We don't hear apostles testifying supernaturally to strangers in their own languages (languages unknown to the apostles), so we say, "tongues are not for today." The rationalistic twisting of Scripture (especially of Paul's epistles) by fundamentalists and evangelicals to make it conform to our own limited experience is sometimes as obvious as Biblical criticism by liberals.

Pentecostalism is somewhat different. As the movement began in the early 20th century, many zealous Christians realized that God still gives grace and graces to believers, but few comprehended how charisma should contribute to the upbuilding of a local body of believers. Thus when someone received "charisma for healing the sick" as promised in I Corinthians 12:9 he or she was often tempted to exploit it to draw crowds, gain fame, and, sadly, to raise money. Pentecostalism came on the scene in a culture of theater-style churches, and adapted itself within that pattern. Most failed to comprehend how each member was given a specific measure of grace for the upbuilding of the body of Christ in a local community. And that only as the body grew to maturity would it be equivalent to what our Lord was on earth in the days of His flesh. So these babes in Christ immediately wanted to see miraculous signs and wonders, ignoring the fact that our Lord didn't start healing the sick until He was 30 years old, fully mature and able to handle the circumstances involved.

Pentecostals in general missed two other important things as well. Not understanding the nature of Christ as a local body of believers, with each one contributing the grace with which God had endowed him, many were taught that every believer should seek every grace. In I Corinthians 12:27-30, the Apostle Paul clearly states that one believer has one grace and another has another grace and so on until all together become equivalent to Christ in that locality. But many Pentecostals insisted that every disciple should "speak with tongues," and then seek all the other "gifts" as well. They generally failed to comprehend the concept of the body in I Corinthians 12:17-19: "If the whole body were an eye, where were the hearing? If the whole were hearing, where were the smelling? But now hath God set the members every one of them in the body, as it hath pleased Him. If they were all one member, where were the body?"

So when Pentecostals extended their denominations to other countries, they established branch churches not unlike those of other traditional missions, except that they had an emphasis on seeing outward manifestations of God's power, primarily "speaking in tongues" and the healing of the sick. And every church was likely to be run almost entirely by one "pastor" who did everything. Few functioned as corporate bodies.

After I returned to the USA from Asia and began a ministry among overseas students, I would usually speak in a different church every Sunday, and frequently on days in between. Often I would tell of my experiences in Asia, such as seeing more than 50 "incurables" instantaneously and miraculously healed of many different types of diseases during a three day prayer conference in Korea. Independent Baptists and other "not for today" rationalists would be very upset by such divisive reports. They didn't appreciate having their church members confused by illustrations of how God was working today as He did in the earliest churches. But Pentecostals would shout halelujah until they asked, "And did they speak with tongues?" When I replied, "Only the Korean tongue," they, too, were upset. Such acts of God were not supposed to happen apart from their system of teaching.

Once when Billy Graham was conducting a crusade in our nation's capital, I participated in a time of fellowship and prayer with a group of Pentecostals. During our conversation, one brother remarked, "You know, Billy Graham is such a wonderful fellow; it's too bad he's not charismatic." That gave me a chance to share what *charisma* really is, as I told that group how our Lord had given Billy Graham a measure of grace greater than all of ours put together. It was the *charisma* of God poured out within him that endowed him to be a powerful evangelist. Without that special grace he would be just another preacher.

To that my Baptist friends would likely say amen, just so long as I didn't quote I Corinthians 12:9 which says that our Saviour also gives *charisma* for healing the sick to other of His servants. Or Romans 12:6 which says He also gives grace for prophecy to reveal secret sins within a local church body.

The point of all this is that because of our traditions we in America and other populations of mainly European ancestry have failed to comprehend what our Lord wants to do among all the nations of the world. It is to build His temple, His habitation, His spiritual house, within bodies of believers among whom He can live and move and have His being. And who will thus corporately bear witness to His living presence within their respective communities. But many of our brothers in Asia and certain other parts of the world have understood these things. So I think it would be much better for the cause of Christ if we would withdraw from the scene overseas, as our Lord caused us to be forcibly withdrawn from China, so He can complete His eternal purpose to have a witness for Himself, a people for His name, among every tongue, tribe and nation.

Now let me tell you what's been happening in China.

CHAPTER NINE

THE MOVE OF GOD IN CHINA

Soon after leaving China I began to receive information from numerous sources about what was happening among the churches there. Some news came from unexpected places. After speaking on a Christian radio station broadcast I received a phone call from a listener who urged me to visit him in the nearby veterans hospital where he was recovering from wounds received during the Korean war. So I went to see him.

His story confirmed my confidence that Christian faith was alive and well in Communist China. He was badly wounded and left for dead when Chinese forces overran American positions in the far northern part of Korea. But when they saw he was still alive, Chinese military personnel picked him up and sent him across the Yalu river to a primitive prison hospital in Manchuria. Among his personal effects which were laid out on a crude box beside his bunk was a pocket New Testament which he had received in a distribution to the troops a few weeks earlier. But he had never read it.

A Chinese physician in Communist army uniform attended him. This doctor, who could speak English very well, asked the prisoner how much he knew about what was in the Testament. He then proceeded to go through it with his patient to show him the way of salvation, and thus led him to Christ. During several months in that hospital, the Chinese doctor was able to guide his new disciple into an understanding of spiritual life within a body of believers that he probably would not have learned in America in a hundred years. In fact, he told me that the reason he called me was that I was the first radio preacher he had heard who seemed to understand how God gives grace by measure to every believer, and that the measure of grace we receive determines our role within the body of Christ in our locality. Now his major problem was where to find a group of believers that might grow together with him "unto the measure of the stature of the fullness of Christ." Thousands of them were meeting together in China, (so the doctor had told him) but where could he find one in America?

As I mentioned earlier, after I returned to the USA I started, in 1953, International Students, Inc., a pioneer foreign missionary ministry to reach visitors from closed lands with the gospel of Christ so they could return to their homelands as His ambassadors. Our initial headquarters was located on Connecticut Avenue in Washington. One night while working late I went across the street to a fast food restaurant to recharge my physical energy. With tray in hand I looked for a place to sit, and chose a table where a very large man was reading a book with his coffee. It looked like a Bible, and upon closer examination I discovered that's what it was. I introduced myself and learned that his name was Soderbaum (after 47 years I can't remember his first name), and that he was passing through D.C. on his way from China to Sweden. As I silently gave thanks for my snack I also thanked my Lord for leading me to a potentially interesting contact. Little did I realize that I had just come upon one of the greatest gold mines of missiological information that I would ever discover. I met with him almost daily for over a month.

It turned out that my new friend was born in China of missionary parents who had gone out from Sweden with the original Scandinavian Alliance Mission. That's the one which now has its headquarters in the evangelical mecca of Wheaton, near Chicago, and is known as The Evangelical Alliance Mission or TEAM.

While growing up on a mission compound in China, Soderbaum was not particularly challenged by Christianity as he came to know it. He sat through boring church services and recognized that those in China were carbon copies of Sunday church services he had attended back in Sweden. He did realize, however, that the free churches his parents attended had more life than those affiliated with the official state church of Sweden. He observed that few Chinese were at all interested in being identified with the foreign colony in their midst. His parents and their associates were able to pull a few congregations together, but only after many years of effort. They did it mainly by picking up destitute children and raising them as Christians. By the time enough of them reached adulthood they could form a church congregation and conduct church services on Sunday mornings under the direction of a minister educated in mission schools.

Growing up as part of the foreign colony in China, Soderbaum became tri-lingual. He was fluent in Swedish, Chinese and English. He was there when "liberation" (as the Communists called it) took place in 1949, and arranged to stay on in China as a representative of the United Nations. He served as an administrator for what became known as UNICEF, handling relief work and related activities. Since he held a Swedish passport he was not looked upon as an enemy when China went to war with the U.S. and its allies in Korea. Soderbaum considered himself to be an evangelical Christian and continued to practice his faith as he understood it.

Then came a new revelation. Three or four years after "liberation" Soderbaum witnessed something that he never dreamed he would see on this earth in all his life. It seemed as though he was transported back in time to the days of the New Testament, and that he was living through events he had read about in the Book of Acts. Indigenous churches moved into the area where he was located in China and he saw "the real thing" in action for the first time in his Christian life. I took extensive notes during our sessions together, and from these notes I want to tell you how our Lord has been building His church in China during the past 50 years.

New churches were formed by migration. When the number of believers grew to more than 50, or even 100, within a particular community, a group of them would sell their few possessions and move to a new location where Christ was not yet incarnate within a local body. There they would find jobs, open shops, or work on farms to support themselves while giving birth to the body of Christ in that community. Each morning at daybreak they would meet together for prayer, praise and intercession. In the evenings they would go house to house, door to door, sharing Christ with neighbors. Some with grace for prophecy would reveal hidden sins in the lives of people they were evangelizing, as our Lord did with the woman at the well in Samaria. When He "told her all things that ever (she) did," her response was, "Sir, I perceive that you are a prophet" (John 4:19). When the secrets of the hearts are thus revealed, people will say, "God is in you of a truth" (I Corinthians 14:25).

Within almost every group of believers who migrated would be some who had charisma for healing the sick, as God promised in I Corinthians 12:9. So the healing of the sick was a major part of our Lord's ministry through each new body in China, as it was through His single body when He was upon the earth. Many Christians in America are afraid of supernatural healings because we associate them with professional healers who rent auditoriums and advertise healing crusades to draw crowds and raise money. These American preachers seldom have healings apart from their big meetings. In China those with charisma for healing go to where the sick are, usually in their homes, and pray for them. And God answers prayer. Even Communist bureaucrats would ask prayer for sick relatives when word spread that God had raised up an incurable in the neighborhood. And as they saw answers to prayer, many turned to the Lord.

Every new church is born in an atmosphere of fervent evangelism. Few Chinese have a sense of privacy as Americans do. Almost every road, street, lane and path has people in it all the time during daylight hours. Rather than sit in their little houses the people are more likely to be outside. Hardly any had home telephones at that time so no one would telephone ahead before calling out a greeting at someone's home. Most Christians are in constant communication with other people all the time, wherever they go. That's how the gospel spreads. And all kinds of sick and afflicted people may be found in every community. When the word gets out that people are being miraculously healed when Christians pray for them, many will bring family members to the Christians for prayer, or ask the Christians to come to their homes and pray for the sick.

The first time I saw God heal numerous incurables in one prayer meeting in Asia, I could not believe what I was seeing. Having worn out several Scofield Bibles as a good dispensationalist, I thought such things were only for the early church, and that God didn't do it any more. But when I saw these miracles happen before my eyes, I realized that my "not for today" theology was seriously un-Biblical. It was based upon my own limited experience, as was the case also with my teachers.

Christians in China have suffered great persecution from their Communist rulers during the past 55 years, but today multiplied thousands of Communist overlords attend Christian meetings. Many turned to faith in Christ as a result of answered prayer for physical healing, either in their own bodies or among members of their families. One of the largest Bible institutes supported by Christian Aid in China today was started by a man who formerly was the top Communist party official in his province. He was converted by a supernatural revelation from the Lord following the miraculous healing of his wife.

The spread of New Testament Christianity in China has been on a scale unparalleled in all of history. After 150 years of foreign missionary activity there, we estimated in 1949 that perhaps a million professing Christians could be found in all of China. And that number was cut in half by the fires of persecution. The wood, hay and stubble was burned up as our Lord allowed the churches to be purified and refined. Then, out of the ashes, the gold, silver and precious stones that remained have multiplied above all we could ask or think. Some estimate that the number of evangelical Christians in China today exceeds 60 million.

Of course not all are still pure after 50 years. Communist bureaucrats set up state control of the organized churches that survived their original purge. They tried to get house churches to register with the government so they could be regulated and controlled. Some agreed but most refused. And erroneous teachings have arisen as might be expected among millions of believers with no centralized authority to give guidance. Still, the growth of indigenous churches in China, and the amazing purity of their teachings and practice, has been a miraculous work of the Holy Spirit that is probably without precedent anywhere else in the world.

During the past 12 years Christian Aid Mission has been sending two Chinese Christians all over their native land to contact and evaluate house churches in every province. What they have found is truly astounding, beyond our wildest expectations.

As the number of believers begins to multiply in a given community, and they come together for daybreak prayer meetings, some have a hard time getting there because they may have to walk (very few Chinese Christians own cars) for 30 minutes each way. So others tell them, "You are walking too far, bypassing too many unsaved people. You should start a new church in your house, or in your neighborhood." And so they do.

Or perhaps a local church will grow so large that no building can be found where all can meet together (meetings are often held in factories or warehouses). That's when a select group leaves together, migrating to another town where they meet together to form a new body. Then when that body grows too large they divide again and some move on to a new location to begin anew. This is one way the churches have multiplied in what may prove to be the largest pioneer missionary expansion in history.

It is completely different from the traditional concept of sending in one or two foreign couples to set up a "mission station" where they might be looked upon as spies sent by the CIA or other subversive agency. What God has shown us in China is yet another factor that has caused me to conclude that it would be far better for the cause of Christ if all colonial type missionaries were withdrawn from every "mission field" country, and our vast financial resources were used instead to strengthen and support indigenous ministries in poorer cultures without colonizing them.

A really significant aspect of at least a million churches in China is that most have no clergy and almost none are organized into denominations. A church is like a home, and a church meeting like a family gathering. Meetings don't need to be scheduled like the Sunday morning ritual originally imposed by colonial missionaries. They take place anywhere, and at any time. Perhaps when new believers arrive in the community from some other place. Or when some member of the "family" is going away. Or a gifted teacher passes through. Or some brother comes along who has special grace and power for healing the sick. Or in times of emergency due to persecution or natural disasters. Or just to get together on a weekend or a holiday for a good time of fellowship.

To a large extent, the great explosion in the number of Christians in China was unwittingly brought about by the Communist revolution, cruel and ruthless though it may have been.

Most Chinese resisted Christianization by foreigners before 1949 because of family loyalty. Children obeyed and respected their parents. Adults honored and esteemed their ancestors. To become Christians would be showing disrespect for family traditions and would dishonor the memory of their ancestors. Solid families were not about to abandon their heritage and join a foreign religion.

The Communists changed all that. Marxism (or rather, Maoism) spread like a new religion. And one major factor of their revolution was to break up families. Many children were separated from their families and turned against their own parents. Often they were called upon to accuse their parents of being capitalist sympathizers, or worse. So a whole generation grew up with little or no respect for their ancestors or family traditions. But most became disillusioned when the utopian society promised by Mao failed to materialize. And thus their minds were open to the spiritual revolution offered by the Christian movement when it came along. All of which leads me to believe that God in His sovereignty knew what was coming in China, and prepared the way for building His church by allowing foreign missionaries and denominations to be removed from the scene.

God knew also that family loyalty was the key element of Chinese society. When ties within biological families were broken up by the Maoist revolution, it left a sociological vacuum among the youth of a rising generation. For millions of young people, that void was filled by the spread of house churches all over China. Reports I have received out of China during the past 50 years indicate that in many communities a majority of those involved within the churches are under 30 years of age. And in thousands of local fellowships, the bond among believers is a replica of the natural family bond that previously existed among blood relatives.

Family members take one another for granted. They enter one another's homes without knocking, or previous arrangement. They know they are welcome to eat with other believers any time they happen to be in their houses at meal time. They are welcome to sleep on the floor with fellow Christians anywhere they go, because all believers are one family in Christ. Thus if a believer has relocated to a new community where he is alone in the Lord, other believers will follow to his community and stay with him (until they find their own housing) to form a new body of Christians in that neighborhood. The fact that few Chinese have cars and that most travel by foot or bicycle contributes to the growth and spread of the churches from town to town and village to village. And the family ties of those who have become spiritual relatives by baptism into Christ are stronger and deeper than were the bonds of blood relatives in previous generations. There is much less quarreling and jealousy.

Before 1949 numerous exclusively Christian communities existed in isolated areas of China. Following the example of the Jerusalem church described in Acts 4:32-35 they had all things in common. Some of these Christian communes grew to about 5000 people. I heard reports that when the Communists discovered them some Party organizers commented that the Christian communes had already achieved locally what the Communists hoped to accomplish within 100 years. In fact, it has been suggested that the disastrous commune system imposed by force on millions of people was an attempt to duplicate what the Christians had already accomplished in several locations. But it didn't take long for the Maoists to discover that they could never accomplish by force among sinful men and women what the Spirit of God had wrought among His children who were baptized with His love and regenerated by His power.

After the Christian communes were broken up, scattered believers who had lived as the family of God within isolated conclaves carried that same loving bond into neighborhood fellowships of believers among the house churches. Although they no longer practiced communal living, almost all continued to experience the marvelous family bond that is known only to those who are in Christ.

House churches are kept purposely small so that within a local body all will know one another intimately. They can meet anywhere. Most homes are small and often have no furniture. But usually about 20 or 30 people can sit together on the floor of the largest room. If the group grows beyond the capacity of the largest available home, they must find another place. Hundreds of churches meet outside in a courtyard of other suitable enclosure, even in cold weather. Others meet in sheds or warehouses or even in limestone caverns. When they come together there is almost always singing from Scripture. The Chinese languages have musical tones, and many read aloud in a sing-song way. Thus Chinese Christians don't need hymn books. They simply sing a great chapter of the Bible. And because Bibles have been in short supply for 50 years, many Christians have memorized numerous chapters, both for their own understanding and also for singing unto the Lord.

At Christian family gatherings in China those who bear heavy burdens share them with the body, and they not only pray for solutions to their problems but also those present are moved to find ways and means to help lift the burdens of others. So no one bears his burden alone. If strangers come in, they are welcomed in love. Should one be a spy sent by the bureaucrats, a prophet may reveal his presence and bring into the open other secrets of his heart. Many Communists have been brought to Christ through the supernatural revelations of believers who have grace for prophecy. And local churches are kept free from secret sins as prophets reveal the hidden things of private lives, just as Peter did with Ananias and Sapphira (Acts 5:1-9).

On special occasions, large numbers of believers from within a given area may come together, with up to 2000 in attendance. One of the big limestone caverns serves as one such conference center. But usually these convocations are held out of doors in fair weather.

How long the resurgence of church growth in China will last, no one knows. As we learn from history, spiritual life in the early churches was destroyed by success in the Fourth Century. Two hundred years of persecution contributed to growth more than holding it back. But coming into favor with the Roman government destroyed the spiritual nature of European churches for 1200 years. We must pray that the same pattern will not develop in China.

From the very beginning the Communist authorities wanted to discredit the influence of colonial missionaries in China. They pointed out that the denominational apparatus with theater style church buildings imposed by foreign agencies had to be propped up by financial subsidies provided by the "rich foreigners." In order to continue, the bureaucrats said, the churches must be "self supporting." Secondly, said the government, Chinese churches may no longer be governed from afar by colonial hierarchies in foreign countries. Henceforth, all Chinese churches must be "self governing." Thirdly, no foreign agents will again be allowed to propagate their religions in China. From then on, all Chinese churches that wished to continue were required to register with the government and be "self propagating."

Under these terms, the Communist overlords allowed certain institutional type churches to remain in existence and a government agency was set up to monitor them. These registered churches were designated as part of a "Three Self" arrangement sanctioned by the government. They conducted "worship services" similar to those introduced originally by foreign missionaries. Some congregations were allowed to use church buildings which had been built by foreign mission groups. Most "pastors" were men who had been screened, trained and appointed by the "Three Self" agency of the government.

In the earlier years of Communist control, the house churches exploded quite apart from the institutionalized "Three Self" churches. Pastors appointed by government agents tended to be liberal rather than evangelical. Theological seminaries were gradually reopened with government sanction, but these also tended to be more liberal than evangelical. However, in recent years hundreds of young scholars coming out of the house church movement have begun to attend registered churches and some have attended seminaries and remained evangelical. The result has been that many pastors of registered churches are now born again, Bible believing evangelicals who are turning those bodies into evangelical social institution churches such as may be found throughout the free world. Where this will lead remains to be seen.

Scores of large churches in various parts of China today have big auditoriums with from 1000 to 2000 believers in attendance every Sunday. Most are registered with the government but some are not. A few have very evangelical Bible institutes active within the church facilities with up to 200 students enrolled with no control by "Three Self" agents. As of the year 2004, through the staff of Christian Aid Mission, I have had personal involvement with 116 mostly unregistered Bible schools and seminaries that have a combined total of nearly 10,000 trainees enrolled fulltime, and 30,000 more in short term and part time study. Already they have sent out over 40,000 missionaries and gospel workers to plant new churches and start new Bible schools in every province of China, including Tibet. Had foreign missionaries remained in China, and if the Communists had not taken over the country, there is little likelihood that Christian faith would ever have spread there to the extent we see today.

We must pray that rapid growth and increasing cooperation with government supervisors will not compromise the building of our Lord's house in China. Many towns and villages are still without a Christian witness, and many thousands of pioneer apostles are committed to reaching them. Those who do not register with the government still face possible persecution, and they need God's guidance as to what they should do.

Meanwhile, let's consider what happened when communism collapsed in the USSR.

CHAPTER TEN

THE RIDICULOUS RUSH
TO RUSSIA

As World War II came to an end in 1945, evangelical and fundamentalist Christians in America began to learn some inside details about the terrible repression of human rights and religious freedom that had been taking place in the Soviet Union. And during the cold war decades that followed, it was generally presumed by many that the torch of Christian witness had been all but extinguished in Russia and its Communist satellites. This attitude was magnified by prominent exponents of Biblical prophecy who (incorrectly, I believe) warned of an impending invasion of the newly formed state of Israel by hordes of Russian Cossacks on horseback.

Very few within the evangelical community had any idea of the actual strength and numbers of Bible believing Christians in Soviet lands. A notable exception was Oswald J. Smith, pastor of the historic Peoples Church in Toronto.

I first met Dr. Smith at a big convention of Youth for Christ held at Winona Lake, Indiana in 1946. Torrey Johnson, President of YFC, prepared us for his coming with keen anticipation. Very few men I ever knew had as great a concern for world evangelism as Torrey did, and I have always been thankful for the positive influence he had in my life. After a stirring message by Billy Graham halfway through the convention, Torrey inspired us even further by saying, "You ain't seen nothing yet; wait 'til you hear O.J. Smith tomorrow night!"

When the time came for Torrey to introduce this man of God, he told us how Peoples Church gave more support to foreign missionaries than any other church in the world, and how its pastor had traveled the globe preaching the gospel on every continent. In true humility Torrey said he didn't feel that any of us upstarts in the YFC movement were worthy to wipe the dust from the shoes of this veteran missionary evangelist who had made such an impact for the kingdom of God. In my heart I said, "This is a man I want to know."

And there began a long and endearing friendship which continued for the remainder of Dr. Smith's life on earth. He became very interested in my ministry, invited me to preach at Peoples Church from time to time, visited as a guest in my home, and served on the Board of Advisers of International Students, Inc. from its inception. We frequently shared the pulpit as main speakers at missionary conferences around the country.

So, what's my point? Dr. Smith told me that in all of his experience, and in all of his travels, the greatest meetings he ever had anywhere in the world, and the greatest response he had ever seen to his messages, were in Russia. He had ministered there frequently during the 1920s and 1930s, and told me how Russian believers were the most fervent, zealous, enthusiastic Christians that he had ever seen in his half century of public ministry.

And the fires of persecution did not consume those precious saints during all the decades of Communist oppression. Their numbers continued to grow and multiply by hundreds of thousands, not only in Russia but also in Ukraine, Latvia, Lithuania, Estonia and other Soviet "republics." Refined as gold tried in the fire, they matured into some of the strongest Christians on earth.

In fact, repression by Communist rulers served to bring thousands of Russian evangelicals to a greater maturity in the faith than they had ever known before. Deprived of traditional dependence upon buildings and paid clergy, and the lifeless formality of church "services," they began to experience life in the Spirit as members of the body of Christ in their respective neighborhoods or apartment buildings.

Around 1970 a technical expert who was also a fervent believer in Christ was sent to Washington to attend a convention as part of an official Soviet delegation. Through a miracle of God's providence he made contact with me and came as a dinner guest to my home. We had many valuable hours together, and on one free night he attended a gathering of believers with me and gave his testimony. But for me the most important thing he did was to tell me what was really going on among evangelicals in Russia, much of which I published in the newsletters of Christian Aid and also in an article in the March, 1973 issue of *Christian Life* magazine.

Following World War II government bureaucrats gradually assumed control of traditional churches in Russia, requiring them to register and gain permits if they wished to continue. A Communist agent would attend every public "service" of the churches that owned buildings, and file reports on what took place. Gradually, the social institution churches withered away, except for a few that the Communists allowed to continue, possibly for their propaganda value in foreign relations.

But the churches did not die. Instead they continued to grow in numbers and in spiritual graces. What died were medieval traditions that have no basis in the Word of God. I am not saying that these traditions lacked spiritual value. Only that church buildings, paid clergy, Sunday services, Sunday schools, denominations and various forms of ecclesiastical hierarchy are not mentioned in the New Testament. Instead, true believers in Russia began to be joined together as the family of God, as they were in China.

Although the Communists gradually snuffed out most church "services," they left open a replacement type of gathering that in the end proved to make a greater contribution to the spiritual life of believers than had the ritual of attending "Sunday services." A big part of every culture in Soviet lands was for various groups to get together for parties. The most popular ones in Russia were drinking parties where the vodka flowed freely to temporarily enliven the atmosphere for song and dance. For born again Christians, lively parties (without the vodka) replaced dead church services, and true religious revival was the lasting result.

They had all kinds of parties on weekends, holidays and often long into the night on normal weekdays. And no Communist spies were ever invited. After all, most parties were private affairs, even within Soviet society. Any group was free to throw a party any time they wanted. There were birthday parties, engagement parties, wedding parties, newborn baby parties, welcome-the-visitor parties, going away parties, anniversary parties, job promotion parties, even funeral parties.

At these get-togethers the believers would sing gospel songs, quote Scripture, give testimonies, pray for one another, and receive teaching from God's Word. One amazing thing about them was that hosts and hostesses replaced traditional "pastors" who had been in charge of formalized church services in previous years. Now anyone who threw a party could lead their guests in praise and fellowship, even in more serious moments of baptisms in bathtubs or sharing a loaf and a cup to remember our Lord's broken body and precious blood shed for our sins.

Hundreds of thousands, probably millions, of zealous Christians kept the faith alive in Russia during the dark days of Communist rule. Two Ukranian missionaries, Slavik Radchuk and Sergei Sharapa, traveled over 30,000 miles through 12 republics in 1984 visiting tens of thousands of believers in hundreds of cities and towns from Moscow to Vladivostok, and from northern Siberia to southern Uzbekistan. Everywhere they went they found eager disciples of the Lord who were holding forth the Word of life in spite of dungeon, fire and sword. Twelve years later Christian Aid would send Slavik on a repeat journey and in every place he found that the faithful had increased in numbers —in Tashkent, capital of Uzbekistan, from about 35 to around 3500. By 2004 this group had grown to more than 50,000 including associated assemblies in nearly 100 nearby locations.

Then came the collapse of the Soviet empire around 1990. Almost overnight a great multitude of evangelical believers could come out of hiding and openly proclaim the gospel throughout the entire country – or what soon became many countries as the various republics gained their independence. One marvelous aspect of this transformation was that the Soviet rulers had required all schools to use the Russian language as their medium for teaching. So 300 million unreached people could now be evangelized with the use of that one language.

Christians everywhere began to hold massive evangelistic meetings. Thousands volunteered to go as missionaries to reach every tribe and nation wherever the Russian language was spoken and understood. In just revolt against restrictions on freedom of thought, speech and religion that had been imposed by the Communists, millions of Soviets were eager to hear something different. Their openness to the gospel at that time was an opportunity without parallel in all of Russian history.

But with the end of state socialism and of artificial props that had supported the economic structure came a total collapse of the economy throughout the region. The Ruble became almost worthless. Widespread unemployment resulted in mass poverty. And those who did hold jobs were paid next to nothing, if they were paid at all. Millions of born again Christians had nothing to contribute for the support of their churches or missionary outreach. So tens of thousands of would be missionaries were stranded in their tracks, with no source of income to buy transportation, food, lodging, Bibles or literature. Since fellow believers had nothing to give for the support of missionaries, one of the greatest pioneer missionary opportunities of all time ground to a halt except, mainly, in local situations. All that those workers needed, on average, was the equivalent of about two U.S. dollars per day and they could have gone almost anywhere God might lead them throughout the former USSR to share the Word of God, win souls and plant churches.

Here is where God's people in the U.S., Canada, Korea and other industrialized countries could have been instruments in His hands to send out thousands of Russian speaking native missionaries to pioneer areas where 300 million unreached people were prepared and ready to respond to the gospel. The harvest was ripe, the laborers were ready, but we didn't have sense enough to see it.

Instead we had the travesty of hundreds of Americans running around the country collecting support of $5000 or more a month each so they could "RUSH TO RUSSIA" as would-be "missionaries."

What did they think they could do, not knowing the Russian language? And how could any one of them justify spending that

$60,000 a year of God's money on themselves when it was enough to provide full support for 100 native missionaries who already knew the language?

In all my 60 years of serving our Saviour I have never seen anything more ridiculous than the way we botched our opportunity to help God's servants in Russia, Ukraine and other Soviet countries reap the gospel harvest while it was ripe. We are custodians of God's treasury. May He forgive us for squandering His resources on the frightfully expensive process of sending Americans over there, when He had already prepared tens of thousands of laborers who could do the job ten times better at one percent of the cost. We know not what we do.

Such idiocy is the legacy we have inherited from blindly following colonial tradition without ever asking whether or not it makes sense or is in accordance with the basic principles revealed in God's Word. Most of us are little different from the hypocritical Pharisees whom our Lord said were blind leaders of the blind. All end up in the ditch.

While speaking at a missions congress in Lima, I was approached by a young Peruvian who gave me his support raising prayer card. He was trying to raise enough money to go as a missionary to Ukraine, but he didn't know a word of either Russian or Ukrainian. No one had told him that God had called and prepared hundreds of Ukrainians to reach their own people, and the cost of this fellow's plane ticket alone would provide full support for any one of them for several years. I tried to counsel him in love by explaining that someone had misguided him with colonial tradition. His native tongue was Spanish, and he should be using that language to share the gospel among those who understand it. Frankly, I wanted to tell him that his idea of going to Ukraine was just plain silly, but I was able to restrain myself from saying so lest I quench his enthusiasm.

The economic nonsense of spending $60,000 or more a year to send some American or Canadian or Korean or Peruvian to the former USSR is just one of the mistakes we have made. There are many others. Like, what we do when we get there. We are virtually helpless in foreign countries unless we are fluent in the local language – both in writing it and speaking it. Probably not one in a hundred of those who have rushed to Russia were really fluent in the language. So where do we begin?

Well, the first thing is to send some good photos to those back home who gave the money. How many times have we seen a snap-shot of some would-be "missionary" waving a Bible in Red Square as if to say, "Look at me! I'm over here on the mission field now." How much better it would be if he had stayed home and supported those who are already there, and whom God has uniquely prepared for His service. Just the cost of our plane tickets would accomplish ten times more for God's kingdom if we sent it to indigenous missions in Russia. The money we spend on hotels, restaurants, taxicabs, sight-seeing and "shopping" after we get there would support several more local missionaries for a year or two. Not to mention the tens of thousands of dollars we receive for "personal support," which includes income taxes, social security taxes, medical insurance and retirement packages.

But having arrived in Russia, we feel we ought to be doing something, so we look up some local Christians and intrude into their space. Their culture and its customs require them to be friendly, but our presence soon arouses suspicion among their neighbors. Perhaps we could work alongside them in some way, we surmise. But we have to have an interpreter, so we monopolize the time of the one who is best educated and most capable in preaching. Instead of giving himself fully to the service of Christ he is now stuck with this foreigner as a virtual servant. Like a houseboy in Africa, perhaps.

As proud Americans we are self assured, confident of our importance. We fail to recognize that the interest shown toward us by Russians is part of their culture, or just curiosity. Or that our presence has stirred up covetousness among Russian believers. They see we have plenty of money for everything we may need or desire. Who wouldn't want to tap into that gold mine, even if one has to fawn over the foreigner in hopes of gaining his favor?

Speaking of money, we don't easily part with it when we go overseas (there are a few exceptions, of course). We say it's o.k. if my support level is $200 per day and I give my interpreter one percent of that. We rationalize our actions by saying it would upset the local economy if he received more than the national average.

When we do use "our money" it is usually to buy power rather than to help provide the needs of God's servants who have next to nothing. Take the case of the Korean group who invited themselves to set up missionary shop in a major city (I'm tempted to name it, but will refrain, just in case this book is ever circulated in Korea) of a former Soviet republic in central Asia. A thriving indigenous church there had 2000 in regular attendance but less than half of them could squeeze into their makeshift meeting hall. On cold or rainy days it was a great hardship for those who had to stand outside. Even if they gave all their income for it, these poverty stricken believers could never buy the necessary materials to construct an adequate auditorium. Almost half were unemployed, and those who did have jobs earned, on average, about a dollar a day. And many were never paid even though they worked long hours on a regular basis.

Apparently the Koreans looked upon them as an opportunity to gain an easy following, even though the local Christians were a fellowship of God's family, held together by bonds of love. So the Koreans devised a plan to lure them away. They put up a large, magnificent (by Asian standards) church building just three blocks from the meeting place of the local Christians. At the time they built it (with funds from the faithful back home) the Koreans had only a handful of followers but, sure enough, in bad weather a few believers from the overcrowded local congregation began to drop in to escape the cold and rain.

Why could not those Korean missionaries have helped the indigenous church put up an adequate building, instead of spending their resources to enlarge their own power base? I'll tell you why. It's because in 90% of what we call "missionary work" our motive is not so much to further the cause of Christ as it is to enlarge our own sphere of influence, power and control. We fail to recognize that our Lord is the Head of His whole body (of true believers) and that we are all members one of another. If we were spiritually minded we would stay at home and use our offerings (which we say are "given to God") to help His servants who are already laboring in poorer countries. We wouldn't go into all the world and divide His body by competing with believers who are native to the land. Or flaunting our wealth as rich Christians living among the poor.

Another tragic failure in the rush to Russia was the fact that American tourist-type missionaries carried corrupt aspects of our culture with them and identified the Christian faith with values and conduct which were looked upon as profane and vulgar by the average Soviet citizen. Our sense of morality and decency has been so cheapened by obscene acts blatantly displayed in movies and television that we often allow ourselves to participate in things that are repulsive to people of other cultures.

During the cold war foreign journalists called Russia a "puritanical society." Although a minority were hedonistic in their conduct, the majority were morally restrained. And Christians even more so. They tend to take seriously the Biblical injunction that women should be dressed in modest apparel. Then along comes an "evangelistic team" from America with young women brazenly displaying their legs and wearing blouses or sweaters that accent their breasts in a sexy manner. To make matters worse, men and women often touch one another in public. Even non-Christians are horrified by such spectacles.

But perhaps the worst part of our culture which we transported to Russia was the type of music we took along. When Billy Graham and I preached at Youth for Christ rallies 59 years ago we had Cliff Barrows as our song leader and George Beverly Shea as soloist. We sang hymns and choruses to tunes that accented the words and messages of the songs. Then rock and roll came into our culture and things began to change.

When the sex-beat rhythm of rock music first became popular in America, I read and heard many objections to it, not just from Christians but from people of all persuasions. But as our society was flooded with it there was no way to shut it out. The general population gradually began to tolerate it.

Then some evangelistic teams began to use it in their meetings. Recently I attended an evangelistic "crusade" to which the evangelist had brought along two semi-trailer trucks full of musical gear that took up a third of the auditorium. The sound was deafening, the beat repugnant, and you could hardly discern a word of the mumbo-jumbo that was being "sung." His argument was that he had to do it to attract young people. But I found through organized inquiry that many who were there, young and old, never went back for a second time because they found the music objectionable. One man told me that to attend even once was more than he could take. So he never went back. He might have been won to the Lord if the music had been more sensible.

If we have to profane our meetings in hopes of attracting young people, what kind of converts do we expect to make of them? I heard Ravi Zacharias speaking on this subject in a radio broadcast. He and his wife had spent five days counseling students at a Christian college. Four out of five, he said, admitted to having engaged in illicit sexual activities. There can be no doubt that vulgar music and lyrics contribute to such depravity.

And if so many people react negatively here, imagine what they think about American Christianity in other countries, especially the former Soviet Union. In 1992 our mission (Christian Aid) received a letter from Moscow signed by Peter Peters, head of the Union of Unregistered Churches and also by Vasilij Ryzhuk, an elder of the UUC. Since it speaks so clearly to this subject, I include it here.

Dear Christian Friends,

For 30 years we have suffered intense persecution, and now freedom is bringing another great harm to our churches. This damage is coming from the Christians in America who are sending us rock music and evangelists accompanied by rock bands.

Our young people do not attend these meetings because we have all committed not to participate. This is a great burden on our hearts. Many come with Bible in hand and rock music. We are embarrassed by this image of Christianity. We do not know what words to use in urging that this be stopped. We abhor all Christian rock music coming into our country.

Rock music has nothing in common with ministry or service to God. We are very, very against Christian Americans bringing to our country this false image of "ministry" to God.

We personally were in prison for 15 years and 11 years for

Christ's sake. We were not allowed to have Christian music, but [while we were in prison] rock music was used as a weapon against us day and night to destroy our souls. We could only resist with much prayer and fasting.

Now, we have a time of more openness, and we are no longer taken to prison. However, now it is Christians from America who damage our souls. We do not allow this music in our churches, but they rent big stadiums and infect teenagers and adults with their rock music.

We, the leadership and congregations of the Union of Unregistered Churches, the former Persecuted Church, have made an agreement to not allow rock music in our churches. We urge you to join with us and certainly do not bring it to our country. Do not desecrate our teenagers with it. Even the unbelievers recognize it is unholy music and they cannot understand how American Christians can be so much like the world. We can give you the conclusion that after Russian unbelievers have attended these rock concerts, they are very disappointed and disillusioned with Christianity.

We call this music from hell. We urge all Americans to stop giving money for the organization of such concerts in Russia. We want only traditional Christian music in our churches. This is the unanimous decision of all our leaders.

The ridiculous RUSH TO RUSSIA fiasco is a vivid example of the carnal nature of so much of our foreign missionary activity. It illustrates where our true interests lie (in so many cases), as we follow the desires of the flesh rather than the mind of God's Spirit. Now let's take a look at Latin America.

CHAPTER ELEVEN

YANKEE GO HOME FROM LATIN AMERICA

About 25 years ago I was invited to visit Argentina and minister in some churches there. Many of them were originally planted by immigrants from England. The report I received was that about a century ago a British firm constructed a railroad from Buenos Aries to Cordoba, and many Christians were among those who went there to build it. In fact, they emigrated with missionary motivation, hoping to be ambassadors for Christ in their places of employment.

Most of the believers who went were in fellowship with assemblies of Christians which outsiders called the "Plymouth Brethren." They had no ordained ministers in their churches, but rather considered that every male believer was eligible to minister, especially those who serve as elders. Upon arrival in Argentina they immediately began to gather in the name of our Lord for teaching, fellowship, breaking of bread and prayers. These assemblies soon became the largest group of evangelicals in Argentina.

I was particularly impressed with their missionary vision. One large assembly (over 1000 in weekly attendance) where I preached in Buenos Aires set up boarding schools in the Andes mountains and in isolated areas of the pampas for children from aboriginal tribes. Otherwise those kids had no opportunity for education. Through this medium hundreds of families were won to Christ and new assemblies were planted among many indigenous people in Argentina.

While sharing God's Word in one of the assemblies I met a man named Alexandro Clifford who spoke the English of his ancestors without flaw even though, I presume, his education had been in Spanish. He shared with me some incidents that had prompted him to write an article entitled *Why Latin Americans Dislike Some American Missionaries*. It appeared originally in a magazine called *Eternity* which at that time was being published in Philadelphia. Later the article was republished in the magazine of InterVarsity Christian Fellowship called *HIS*, and was then reprinted for wider distribution by International Students, Inc.

As Clifford talked with me I began to realize that I was personally acquainted with some of the American missionaries described (but not named) in his article. Then and there I began to understand why so many evangelical Christians in Argentina, Brazil and other South American countries had joined the "Yankee go home" chorus which was being chanted by university students in several countries.

Clifford's article is so relevant to the actual situation that I want to include portions of it here. I have edited it for brevity, but no words are added except those in brackets, for clarity.

Why Latin Americans Dislike Some American Missionaries

I cannot think of any believers spitting at an American missionary, or throwing rocks at him, yet I have seen mature Christians tremble with indignation at things done and said by some missionaries who have come from the United States to civilize and Christianize us.

I am a native of one of the South American republics. We have had gospel work here for nearly a century. There is a strong national church with extremely capable national leadership. But some Americans are not aware of this fact. This is how they start work:

Someone in the States forms a "Gospel Mission for the Enlightenment of Pagan Argentina," or Uruguay, or Peru. Then he visits the capital of the republic. He is probably surprised to find a progressive modern city. As to the culture of the people, he cannot say much, as he knows no Spanish and less than nothing about the cultural heritage of Spanish America.

In the capital city, he gets in touch with a colleague who is director of "Biblical Bundles for Benighted Babies of Latin America, Inc.," hears colorful stories of his success, and promptly cables home: "Your director in front line of battle. Marvelous opportunities. Souls perishing. Light must be sent." It is quite true. Souls are perishing just the same as in the United States. And after all, what is a front line of battle?

After two or three days in a luxury hotel, the director flies home. He is now able to write a pamphlet and several "prayer letters." Oh these prayer letters! Some of them are so unfortunate! And it is even more unfortunate that they often fall into the hands of native believers who read English. In these cases, the native's sense of humor may save him from becoming embittered and anti-American. But not all natives have a sense of humor.

When the prayer letters have "stirred up enough interest" (missionary jargon for "brought in enough funds"), the director general and his family, plus a six months supply of bubble gum, several cameras, a trumpet and a marimba, descend on a Latin American city. The gospel has been preached there for perhaps 50 years. There may be two, three or even 30 evangelical churches. But the director never thinks of these, or at least never refers to them in his prayer letters. In them he is alone in vast mysterious South America.

Some years ago I saw a map which circulated quite extensively. The missionary who distributed it lived in a small town in one of the republics. The map showed a very dark South America with four rays of light in it: Rio de Janeiro, Buenos Aires, Lima, and the town where this missionary worked. The whole thing seemed calculated to leave the impression that some work was being done in the coastal cities but that the interior was completely neglected except for the efforts of that one lonely missionary family.

The director general, of course, cannot afford to ignore the local Christians entirely. One of them helps him to get a house. Another sees him through the maze of [bureaucratic] red tape which exists in most of our cities. Another gives him Spanish lessons free of charge, but finds it a difficult job as the director general knows nothing about grammar. Then of course it is easier to find a ready made church, composed of a few disgruntled Baptists or marimba-loving Methodists, than to start from scratch. And these members give plenty of ammunition for prayer letters.

There is an element of farce about the whole situation. But even farces can become painful. To have the crude spectacular circus tricks of some American religious groups presented to us as ideals to be followed is hardly the thing that will appeal to the spiritual descendants of the Spanish mystics and reformers. At times it is almost more than we can bear. These friends do not know that we have had a complete Spanish Bible since 1569. I remember that some American missionaries have actually attempted to give nation wide [radio] addresses on the evils of [modern English translations] without realizing that the problem of an English translation means nothing to people who read their Bibles in Spanish.

Most Latin American audiences, at least in the cities (and the missionaries I am writing about do not go elsewhere), will include a few professionals and a good number of bright young students. These people are well read, alert mentally, and in touch with current events. Their conversation is stimulating, and the younger folk are always asking questions. What can a missionary who has never even heard of, let us say, Thomism, Existentialism, Relativity, Engels or Sartre, have to say to these students when they bring him their problems? I know the answer: "We are not here to teach worldly philosophy but to preach the gospel." But how are they going to reach people, and how are they going to keep them, if they cannot even speak the elementary language of an educated man?

In talking to a missionary one day, I happened to mention the Copernican theory. He looked blank, asked me to repeat what I had said and then replied in a kindly superior way: "That word is pronounced Capernaum, brother."

The message of some of these men is in my opinion unscriptural. It could be summarized thus: "Believe in Christ and all your troubles will be over. If you are faithful, God will prosper you materially. Look at us. The Lord has given us cash, cars and comfortable homes." This doctrine may go in some circles in the USA, but does not appeal to mature Latin Americans, though it may gather a few "rice Christians" round the missionary. (Let me say in passing that I belong to a conservative church and have no leanings toward liberalism. It is not the fundamentalism but the infantilism of these missionaries that I sincerely object to.)

Jokes about Texas are an essential part of most addresses. We smile at them because we are expected to but, as Queen Victoria would have said, "We are not amused." And when the missionary tells us of his heart-rending sufferings while visiting some other mission field, we are not impressed. We know what his standard of living is in our city, and while he is talking we cannot help wondering what tales he will tell folk in the States, on his first furlough, about his suffering among the savage denizens of Buenos Aires, Lima or San Jose.

It sounds like a line from Walt Whitman, but it isn't. It is one of the most important lines of many American missionaries. "Our work, our family, our helpers, our trumpets (they blow their own), our native flock" (often non-existent or borrowed from some other mission) must be photographed from all angles, with colored filters to give the right tropical effect. Examples?

A group of young people from several churches attends a service at the [U.S.] Mission one evening. They are asked to stay for some hymn singing. Suddenly a camera appears and flash bulbs start popping. The picture appears later in a prayer letter as "our Choir."

A gifted young native preacher holds special gospel services, attended by an American missionary. Dozens of photos are taken. A prayer letter appears, beautifully illustrated. Nothing is said about the native preacher, though the gospel campaign is mentioned in detail. The American missionary is quick to explain that "back home nobody knows or cares about the native, so why mention him? They are interested in what I am doing, and would probably think it strange that somebody else should be doing the preaching." Many of these native helpers and pastors are very godly men. Only godly men could stand some of these American missionaries.

A paragraph in a mission paper was brought to my attention by a native worker. It was under a large photograph of a missionary kid, and was a special appeal to raise enough money to send her to an American kindergarten. The sum requested was more than what the native worker, a married man with a family, received in a year. And in this particular case, if it had not been for the native helper, there would have been no way of justifying the existence of the American missionary.

A complaint which is voiced continually by the missionary: "Why is Pedro always grumbling about the cost of living? I try to explain the him that everything is so much cheaper here than it is in the States, but he just refuses to understand." The speaker spends more money a week on candy and canned fruit juice than Pedro receives as his monthly salary. And Pedro has a wife and six children.

Have American missionaries unconsciously slipped into the role of the Master Race, left vacant by Adolph and his followers? Some of them make us wonder.

One thing which Clifford mentioned is especially pertinent. It's those news and prayer letters which U.S. (and other) foreign missionaries send home to their supporters. Over the years I have made it a point to get on as many missionary mailing lists as possible because those letters keep me informed as to how colonial missionaries operate. Once in awhile I receive one that actually tells something about how the kingdom of God is progressing in a particular location. But nine out of ten say nothing about the body of Christ in the locality where the missionaries are stationed. Rather, they are filled with pictures of the kids, where they go to school, what they got for Christmas, where the family went on vacation, how they solved the problem with their air conditioners, or their house, or their cars, or their plans for furlough, you name it. The focus is almost always on the missionary and his family. It is very seldom about spiritual progress among believers where the foreigner is supposed to be serving the Lord.

Clifford aptly pointed out that if the letters do say anything about the work of God it is likely to be in colonial possessive terms:

"*Our* work, *our* family, *our* choir, etc." I have seen letters that speak of "our nationals" when referring to Christian citizens of other countries. They also speak of "our churches, our Bible schools, our special meetings, our students, our Sunday schools, etc. etc."

This focus on the family of the missionary has a spiritually destructive effect on the members of evangelical churches in America which support these missionaries. Whereas our primary concern should be about how our Lord is building His church among every tribe and nation, and on the welfare of our fellow believers in places of poverty and persecution, our attention is diverted instead to a preoccupation with "our missionaries" who are likely to be hindering more than helping the cause of Christ in the places where they have gone. I see no hope for an end to this distorted view of the kingdom of God until we phase out the "going and sending" traditions within our churches, and focus instead on the welfare and work of the body of Christ in all those places we mistakenly call "the mission field."

Very few North Americans who go south of the border as missionaries ever become fluent in Spanish. I say this on the authority of Zulay Carmona, known among evangelicals as "the great lady of Costa Rica." She once taught Spanish to would be missionaries at the big language school for foreign missionaries which for many years has been located in her country. She told me that one reason she gave it up was because most of her students were hopeless as far as their ever learning Spanish was concerned. She also said another reason was that she felt hardly any of them would be of any positive value to the cause of Christ in Latin America.

Zulay developed a close friendship with Sheila Hargreves from Pennsylvania while the two of them were young missionaries working at Radio Station HCJB in Quito. A few years later Sheila visited Zulay in Costa Rica, and her time there coincided with a Christian student conference in Panama which Zulay planned to attend. Sheila was anxious to go also, but Zulay begged her not to. "If a North American comes into that conference," Zulay said, "the Communists can exploit the incident to claim that all Christian students are agents of the Yankee imperialists." So Sheila wisely stayed in Costa Rica until the conference was over. But many other

North American missionaries have stupidly intruded into sensitive situations where their presence caused great damage to the witness of Latin American Christians.

Very few North American missionaries are willing to face reality regarding language deficiencies. Once during missions week at a Presbyterian (PCA) church I heard a missionary of that denomination suggest that more of their young people should go to Mexico, as he had done. When time came for questions, I asked him if he was giving the same message in Mexican churches. Was he urging Mexican young people to go to the USA as missionaries? His reply was that there would be no place for them here because they wouldn't be able to learn English. He failed to comprehend that what he was saying was tantamount to arrogant pride and race prejudice. He implied that Anglos from the USA could learn Spanish but Mexicans couldn't learn English. He might as well have said, "We are superior, they are inferior." I agree that Mexicans do have difficulty learning English well enough to use it fluently in a small town in Iowa, but Anglo kids from Iowa have even more difficulty learning to speak Spanish as a Mexican does.

The actual motivation of this missionary was obvious to me, but I doubt that many others caught the significance of his response to my question. He was not being guided by common sense or spiritual wisdom. Rather, it was the inbred compulsion to perpetuate missionary colonialism in our denominations. Out of one side of our mouth we say it's our responsibility to keep on sending our church youth to Mexico, but from the other side we admit it makes no sense for Mexican youth to be sent to the USA as resident missionaries (unless, of course, they work among Hispanics).

While in Brazil about 25 years ago I visited the headquarters of an indigenous ministry that had hundreds of missionaries within its fellowship. The auditorium of their mother church could seat 25,000 without crowding. The head man of this church, was not called its pastor. Rather, I was intrigued to see in their publications that his title was "missionary." It was even more fascinating to learn a little about his background. As a zealous young Christian but without resources he had joined a large denominational mission from the USA. It was pouring funds and personnel into his country, sparing no cost to have a presence there. They offered to support him (at five percent of the amount being paid to the Yankees) if he would serve as one of their "native workers."

The Yankees treated him as though he were a child, or perhaps it was more like a slave. They insisted on exercising complete control over his life, forbidding him to have any form of ministry without approval of his American supervisors. But there were times when the Spirit of God witnessed with the spirit of this young Brazilian that he should proceed to witness for Christ, speak at meetings, distribute literature, or minister to a soul in need without specific directions from one of his foreign bosses. For so doing he was slapped with an injunction intended to teach him submission to those in authority. Part of the discipline included an order that he was not to speak (preach) in any public meeting for one full year.

Like the early apostles, this modern one had to choose whether to obey God rather than men. So he left his colonial masters and launched out on his own, by faith, as a missionary to the unreached. About 100 of his fellow Brazilians left with him, even though it meant they would no longer have financial support of any kind. While the Americans with whom they were formerly associated continued to live in comparative affluence, these pioneer apostles often went for days without food, slept outside on the ground, and walked up to 30 miles in a day because they had no means of transportation. But God was with them, and through their self denial many souls were won, churches were planted, offerings were received and, eventually, their basic needs were supplied. From that austere beginning this team of consecrated apostles grew to become one of the largest missionary ministries in all of Brazil. Their goal has been to plant a witness for their Lord in every town, village, tribe and nation throughout that great country.

This tremendous ministry could never have happened if that zealous young worker had remained with the foreign denomination. Think of how much better it would have been for the cause of Christ in Brazil if all those rich Yankees had gone home and diverted their extensive wealth to supporting indigenous ministries instead, including the one they rejected.

Probably one of the poorest countries in the western hemisphere is Haiti. There I was a guest in the home of a fellow Baptist who had formerly been the pastor of a large church in the USA. In that comfortable position he had received a generous salary and lived in a beautiful parsonage with his family, enjoying the good life to the full. But it was not enough to satisfy the deeper longings of his heart as he read of the sufferings of our Saviour and the sacrifices of the original apostles of the cross. So in due time he made the supreme sacrifice himself. He gave it all up and "went off to the mission field."

Well, he gave most of it up. His parishioners sent him out with two cars, window unit air conditioners, furniture for an eight room house, toys and electronic gadgets for his four children, and enough household supplies to last them until furlough. He rented a house in Haiti about equal in size to the parsonage he had left, and moved in as soon as he had unloaded from an ocean freighter several shipping containers packed with all their stuff.

But he and his family were making a sacrifice, nevertheless. Their house had running water, but it went on and off from time to time. As did the electricity. And the sewer drains were often clogged. Even though they boiled their water before drinking it, and carefully cooked everything they ate, family members started getting sick one after another soon after arrival. Even going over their kitchen daily with a disinfectant didn't solve the problem.

Anyway, here was this self-sacrificing family now "out on the mission field," ready to serve God. Or, at least, this Baptist pastor turned missionary was ready, but not the members of his family. They were all busy with their own personal agendas. But what would he do? He could not speak either French or Creole, the two local languages. And even if he could, he actually had little time for religious activities. Almost all of his time was taken up looking after his family, especially taking one after another of his children to doctors and hospitals miles away. Hours and hours had to be spent taking care of their house and cars, exchanging money, negotiating with and transporting domestic employees, arranging enrollment and communicating with private English language schools for his kids, arguing with the landlord about maintenance and repairs for the house, negotiating for services and paying bills in person (rent, water, sewer, electric, phone), plus daily shopping for groceries and household supplies. Just getting a tank of gasoline required almost an hour. His wife could use her car to do some of these things, but she was also sick frequently. The day began with driving 30 minutes each way to take the two older children to an English high school. A second hour was needed to take the two younger ones to another English school 18 miles away. Then this faithful missionary would spend the rest of the morning on personal and family living details. In early afternoon he would drive for an hour picking up and bringing home the younger children, after which he would drive another hour to retrieve the older two.

This went on five days a week. Saturday was reserved for family time together: a trip to the beach, picnic in the hills, athletic events, sight seeing or other activities. On Sunday morning the family drove two hours each way to attend an English language church together, so after a mid-afternoon dinner the day was done. When she wasn't sick, the wife's days were taken up mostly with trying to supervise domestic employees in shopping, food preparation, laundry, cleaning and other chores around the house.

The only actual "missionary work" this martyr was doing at that time consisted of trying to teach English to his household employees, and some family members of their employees, by having a translator on hand while reading the Bible to them. What a waste of time and talent. But it has been repeated a thousand times because of the guilt trip which has been laid on so many American Christians by the "go to the mission field" philosophy that has been disseminated in evangelical churches by colonial missions.

Early in my Christian life I and my contemporaries taught that full consecration to the Lord would eventually lead us on to the ultimate sacrifice of "going to the mission field." Anything less was second best. We mocked those who were hesitant by quoting Isaiah 6:8, "Here am I, Lord," and then adding sarcastically, "Send my sister." I had to live in Asia for three years before I realized that my original approach had been unwise as well as without Scriptural precedent.

It's a tragedy that no one told that Baptist pastor (while he was still in the USA) about indigenous missions. Had he known what they were doing, he would not have wasted the most productive years of his life by giving up his church and going overseas. He was in a position where he could have inspired his church's members to support perhaps a thousand of the native missionaries who are now on the field with no support in Haiti and other countries. Instead, he became dependent himself and those truly effective servants of our Saviour whom he could have helped were left with nothing.

A short distance from this American's house I visited the headquarters of an indigenous ministry which had around 90 missionaries on the field. It was started by Haitians, led by Haitians and staffed by Haitian missionaries. Most of those native missionaries lived in one or two room houses with little or no furniture. None of them had cars, although the mission did have one dilapidated vehicle (bought used from a U.S. mission) that served all of them to the extent possible. On average these missionaries received less than $30 per month in personal support. Most were graduates of the combination Bible institute and missionary training center being operated at the mission's headquarters. I met with about 30 new missionaries in training while I was there.

I also visited several churches which had been planted by missionaries of this ministry. Since the believers nearly all lived in one room houses that were too small for group meetings, each local church had to construct its own meeting place. Those I visited all had mud walls, dirt floors and thatch roofs. None had chairs, but there were a few unfinished boards mounted on short "tree stump" posts that enabled some of the older persons to sit about one foot off the ground.

The entire income of this mission, including the Bible school with room and board for students, and personal support plus ministry expenses for 90 missionaries, was less than the total budget of that one Baptist minister from the USA who had made the supreme sacrifice of "going to the mission field." To say this makes no sense is to put it mildly. Nothing short of a complete reformation will bring the foreign missionary movement into conformity with the basic principles of the Word of God.

What has been evident in Latin America is even more so in Africa, as we shall see in the next chapter.

CHAPTER TWELVE

WHITE MISSIONARIES SHOULD STAY OUT OF AFRICA

My first doubts about whether there was a need for foreign missionaries to stay on after churches have been started in a given country came near the beginning of my Christian experience. As I said earlier, while working with IVCF, traveling all over the USA as an evangelist among university students, I was continually trying to recruit volunteers for missionary service overseas. But one day a student from Ethiopia took the wind out of my sails. He said it would be better for the cause of Christ if no more white missionaries went to Africa. The churches would grow faster, he said, if the foreigners weren't there.

Then he told me something that had happened in Ethiopia. From what he said I gathered that some Baptist missionaries had gone there and started a few churches before Mussolini sent Italian troops to occupy Ethiopia in 1937. Foreign missionaries from countries unfriendly to Mussolini were forced to leave. In keeping with colonial thinking, the foreign Baptists quite naturally presumed that the infant churches they had started would all die out once their missionary parents were removed from the scene.

Why? Because as long as the foreign missionaries were there, Ethiopian natives showed little interest in the churches. They attended Sunday services somewhat grudgingly. They wouldn't give of their meager financial resources to support the white man's church. Hardly any of them demonstrated initiative toward leadership. The few who professed to be Christians tended to be lackadaisical about the whole thing, and did little unless prodded by the missionaries.

But when World War II was over and the Italians were gone, a few Baptist missionaries returned to Ethiopia. They were probably expecting to find that their fledgling churches would be no more. Instead, they found that the number of believers and churches had increased a hundred fold. And my new friend from Ethiopia told me it would have been better all around if the foreigners had never gone back. But that's another subject.

I want to deal with why nothing much happened until the foreigners were all gone. I believe it's because white men in black Africa cast a shadow. Their presence is intimidating to many Africans. Local men will not step forward in leadership as long as the dominant foreigners are there looking over their shoulders. The foreigners treated Africans like they were children, or worse yet, servants (slaves?). And Ethiopians had no motivation to give money to a church run by foreigners who were a hundred times richer than they were.

But let the foreigners be removed from the scene and everything changes. Once the overbearing shadow is gone, local believers will assert themselves and take initiative. With no rich foreigners around, whose individual salaries are triple the entire church budget, the local Christians are less reluctant to give what little they have. And as leaders emerge from the ranks they are no longer timid about innovation. Their ministries can move ahead as the Spirit leads, and multitudes will follow.

The experience of the Sudan Interior Mission in Ethiopia was similar to that of the Baptists. They had 47 disciples there when they had to leave in 1937. Upon returning after the war they found over 10,000 new believers. I don't believe it would ever have happened if the foreign missionaries had stayed around during those eight years. Raymond Davis, head of SIM, wrote a book about it called <u>Fire on the Mountain</u>.

For several years one of the Board members of Christian Aid

was Dr. Jon Bonk who grew up with his missionary parents in Ethiopia and later worked there as a foreign missionary. He told me that of all the missionaries he ever knew in Ethiopia, by far the most effective one was an Ethiopian named Ato Makay of the Wolaitta nation. Although his personal support was less than two percent of that of most foreigners, his work was more effective than a dozen of them put together. He started scores of churches among many different tribes. He could learn the languages of his neighbors very easily because they were similar to his own. He moved among nomadic people teaching them how that instead of moving about continually they would do better to stay in one place and grow vegetable gardens. As a result, their food supply was greatly increased and they developed stable communities centered in the Christian faith.

Inspired by Ato's success, many other Wolaitta men also went out as missionaries among various nations of Ethiopia. A Ph.D. thesis concerning them was recently completed at the University of Aberdeen in Scotland. In deference to colonial tradition, the author titled it *The Wolaitta Evangelists*. Those pioneer apostles should have rather been called "missionaries" instead.

In 1966 I attended a "world congress" of evangelical leaders in Berlin, sponsored by Youth for Christ, the Billy Graham Evangelistic Association and similar organizations. It was largely dominated by Americans who called for sending out more white missionaries to "all the world." Delegates from other countries who had different ideas were restricted to smaller workshops and discussion groups. Two native missionaries from West African countries had an opportunity to share their convictions in one session I attended. From notes I took, this is a summary of what they said:

"We thank God for the white missionaries who brought the Word of God to our people a hundred years ago. But the situation is completely changed now. We want to evangelize our countries, but we can't do it as long as you white missionaries remain there. Our people mock us. They say, 'Are you still working for white men? Don't you know we have independence now? But we still see these white people sent here by their governments. Why do you keep working for them?' And so they won't listen to our preaching and accept our message because they associate us with colonial rulers of the past. We would have much more freedom in our work if all white missionaries left our countries in West Africa."

You can imagine how popular those brothers were among ambitious American mission executives at that conclave. It was easy to see why indigenous leaders from "mission field" countries were not given much of a voice while there.

In 1974 I attended another world congress in Lausanne, sponsored mainly by the same organizations as the one in Berlin. Among the many delegates were 200 from all over Africa. They represented very diverse ethnic, denominational and organizational backgrounds, but all were more or less evangelical Christians. Before formal sessions began at the congress, all the Africans got together and agreed to present a united petition to the organizers. It called for a moratorium on foreign missionaries being sent to Africa from other parts of the world.

In a plenary session Billy Graham stood before the whole congress and openly denounced the position of the African delegation (without naming them specifically). The basis of his disagreement with them was the Word of God (as he understood it). "We are commanded to go," Billy said, "so we must keep on going even if some of our brothers say they don't want us to come" (or words to that effect, as I recall). I had worked with Billy Graham for four years in Youth for Christ days, and he provided my personal support while I served as a missionary in Asia. A dearer friend I never had. But I had to tell him he had missed something in his declaration. Our Lord told His disciples to go (from Galilee) to Jerusalem, not to foreign countries. But I fear that neither Billy nor any of his associates understood the missionary strategy of the New Testament at that time.

But Howard McFarland and his wife, Charlotte. understood it. They went to Belgian Congo as missionaries in 1954. After independence came in 1960 they were faced with a tough decision. After much prayer, Howard and Charlotte both felt they could be most effective for the cause of Christ in Africa if they devoted the rest of their lives to reaching African students in U.S. universities. At that time, probably 50% of such students were active in

Communist cells. And they would be the top leaders of their respective countries upon their return. As was Kwame Nkruma when he returned from Pennsylvania to the Gold Coast and gained its independence. Once he became Prime Minister he declared that the new nation he called "Ghana" should become a Marxist state. But when Howard returned to the USA and began his new approach to impacting African countries for Christ, very few of his supporting churches continued to contribute toward his ministry. I suppose they presumed he wasn't a foreign missionary any longer. He soon learned that being a foreign missionary in a way differing from the colonial pattern of the 19th century was going to be difficult indeed.

When I have visited Africa, most of the church leaders with whom I have had fellowship knew before my coming that I was not in favor of sending any more foreign missionaries to their respective countries. So they haven't hesitated to tell me how things go better for the cause of Christ if the foreigners aren't there. Of course many of them are leaders of completely indigenous works with which no foreigners have ever been involved, but others have had their roots in the colonial missionary enterprise of the past 150 years. I have received some interesting comments from the latter group.

First of all, leaders from Christian families which are second, third and fourth generation Christians are deeply grateful for the pioneers who came to their countries and put the Word of God in their languages. They appreciate the schools, medical facilities and other good things which were established in their countries, even those that were eventually taken over by non-Christian governments. They are thankful, too, for churches that were started and Christian standards that were introduced. But things stop right about there, because it's mainly concerning local churches that Africans are glad when the white people are gone.

You see, the foreigners started churches just like they had at home. They often helped the Africans pay for church buildings patterned after those in America, Canada or other industrialized countries, but on a simpler scale. There would be chairs or benches to sit on and frequently a pump organ to provide music for the singing of hymns translated from English. The Sunday service, as might be expected, would be pretty much like those in the missionary's home town. There would be a few hymns, prayer, offering, special music, Scripture reading and a sermon followed by the benediction. African Christians, like sheep, would dutifully attend these rituals and sit through them quietly, in spite of their strangeness. Now and then they could persuade their relatives to attend also, and in spite of the formality some would accept Christ. But few of them ever grew to spiritual maturity. However, once the foreigners were gone, things really changed.

Out would go the benches. Out would go the pump organ. And in would come the drums. Hymn books would be respectfully stowed away. And African meetings would begin. In village celebrations for many centuries, Africans have always danced. Not the vulgar man-with-woman dancing of Europeans; or the obscene simulated sex gyrations of the pelvis so common in America; but the joyful stomping of feet in rhythm with the clapping of their hands. It's their way of expressing joy and enthusiasm. At the same time, they sing, not stilted translations of English poems, but Bible verses and expressions of praise repeated over and over in rhythm till everybody knows them. The illiterate can then go home singing just as freely as the educated. And keep singing God's praises until the next meeting.

As independence came to one African country after another, and the foreign missionaries were eased out, thousands of churches were Africanized. And attendance exploded. As did the spiritual life of the members. While the foreigners were there they tended to resist the Africanization of their branch churches. Every preacher was required to wear a coat and tie when entering the pulpit. Women were given "potato sack" dresses to pull over their bodies before entering church "services," no matter how hot it was inside. Once it was over they would hurriedly go outside, pull the dresses over their heads, roll them up in a ball, and take them home to have on hand for the next Sunday. Many foreign missionaries had said the use of drums, clapping of hands or dancing in church were "heathen" practices. And in so saying they held down the life and growth of the churches. But once the colonial overlords were out of the way, indigenous Christianity really took off in many African countries. Preachers dared to enter their meetings in comfortable tribal dress rather than wearing a "choke strap" (necktie). Women left the potato sacks at home and dressed in normal African attire when they gathered at church meetings.

One thing the original missionaries had introduced was retained, however, and that was the Sunday sermon – but was it ever changed! With no white people there to inhibit them, African Christians were free to be cheerleaders for their preachers. Even in churches that were originally Baptist or Presbyterian. Every good exhortation, or exposition of truth, was supported with enthusiastic shouts of approval from those standing up to praise the Lord or seated on the floor. And when a climax was reached in the message, the whole congregation would burst out in spontaneous song. A really good preacher might be interrupted three or four times with supportive songs before he got through. Preaching became as exuberant as a ball game, and could go on for over two hours without boredom.

When our Lord was born in Bethlehem, He was made in the likeness of the men of that time and place. When He was born in Ephesus, His body (of believers) grew as a company of Greeks, recreated in God's image. He increased in wisdom and stature and in favor with those among whom He lived (Luke 2:52). When He has more recently been born within a body of believers in a particular village of China, He has developed after the pattern of a joint family of from 20 to 50 adults and children. And in African towns and villages, He has entered freely into the life of those communities without much alteration of their tribal customs. He has replaced their animistic beliefs in many spirits with the presence and power of His one Holy Spirit. As individual lives have been thus transformed, warfare, diseases and sexual promiscuity have diminished, and new life prevails in thousands of Christian communities.

My purpose in saying these things is to point out how God leads his children onwards in spiritual growth that is expressed in the context of their respective cultures. The continued presence of foreign missionaries tends to bend the local culture out of shape, and inhibits healthy growth of the churches. As I will explain in the next chapter, when the suffocating effects of foreign organizations are removed and the Spirit of God is moving, He will in miraculous ways cause His church to grow and spread spontaneously from people to people and tribe to tribe.

CHAPTER THIRTEEN

THE GOSPEL SPREADS FROM TRIBE TO TRIBE

Can it be that the Spirit of God sometimes waits until the foreign missionaries are out of the way before doing a spectacular work among unreached peoples? It certainly seemed that way in regard to aboriginal nations in the mountains of Formosa (now called Taiwan) 60 years ago. I visited churches among some of those peoples in 1951, and had to agree with my host, James Dickson, that what had happened was truly *Stranger Than Fiction*. That's the title he gave to a booklet he wrote describing the amazing work of God that took place while he was back home in Canada during World War II.

At that time, churches were quite well distributed among the general Chinese population of the island. Numerous foreign missionaries worked among them, and jointly with some Chinese churches they operated separate Bible schools for men and women in Tamsui. The ruling Japanese authorities tended to be tolerant of the churches, but after Japan went to war with America on December 7, 1941 all foreign missionaries were required to leave.

Aboriginal tribes living in isolation high in the mountains were never completely conquered by the Japanese, although some at lower elevations concluded a truce which allowed Japanese representatives to enter mountain villages and open schools and police stations. One objective of the Japanese authorities was to end tribal warfare and stamp out the aboriginal practice of head hunting. Some tribes required a young man to collect a human head before he could be married and to produce fresh human blood to be drunk during his wedding ceremony. These tribespeople had a formula for shrinking heads which I seriously doubt any modern pharmaceutical company can duplicate. Collecting heads was also a means of gaining status among the tribes. I still have a photo of one chief who personally cut off 60 human heads and shrunk each one down to the size of a baseball. A favorite collector's item was the head of a Japanese policeman. One reason why the more isolated tribes were never subdued by Japanese forces was that tribal scouts would hide in trees and shoot intruding soldiers in their necks with deadly darts from blow guns.

The first tribe to conclude a treaty with the Japanese was the Tyal nation, and the negotiator was a highly intelligent woman named Chi-oang. In addition to her own language she became fluent in both Japanese and the Chinese dialect which was spoken by the Taiwanese majority. She could converse in several of the languages of other aboriginal tribes as well. As an unofficial ambassador representing the tribes to the government, Chi-oang became very well known and highly respected. And through association with local Chinese churches, she became a Christian.

During a visit to the east coast of Taiwan in 1929, James Dickson met Chi-oang and persuaded her to attend the Women's Bible School in Tamsui. She really stood out there because of the broad blue tattoo marks of her tribe upon her face. She completed the two year course successfully and then returned to her people in the mountains. She took along several sacks of Bibles and New Testaments in Japanese, which many of the young people in different tribes could now read, since the government had opened numerous schools among them using their official language.

A young Tyal man named Dowai also attended Bible school in Tamsui for two years. He, too, took along sacks of Japanese New Testaments when he returned to the mountains. Soon word filtered out to the Chinese churches that some of the aboriginal tribespeople were turning to Christ. But that was just at the time when all the foreign missionaries had to leave. They presumed, as James Dickson told me, that nothing much could take place among the aborigines without their guidance. The surprise of his life awaited Dickson upon his return in late 1945.

Tens of thousands of tribespeople had turned to Christ and formed churches. The movement began small, with those who found Christ telling family members, and they in turn telling others. As the word spread, numerous tribal leaders went to Chi-oang for teaching, then took the word back to their villages.

As the number of believers grew, Japanese police began to persecute them. With the war on, Japanese soldiers and police had orders to impose Shinto on all the Emperor's subjects. It was a sort of super patriotism with shrines for showing reverence toward the Emperor as "the son of heaven," or an incarnation of the sun-god. When Christian faith began to spread from village to village in the mountains, it quickly out-flanked the Shinto shrines. So loyal Japanese police felt they had to stamp it out. Bibles were collected and burned. Leaders and teachers were beaten unmercifully. Chi-oang had to be carried far up into the mountains by a group of young men from her tribe, and hidden from village to village to avoid arrest. But Dowai was arrested and put in prison, after leading many young Tyals to Christ.

Although the persecution was severe, it actually served for the furtherance of the gospel. Most of the mountain tribespeople shared a strong dislike for their ruthless rulers, and had no interest in bowing at the Shinto shrines. The new message about the King of all Kings and eternal life through His salvation was a powerful alternative, and tribes that had previously been fighting each other were drawn together by this redeeming grace. Thus the gospel spread from tribe to tribe.

One of the first young men gifted as a soul winner in the Ami tribe was arrested and beaten by the Japanese, then forced to serve in their army. They shipped him off for duty in Hong Kong, and while stationed there he met another soldier who was a Taiwanese aboriginal from the Sesset tribe on a different part of the island. He accepted Christ and after the war went back to start the first churches among his people of the Sesset nation.

In many cases among these tribes, entire villages turned to Christ and the elders of a given village would serve as elders of the church. All the people would get together and construct a simple bamboo meeting place with dirt floor and thatched roof. In most cases the ones I saw while visiting them appeared to be the finest buildings in their respective villages.

Fortunately there were no foreigners around to tell these simple people how to have "church services," so they figured that out for themselves. In every village the day would begin with family prayers attended by all, and then at the end of the day they would come together again to worship God as a group. At these simple gatherings they would sing songs (which gifted believers had composed) interspersed with prayers of intercession and thanksgiving. Those with special concerns would ask for intercessory prayers, and when a special blessing occurred an account of it would be shared so all could rejoice together.

Chi-oang became known as "the mother of 10,000 souls." She taught her disciples that one day in seven should be dedicated to God, so on Sundays entire villages spent the whole day together as a church family. How would they spend a whole day together? If some foreign missionary had been guiding them, they would have been instructed to have a dull one hour "church service" and that would have been it. After all, what more could they do, especially when nearly all the adults were illiterate?

One characteristic of illiterate people, especially those who live in isolation from modern technology, is that their capacity for memorization far exceeds that of their cousins in industrialized countries. Our brains have been gorged from childhood with movies, radio, TV and print media images, and all that clutter reduces our capacity for memorization. Many of the greatest preachers in rural Africa today are illiterate, but can quote whole chapters of the Bible from memory. That's what happened in the mountains of Taiwan.

Young people would read the Scriptures in Japanese, then make free translations of it. Older people would then learn it, and choice portions would be set to music and chanted. Thus gospel songs were born in the tribal languages. While visiting among them I was greatly blessed by their enthusiastic singing. The highlight of their all day Sunday meetings would be dramatizations. First a Bible story or parable would be read and translated. Then it would be dramatized. For example, let's say it was the parable of the Prodigal Son. An older man would act out the role of the father, a young man would be his son. Others would enact the parts of people met by the son in the far country, including the villain who owned the swine that the wayward son had to feed. All the church would join in the celebration when the prodigal came home, except the one chosen to be the jealous older brother.

Other favorite dramatizations were the story of Joseph in the Old Testament, Daniel in the lion's den, events on the day of Pentecost, Paul and Silas in prison in Philippi, and similar stories. What God did in those isolated mountain villages demonstrates how our Lord is the head of His church, and that He works in unique ways among His people by His Holy Spirit. Not in a thousand years would a properly educated American missionary dream up a plan whereby an infant church of largely illiterate believers would learn God's Word by dramatization.

Entrance of the gospel of Christ transformed many aspects of the daily lives of the aboriginal tribes of Taiwan, without upsetting their basic culture. Headhunting, and killing others with poisoned darts, was stopped completely. They also discontinued the tribal tattoo identification marks which had disfigured their faces in previous years. Drunkenness from alcoholic beverages was stopped as was the use of hallucinatory herbs, especially those that were addictive. Men began to share in daily work, and ceased to take advantage of their women, who formerly had been forced to do all menial tasks. When the men joined in water procurement, housing construction and agriculture the standard of living shot up remarkably in every village. As the gospel spread from tribe to tribe, tribal warfare ceased and peace reigned for the first time in those jungle hills and valleys.

Improvements in the economic conditions of the villages took place through utilization of their own ingenious means of food production, developed over hundreds of years, and not by imported schemes which are alien to the climate and local ecology. I met a

Methodist missionary in Korea who was trying to teach Koreans how to raise rabbits for food. But she seemed oblivious to the fact that her little bunnies might eat every edible plant in their vegetable gardens. And a Presbyterian missionary there was trying to teach Koreans to grow apples, not realizing that the precious land area used for five or six trees would be enough to support an entire family by growing vegetables.

Some argue that, no matter what, foreign missionaries are necessary to provide medical care for Christians in isolated regions like the mountains of Taiwan. It is true that medical emergencies do occur, and occasionally someone will die prematurely when their life could be saved. But far worse than the occasional death or disfigurement of a young person is the terrible toll that is paid when the white man's diseases are introduced. Time after time some well meaning missionary has penetrated an unreached tribe and introduced measles or flu or chicken pox or pinkeye or some other microbe to which the tribal people have no immunity. Half the tribe may be wiped out within a year. It has been said that far more native people in North and South America were killed by European diseases than by the guns of the conquerors. Tuberculosis was unknown among the aboriginal tribes of Taiwan until the foreigners came, and then it killed thousands. One of the first overseas projects taken on by Christian Aid was a TB hospital for victims of the disease among these mountain people. It was set up and operated by Dr. Wei Sia, a native Formosan, after he completed advanced medical training in the USA in 1954. He was one of the most self giving Christians I have ever known.

Our insistence on sending in foreigners to initiate and propagate the Christian faith in pioneer areas demonstrates a lack of faith in the power of the gospel and the work of the Holy Spirit. Take Indonesia for example.

While on a plane flight years ago I had a long conversation with two army officers from Indonesia who were on an overseas assignment. One was a Muslim and the other a nominal Christian (Dutch Reformed). I asked, "How many Christians live in the islands of Indonesia?" The answer: about 100,000.

"How many Muslims?" About 100 million (at that time).

Why the difference? That's what we talked about.

The first Protestant Christians began to arrive in the islands soon after the incursion of the Dutch beginning in 1602. All were Europeans. For natives of the islands to accept the religion of the foreigners would cause them to lose face among their friends and relatives. So they generally resisted it.

Islam also began to appear in the islands in the early Seventeenth Century. But it was not introduced by foreigners. Indonesian traders discovered the book (Qur'an) about God and the man who was said to be His prophet (Muhammad) while away from home in Malaysia and India. To them it was a priceless treasure which they proudly brought home and shared with their families, friends, customers and neighbors. When these polytheistic idolaters heard of the one God who had created heaven and earth it was also a great discovery for them. To have a share in this new knowledge was to gain face among friends and families. So Islam quickly took root and spread rapidly through the islands.

Is not the Bible and its message more powerful than the Qur'an and the sayings of Muhammad? And does not the Holy Spirit apply it to human hearts while Islam is dependent upon the works of man for its propagation and acceptance?

Obviously, the spread of the Christian faith among the people of Indonesia was hindered by its identification with foreign invaders. But Islam was introduced and propagated solely by natives of the land. Too bad we Christians didn't learn these principles four hundred years ago.

Our role should be limited to reaching people while they are away from home, then getting behind them with financial support when they go home to spread the faith among their own people. When we serve as the supply line for God's servants in poorer countries, we will see the gospel spread in His way from tribe to tribe throughout the world. And once indigenous churches take root among any people, no matter how primitive we may think they are, within one or two generations they will have their own teachers, schools, translators, physicians, nurses and technicians to accomplish anything and everything that we could do for them. And they will do it far better than we ever could in the context of their culture, at a fraction of the cost.

One great example of how our Lord builds His church among unreached people without the involvement of foreign missionaries has been demonstrated in the kingdom of Nepal where thousands of churches have been planted among 70 tribes and nations during the past 50 years. In the next chapter I want to tell the amazing story of some of the pioneer native apostles whom our Lord used to build His church in that land which has never openly admitted foreign missionaries, even to this day.

CHAPTER FOURTEEN

CHURCH GROWTH IN CLOSED LANDS

One of the big arguments used by traditional missions to perpetuate their existence as "sending" agencies has to do with "unreached people groups." Over and over I have heard or read statements coming from executives of traditional missions to the effect that the so called "nationals" in "mission field" countries have no concern for reaching the unevangelized tribes and nations within their respective countries, or in neighboring countries. Those conclusions are based on observations of branch churches of colonial missions, which do tend to be apathetic as long as the rich foreigners are around. "Let the foreigners do it," say the hired clergy of branch churches associated with foreign denominations. "That's what they're getting paid all that money to do."

While I agree that colonial branch churches tend to lack missionary vision and motivation (with a few notable exceptions), the exact opposite is generally true of indigenous evangelical churches (and their associated missionary ministries) that have never been affiliated with foreign colonizers. The consuming passion of several thousand indigenous missions is to plant a witness for our Saviour among those people and in those places where as yet He has no people for His name. And they are ten to one more effective at doing it than are missionaries from industrialized countries.

One notable example of how God works apart from traditional missionaries sent out from wealthy countries may be seen in the isolated, landlocked country of Nepal, nestled among the high Himalaya mountains between India and China. Until 50 years ago there were no roads into that country, and foreign visitors were not allowed. The Hindu king had absolute power, and his subjects were forbidden to change their religion. I believe this rule might have been intended to maintain the status quo between the Hindu majority and the Buddhist minority. Some foreign missionaries had stations along the Indian border from time to time, but none have ever been allowed to enter the country recognized as missionaries. Several foreign agencies formed a consortium called the United Mission to Nepal which concluded an agreement with the Nepalese government by which they were allowed to do social work (mainly schools and medical clinics) within the country. But in order to gain admittance, all UMN representatives had to sign a document by which they agreed that they would not try to propagate their religion while in Nepal.

Of far greater significance for the cause of Christ in that country was the marriage of John and Edith Hayward in Canada about 80 years ago. Edith had been a student at the Christian and Missionary Alliance Bible Institute, where she told her classmates that she planned to be a missionary to India. But then she met John Hayward of Winnipeg, and was led of the Lord to become his wife. Her roommate at the Bible Institute refused to be her bridesmaid. The reason given: "You have given up your call to be a missionary." Little did she realize that, as a result of marrying John Hayward, Edith's influence for the cause of Christ in India would eventually be greater than that of any other Canadian who ever lived. Yet she never went to India. Nor did she go to Nepal, but she became the spiritual grandmother of thousands of believers there.

The story began in the Winnipeg YMCA gymnasium in December 1929. While John Hayward was getting a workout he noticed Bakht Singh, a Sikh from the Punjab area of northern India, who was studying agricultural engineering at the University of Manitoba. John asked this stranger how he was able to maintain such an excellent suntan so late in the year. Bakht Singh replied that he was born with it, and so began a casual friendship. In due time, John invited Bakht Singh to his home for dinner and during family Bible reading that evening Edith Hayward began her astounding career as a pioneer missionary to the unreached people of India and Nepal.

The Haywards invited their new found friend back frequently, and eventually gave him a New Testament. Bakht Singh did not tell them what had happened when a British missionary gave him a leather bound Bible back in Punjab. He associated that missionary with the British rulers who had conquered India, "So this Book must be part of their propaganda," he said to friends. Whereupon he tore out all the pages and burned them. The fine leather cover he kept to put other papers in. I was moved to tears when I first heard Bakht Singh tell about this incident.

As the Great Depression crippled the economy of British India, Bakht Singh's previously prosperous father was unable to continue sending funds to his son in Canada. But the Haywards came to the rescue. They invited Bakht Singh to live with them in their home in order to continue his education. Out of courtesy he reluctantly sat through Bible reading and prayer at the dinner table every evening. Sometimes discussion of the Scripture would take place, and Bakht Singh would argue vehemently against what the Haywards were trying to teach him. This went on for about a year, and then the Spirit of God broke through Bakht Singh's shell of resistance. Alone in his room one night he saw the Lord, accepted Christ as his personal Saviour, made peace with God and was born again. He really surprised the pastor of a Baptist church attended by the Haywards when he showed up in the middle of the week requesting to be baptized.

On April 6, 1933 Bakht Singh arrived back in Bombay and was met by his parents from Punjab. They begged him not to tell anyone of his conversion lest he bring disgrace on his family among the Sikhs. When he refused they told him he could not come home with them. So they left him alone in Bombay. Twelve years later Bakht Singh would baptize his earthly father and hear him say, "My natural son has become my spiritual father in Christ."

With a university degree after study in both England and Canada, Bakht Singh could easily have found favorable employment. But he wasn't interested. He struck out, house to house, door to door, village to village, preaching Christ. First it was to very small groups, then to hundreds, then to thousands all over India. He is credited with being the spiritual father of many thousands of local assemblies of believers in his native land.

In the early years of his ministry, Bakht Singh would gather a team of about 20 disciples and go to a town where there was no church. To get there they would hitch rides on bullock carts, which were to India in those days the equivalent of what trucks were in more industrialized countries. About all they had to take along would be a big bag of rice, and twice a day they would build a fire out of grass and twigs to boil enough in their portable pot for each man to have a little. Any other food they ate would be courtesy of the Hindus or Muslims with whom they were sharing God's Word.

When they reached a given town they would borrow or rent a vacant lot and erect a simple pundal (brush arbor) of palm fronds. There they would sleep on the ground at night, while during the day the team would fan out house to house and in the market places sharing the gospel. Preaching meetings would be held every night at the pundal. Since monsoon rains last only about three months, they had nine months of dry weather every year for apostolic work planting new churches. Their favorite months were April to June when temperatures rose above 100 degrees every day. Few people could keep working in the oppressive heat, so Bakht Singh could find an audience anywhere he went.

I traveled over 5000 miles throughout India in 1948 visiting foreign missionaries who were still there. I met dozens of them who had spent several years in Hindu communities trying to get churches started, but without success. Bakht Singh and his teammates would have a congregation of up to 200 disciples meeting together after only two weeks in a predominately Hindu town or large village. He would leave two teammates behind to meet with them daily for prayer, and for several hours on Sundays to build them into a viable church after he and his team had moved on to the next town. They would take along two new disciples, who would grow in grace and knowledge quickly, then within a few weeks or months return to their original homes where each would serve as an elder or teacher within the church that had been formed there by the team.

Edith Hayward was an integral part of these teams, though still home in Canada. Every month Bakht Singh would send her a letter giving reports of his ministry and she would mimeograph it to be distributed among her Christian friends. In response many would give her a dollar or two which she sent on to her co-worker on the India field. Bakht Singh's tremendous ministry was made possible in large part during those early years by the faithful support of praying friends in Canada recruited by Mrs. Hayward. She thus inaugurated a form of foreign missionary operation which has recently been shown to be more effective than any other. Organizations which follow her example, such as Christian Aid and Partners International, are today sending support for indigenous missions which have deployed over 100,000 missionaries to serve Christ in poorer countries.

Although he held an engineering degree from the University of Manitoba, Bakht Singh never attended a Bible school or theological seminary, yet he had a working knowledge of the Scriptures which exceeded that of any professor I have ever met in such institutions. He memorized hundreds, if not thousands, of verses in the King James English. And not having to unlearn a lot of medieval theological traditions, Bakht Singh very quickly grasped the meaning of the local church as the body of Christ in a given community, as revealed in the epistles of Paul. As I came to know him and sat under his ministry, I was astounded at the similarity between his teachings and those of Watchman Nee in China. Believing that God gives graces to every believer to be exercised for the local church body, neither had any place in their assemblies for ordained ministers.

Since he had not been brain washed by rationalistic Scripture twisters who interpreted God's Word in the light of their own limited experience, Bakht Singh's ministry was not crippled by the "not for today" heresy. He prayed for the sick, and God answered prayer. Mrs. Samantha Vedanayagam told me how her father was deathly sick in a hospital in Madras when the Christians offered to pray for him. The family gave permission and she said the whole building seemed to vibrate as Bakht Singh prayed with power. And her father took up his bedding and walked out of the hospital, to serve the Lord for many years. Thousands of Hindus, and Muslims also, have turned to Christ as a result of miraculous healings in answer to prayers by indigenous church leaders such a Bakht Singh.

On the other hand, Bakht Singh was not a Pentecostal. He believed the Scripture that teaches how God gives different graces to each believer, "dividing to every man severally as He will" (I Corinthians 12:11). He did not try to channel all of God's graces through the single ecstatic experience of "speaking in tongues."

While sharing a time of prayer with Bakht Singh over 40 years ago, I made intercession for the closed countries between India and China: Nepal, Bhutan, Sikkim and Tibet. I prayed that our Lord might yet have a people for His name within each of them. After we had prayed, my dear brother said gently, "You should not pray for those as closed lands; rather, you should remember the saints of the Lord who bear witness for Him there."

I was astounded. This was still early in my Christian experience, and I knew that no European or American missionary had ever worked in any of those countries. To some extent, I was still at that stage where I thought that if we didn't do it, nobody would. "What?" I asked. "Do you mean that believers are located in those places now? Did you send missionaries there?"

Again my Indian brother responded gently. "No, that's not our way," he said. "That's your way, and the British way, and the Canadian way, and the Australian way." Then he told me how visitors and traders from all those areas came into India, and how Christians in local assemblies were alerted to be on the lookout for them. While other Indians might sometimes take advantage of them or treat them in an unfriendly manner, the saints of God showed love and kindness to strangers in their midst. And won many to Christ. In fact, I met a score of them who were staying temporarily as trainees (along with about 80 Indians) at Bakht Singh's home base in Hyderabad. After a few months of discipleship they would return to plant churches in their homelands, or serve as teaching elders in assemblies which had already been formed.

Many citizens of closed lands go abroad seeking employment, and that provides an excellent opportunity for missionary minded Christians to recruit native missionaries. Large numbers of Nepalese, called Gurkhas, found employment as mercenary soldiers with the British forces for 100 years, and later in the army of India. One such Gurkha was Prem Pradhan, who served in the Royal Air Force during World War II, and then was commander of a tank regiment in the Indian army after India gained independence in 1947. In June, 1951 Prem took his annual leave so he could visit his family back in Nepal. While passing through Darjeeling he heard some street preachers say, in the Nepalese language, "It is appointed unto men once to die, but after that the judgement" (Hebrews 9:27). They were from a local assembly started by Bakht Singh. As a Hindu, Prem believed he would die and be reborn many times and in many forms. So what new teaching was this? He went to see the street preachers so he could inquire further.

Within a few days those native missionaries had won Prem to the Lord, baptized him and sent him out to tell others of salvation in Christ. In fact, when he shared the good news with his family back in Nepal and gave them Nepali New Testaments, he was put in jail for three days. Such activity was not allowed in his country. That was the first of 14 imprisonments that Prem would suffer, including one term of five years (reduced from a six year sentence).

Prem returned to his post in the army, taking along an English Bible (KJV) which he read through 12 times during the next three years. He grew in grace rapidly, as he met together at every opportunity with fellow believers in local assemblies started by Bakht Singh and his fellow apostles. Then in 1954 Prem resigned his commission and returned to his homeland as a missionary among his own people. Without any instruction from missions professors or missiologists, he was given wisdom from the Holy Spirit how to plant churches in a totally alien environment. Had someone of European ancestry had a chance to "train" him, I fear he would not have been nearly as effective. His fellowship with Bakht Singh and other Indian believers had served to bring him toward maturity in Christ, but in the completely virgin field of his homeland he would receive wisdom from God which no man could have given him. However, I should mention that he would later spend one year at the OMS Bible school in Allahabad.

Prem walked hundreds of miles over the mountain trails of his country, since there were no roads at that time. He often slept in temples, and sometimes in trees. Occasionally a Hindu family might let him sleep on the dirt floor of the lower part of their hillside house, where they kept their animals. If they knew what he was teaching, they could not invite him to sleep with the family on the hand hued log floor of the upper room lest their family gods (idols) become angry. An entire family he stayed with turned to Christ when a lady whose right side was paralyzed rose up and walked after Prem prayed for her. A Buddhist lama who knew this woman saw what had happened and knelt at Prem's feet, saying, "You are a great lama." Then he offered money if Prem would teach him the "magic" by which this paralytic was healed. But Prem led him to Christ without money and without price. After Prem baptized him that former Buddhist was killed by other lamas.

When Prem would arrive at a village he had never visited before, men of the village would be sitting around talking. Naturally, they would inquire of the stranger, asking who he was, where he was from, and what was new. Prem's reply, "I learned a new thing. A man died and rose again." Their curiosity awakened, the men would then learn immediately of the Lord Jesus, resurrection and eternal life.

Prem Pradhan's introduction of Christian faith into the hostile environment of his native land brought untold suffering to him and his disciples. Younger people were put out of their homes. Older families had their property confiscated and were expelled from their villages. The first assembly halls to be constructed were burned by the Hindus. And since most churches were located in rural villages, the believers had no source of cash. None held paying jobs. They exchanged goats for clothing or chickens for salt within the barter system by which the Nepalese economy functioned. Financial help was desperately needed to care for refugees, pay for building supplies, support schools (there were few public schools at that time) which Prem and his co-workers started, and for many other purposes.

But would any foreign agency help meet the urgent financial needs of these infant churches? Not on your life! All followed the competitive free enterprise model. None would share their wealth simply because they were fellow members of the universal body of

Christ. The mission boards associated within the United Mission consortium were eager to collect and spend $60,000 (adjusted for inflation) a year each sending American families there to do "social work," even though each one signed an agreement with the Nepalese government that they would not "propagate their religion" in Nepal. If they were caught doing it they would be put out of the country. But here were all these Nepali Christians openly spreading the gospel and paying the price for so doing, yet hardly any of the foreign agencies would share their largesse with the Nepalese believers. If the millions of dollars expended for the support of these "social workers" had been made available to the Nepalese churches, far more would have been accomplished for the cause of Christ in that land.

Although foreign mission board executives could not enter Nepal as missionaries, many went as tourists, and some of them contacted Prem Pradhan. Half a dozen leaders of independent inter-denominational missions made him offers: "Just join us, and we will help you financially." Some Lutherans made the same offer. As did Baptists. And Presbyterians. None seemed to be able to think in New Testament terms, that Christians should help their fellow believers solely on the basis of being one in Christ. All were locked in to colonial tradition of every agency seeking to build its own empire and expand its territory. If anyone could gain a following he could put a star on his world map back home, and proudly say, "We are in Nepal now!"

Had Prem accepted any of these offers it would probably have cost him his life. During his five year prison term he was taken to the King's palace for interrogation. The first question: "Where are your headquarters?" Prem could honestly answer, "In Heaven." Had he been affiliated with any foreign agency he would probably have been executed.

Early on, the only U. S. or Canadian mission that contributed financial support on a regular basis to the ministries of either Bakht Singh or Prem Pradhan was Christian Aid (although some individuals and a few churches sent help directly). Christian Aid sponsored Bakht Singh for visits to the USA in 1959 and subsequent years, while Prem was brought over several times after 1967. While I had

Prem with me in Canada in 1970 I took him to visit John and Edith Hayward. Upon entering their house I said, "Mrs. Hayward, meet your grandson."

Many church congregations were thrilled to hear how our Lord was building His church in Nepal and India, and joyfully gave love offerings to help our fellow believers there. But, as I explained in Chapter Seven, missionaries "on furlough" and administrators of colonial missions have expressed vehement opposition to any financial help being given to ministries based in poorer countries. "Let them be supported within their own countries," is a chorus repeated over and over like a broken record.

Almost all of those U.S. missions raise support in other industrialized countries. But the colonial tradition of trying to make their branch churches self supporting in poorer countries is so strong that they are blinded to the fact that indigenous missionary ministries based in those countries should find support abroad on an equal basis with mission boards based in affluent countries. Any other policy is sheer selfishness based on pride and bigotry. "We are superior," the attitude says. "We are deserving of your missionary dollars. But these 'nationals' from third world countries are like inferior children. If you give them money you will spoil them; possibly make them dependent upon you [as we are] for continued assistance."

Several missiological lessons can be learned from indigenous ministries like those headed by Bakht Singh and Prem Pradhan.

First of all, growth of indigenous churches in Nepal has been almost entirely the result of witness from native missionaries and individual local believers. Their development demonstrates the falsehood of colonial mission executives who say the "nationals" don't plant churches among unreached people. The number of believers in Nepal has grown from zero to 600,000 in the past 50 years, and foreign missionaries are still not legally admitted. Believers have been won and churches planted among every one of the 70 or so tongues, tribes and nations there.

Secondly, church growth in Nepal has not been by frontal assault of invading a different culture. Other key men besides Prem found the Lord while away from home and returned to plant churches within their respective tribes. I visited Prem in the Jaliswar prison in 1973 (serving a 50 year sentence, later commuted) and he told me that being there was a great opportunity for him. All prisoners were crowded into a common hold where Prem had a captive audience for Bible classes. But the great thing about it was that his fellow prisoners came from many different tribes and nations. Some of Prem's most effective missionaries were men he won and discipled in prison and then sent back to their respective tribes with the gospel after they were released. But they didn't start branch churches of some denomination. They began and continued the body of Christ in that locality. Prem would not send a Gurung to invade the Tamang nation. Rather, he encouraged the Gurung believers to reach Tamangs who were away from home, and then send them back as apostles to their own people. The same was true regarding most of the other nations among whom he and his disciples planted churches during his lifetime (Prem went home to glory in 1998).

Third, financial support sent to indigenous missions serves to strengthen and greatly multiply their outreach and effectiveness. It does not in any way lessen or reduce the sacrificial giving of the people in their churches. Bakht Singh and Prem Pradhan both lived in utmost simplicity. Neither owned a private home or personal property. Everything was shared with their respective missions. Prem slept on the floor of a school building during the last ten years of his life (even when a guest in my home in America he would sleep on the floor). I visited the closest thing to what Bakht Singh might call "home" in Hyderabad. It was a tiny room in the main building of his home church training base. It had one single bed, a small desk and a chest of drawers.

Colonial mission executives have continually spread the idea that sending financial aid to missions based in poorer countries will cause dependency and deter their own people from giving. That happens only when a comparatively rich foreigner is living in their midst. Time after time I have seen the poorest people in the world give sacrificially of everything they have to support their churches and send out missionaries. A little help from abroad tends to cheer them on and inspire them to give even more.

It enabled Bakht Singh to build dormitories and other facilities in Hyderabad so he could keep over 100 trainees in residence from various parts of India and surrounding countries. Help from abroad enabled Prem to build schools and pay teachers for the education of thousands of Nepali children (especially those from high in the mountains) who otherwise would never have had a chance to learn.

Nepalese Christians voluntarily supply all the labor to make bricks and construct meeting halls and school buildings, but while living on a barter system with no paying jobs there is no way they can come up with money to pay for importing structural steel, cement, glass windows, nails, carpentry tools and sheet metal roofing from India. So when funds arrive from fellow Christians in America, it helps them appreciate the oneness of the universal body of Christ. It also brings a capstone of joy to their sacrificial gifts and labors which would have remained unfinished had not fellow believers far away joined hands with them in supplying materials for completing their projects.

The missionary gifts and offerings of God's people in industrialized countries will accomplish from 50 to 100 times more for the kingdom of God if sent to indigenous ministries rather than being invested in the much more expensive and far less effective tradition of sending Americans, Canadians, Koreans, Europeans, Australians or others overseas to work in foreign countries.

Around 1955 I shared in the annual missionary conference of a church in Michigan. Among the "candidates" there for consideration was a fine young fellow who had received a "call" to be a missionary to India while he was attending Moody Bible Institute a few years earlier. To be better prepared he had then gone to a Christian college and after that to a theological seminary. Along the way he had gotten married and now had four kids. Meanwhile, India had gained independence and didn't want any more missionaries. But he was sure he had been "called" years earlier while in MBI. So he was going right ahead with plans, sure that miraculously "the door would open." What he was seeking was (in 2004 dollars) $60,000 annual support, $20,000 for equipment and supplies, $10,000 per year to put his four kids in English language boarding schools and $8000 for passage money to ship the whole lot and his family to India. If he could obtain a visa to get in.

I asked what he would be doing once he got there and he replied that, of course, he would have to spend the first two or three years in language study. Then he might be able to do some "real missionary work" for about a year, after which it would be time for him to come back home again "on furlough." That is, if he or his wife or one or two of their kids didn't first get so sick that they had to come home earlier. I figured it up for him: he was going to spend over $300,000 (in 2004 dollars) of God's money so he could possibly do about one year of "missionary work" somewhere in India. If he could get a visa to get in.

I asked what he planned to do if he didn't get the visa. He had no alternative plan. So I gave him a suggestion. Why not keep right on doing "deputation" to raise money for missionary support and equipment, but then send it to an indigenous ministry instead of using it all for his own family. What this dear brother's mission board was going to spend to send this one family to India would, in the hands of Bakht Singh or other indigenous mission leaders, provide full support and transportation for more than 50 missionaries who were already there. They would already know all the major languages of India, and any one of them would accomplish ten time more for the kingdom of God than this brother ever could within that culture.

Obviously, he had never thought of such a thing. During ten years studying "missions" in three evangelical institutions, the only thing he had ever heard was the 19th century colonial concept of "going." Not one of his teachers had ever enlightened him concerning the fact that all true believers are one body in Christ, and that if God was truly "calling" or leading him to further His eternal purpose in a foreign country it should be by helping our fellow believers who are serving Him there. Being bound by the colonial traditions of another century, most mission boards, denominations and evangelical organizations in industrialized countries just keep on perpetuating this tragic misuse of God's resources. Most tend to ignore the needs of our fellow Christians in poorer countries because, I believe, we are so preoccupied with doing our own thing, and want to perpetuate our respective organizations.

For more about wise and unwise allocations of God's financial resources, read on in the next chapter.

CHAPTER FIFTEEN

LET'S REDIRECT OUR MISSIONARY GIVING

O nce at the missions conference of a large metropolitan church I shared speaking responsibilities with the head of a major American mission that worked in Africa. He was seeking financial support for his mission so he could send more white missionaries to black Africa. My objective was rather to encourage that church to support indigenous missionary ministries based in African (and other) countries.

One session was an open forum where each of us could present our case and give opportunity for questions. As might be expected, my good friend who headed the traditional mission took issue with what I was saying, because I commented that what he might spend sending one American missionary to Africa would provide full support for 50 African missionaries who were already there. And the Africans already know the local languages, whereas the Americans would have to spend most of their first term trying to learn a tribal language. And historically, over 50% of traditional missionaries who have gone overseas have failed to go back again for another term after their first "furlough."

"But you can't trust the Africans," said the mission executive. "After 100 years of working in Africa, we still have no African we can trust with handling money."

I responded that if his mission stayed on another hundred years they still wouldn't. Why? Because the presence of the rich foreigner breeds covetousness. Compared to the average African, a typical American missionary is fabulously wealthy. Equivalent to a multi-millionaire. Any followers he is able to win would quite naturally want to tap into the gold mine he represents.

When colonial mission leaders say, "You can't trust the nationals," they are speaking out of their own sad experience. For two centuries comparatively affluent foreign missionaries have tried hiring Africans (or Asians) to work for them, and the arrangement has always been fraught with deception, or at least with disappointment. In his book, *Missions at the Crossroads*, my good friend [the late] Stanley Soltau quotes an Asian worker as saying, "The most shameful experience I have had comes month by month when I receive my salary from a foreigner." Then he cites the case of when one of them comes to the foreign missionary "with the plea that he is unable to live on the salary he is receiving because of the high cost of living, or because of the increase of his family, and asks for more." Mission policy dictated that "national workers should be paid so much and no more." So, no increase. But then, Dr. Soltau comments, the "national" might ask his overseer, "How much do you receive?" Knowing full well that the foreigner received many times more than he does, the local worker might say, "Supposing you received just $10 or $20 less a month and give that amount to me. Wouldn't that be fair? Are we not both brothers in Christ?"

As long as the American, Canadian, Korean or European missionary is there, he creates an intolerable situation. Sure, we say, it's o.k. for him to be supported at $60,000 a year, but you can't think of giving that amount to a "national." He would then be receiving 50 times more than other "nationals" in the same country. Implied in that policy is the presumption that the American is superior to the "national" and therefore deserving of more income. But such an implication is simply not true. Within the context of his own culture, the so-called "national" is likely to be ten times more effective than the foreigner, and may also have higher intelligence.

In 1951 I worked with Dr. Roy Hasegawa in Japan. He spearheaded a pioneer evangelistic outreach among university students in the Tokyo area and beyond. He had no direct involvement with any Japanese churches that could provide his support, but he did receive $30 monthly from Park Street Congregational Church in Boston. I compared him with some U.S. missionaries who were receiving 20 times that amount. He appeared to me to be more intelligent than most of them. His command of the Japanese language was far greater than any of theirs would ever be. He was also better educated in English than some of them, having attended college and seminary in the USA during World War II. He and his wife used his ancestral home as a Bible school, and she had to work two jobs to help keep the work going.

I wrote to my good friend Harold John Ockenga, pastor of Park Street Church, and urged him to increase the support his church was sending to Roy. Dr. Ockenga sent me a blistering reply, saying that we should not even think of supporting a "national" on a level above the average income of the general population within that country. He was repeating the standard policy of colonial missions at that time, even though I had mentioned in my letter that Roy was doing more and better work than any of the Americans who received 20 or 30 times more support than he did. That attitude of superiority, shared by virtually every foreign missionary I met in Japan, is, I believe, a major reason why foreign missionaries were so ineffective there. Subsequent events have demonstrated that, if anything, the average Japanese citizen is superior to the average American in many ways: in learning capability, work ethic, techno-logical achievement and industrial production. Japanese industry has put many American competitors out of business in world markets for cameras, copiers, autos, electronics and other products. Of course wages there now are on a par with those in the USA, but in 1951 the average Japanese worker earned about a dollar a day.

The millions of dollars expended by traditional missions send-ing American missionaries to Japan would have been used far more effectively after the war if applied to the support of indigenous ministries inside Japan, and used also to reach Japanese students and business men with the gospel while they were away from home on temporary assignments in the USA and other countries. But traditional foreign missions generally ignored this alternative, and

continued on their obsolete course, perpetuating colonial missionary methods of the 19th century. Their impact in Japan has been
somewhat insignificant as a result.

One key to this matter of support for indigenous ministries
centers on whether any resident "rich foreigners" are involved in
the local distribution of it. If so, it is likely to be regarded as paternalistic colonialism and trouble will follow. But if no resident
foreigners are involved, and the support is handled entirely by
native Christian leaders who all live on the same economic level
and are accountable to one another, that support will multiply their
work many fold. I have yet to see a case of corruption or financial
abuse when support from God's people in industrialized countries is
sent to well established indigenous ministries based in poorer countries, where responsible leaders are open and honest in the handling
of all funds received from all sources, foreign and domestic, and are
accountable to one another.

When William Carey went to India in 1792, no Indian missionary society was there to do the job. Today more than 4000 evangelical missions based in India have sent out an estimated 100,000
missionaries to plant churches among almost all of the 1600 tribes
and nations of that sub-continent. Those with regular support
receive on average about two dollars a day, but thousands more
have no guaranteed income. Similar situations are true elsewhere in
Asia, Africa, Latin America, the former USSR and Eastern Europe.

Why have traditional missions not used their billion dollar
donor base and huge fund raising capabilities to support highly
capable native missionaries who serve with indigenous missions in
poorer countries? Some say it is because most denominational leaders and mission executives are committed only to extending their
own operations into foreign countries, like Ford and GM or Coke
and Pepsi.

I know of one agency that collects multiplied millions of dollars
each year to put on "training seminars" for Christian leaders from
poorer countries. Many of these leaders contact Christian Aid to
request the financial assistance they need to attend those seminars
in various places. Attendees are "challenged" to go home and work
hard spreading the gospel. But the official policy of the sponsors is

to never give a dime to any "national" to help him get the job done.

I am familiar with a certain denominational mission which used to work in a particular country and then their missionaries were all put out. They left behind hundreds of believers, many of whom are now serving as missionaries. This denomination has a large sum of money designated for missionary work in that country. But I have been given to understand that they will not give any of it to the servants of Christ who live there. All is being held back until maybe some day they can send American missionaries there again. Meanwhile the native missionaries must carry on as best they can in the face of indescribable poverty and deprivation.

The few agencies that send financial help to indigenous missions have often been verbally abused. Christian Aid and Partners International have both been supporting mission boards based in poorer countries for half a century. And both have been severely criticized by the evangelical establishment for so doing. These two agencies recognize that we are one body in Christ with our fellow believers in lands of poverty and persecution. Most of what was said in the New Testament about giving concerned the responsibility of Christians in one region for sending financial help to fellow believers in other areas, particularly to those who were going through trials and tribulations caused by famine or oppression from unbelievers (read I Corinthians 16:1-3, Romans 15:26 and II Corinthians 8:1-4). That's what American mission organizations ought to be doing. And they certainly should not oppose and criticize the agencies that recognize the spiritual unity and equality before God of all who are truly in Christ.

One of the graces mentioned in Romans 12 is grace for giving. And the giving mentioned in Romans 15:26 and I Corinthians 16:1-2 was for the purpose of helping fellow believers far away where they faced poverty and persecution. Two entire chapters, II Corinthians 8 and 9, are devoted to explanations of why Christians who have more should share their bounty with the saints who have less. Industrialized countries are God's treasuries. Our vast wealth should be used to support and strengthen the work of our fellow believers in poorer countries, without colonizing them. It should not be squandered on expanding our operations to other countries, especially if our activities compete with true believers who are already there.

Our Lord spoke of the poor widow whose offering of two mites cast into the temple treasury was, in the sight of God, more than all of those given by the rich men who were also casting in their gifts (Luke 21:1-4). Let me tell you of the railroad worker in Canada whose single sacrificial gift in 1951 went further in God's kingdom than the contributions of hundreds of others combined.

The story begins around 1949 when a zealous young Christian named Nicholas Bhengu received a scholarship for study at Taylor University in Indiana. He came from the Zulu nation in southern Africa. His personal testimony was effective and powerful, which resulted in frequent invitations to speak at youth conferences and other church meetings. As the word spread he was invited to speak at ever greater distances from the Taylor campus, including the annual missionary convention at Prairie Bible Institute in the Canadian province of Alberta.

Most of the other speakers were U.S. and Canadian missionaries "on furlough." They shared all the problems they were having in their work in order to generate prayer support and also, I think, to gain sympathy and thus encourage more contributions from the faithful. If you have ever attended a missions conference, I am sure you've heard a long list of problems enumerated.

1. Preparation. Education is essential, and expensive. Some go out with only a Bible institute diploma after high school, but most mission boards require four years of college and even a seminary degree in some cases. Many candidates have to work two or three extra years to pay off their education debts before they can go overseas.

2. Deputation. Many boards require each missionary to raise his or her support before "going out to the field." That may take another year or two, because many churches must be visited, and if the candidate is married with children all that travelling creates horrendous family problems. And is also very expensive.

3. Passports, Visas, Equipment, Shipping and Customs. Every country requires that foreign persons have a valid passport in which their embassy inscribes a visa to permit entry. If the occupation in

the passport is listed as "missionary," visas will be refused by many countries. So a "little white lie" has to be told to cover up the real reason why the missionary is going to a particular country. Then there is the matter of gathering equipment and supplies and shipping the whole lot overseas. Getting it all through customs inspectors, many of whom will hold them up until bribes are paid by the "rich foreigners," can be an exasperating struggle. A friend of mine who was shipping out from New York had $60,000 worth of "equipment" packed into a big van which he was taking with himself and his family "to the field" by an ocean freighter which also carried passengers. He had to leave it in a parking lot overnight and when he returned next morning a window was broken and the van was empty. That loss forced him to postpone his departure date and start over, so he could collect "equipment" again. A young couple I knew went out to India 50 years ago with 24 barrels (steel drums) full of all their personal things, for which they and their supporters had expended thousands of dollars. After much effort they succeeded in clearing all through customs in Bombay, then consigned the barrels to a freight forwarding company for shipment by train to the station of their mission board many miles away. But not one barrel ever arrived. On top of such tribulations, thousands of American missionaries have gotten settled in for a year or two and then the host government refuses to renew their visas. So out they go, after selling all their equipment and furniture to the highest bidder. Few will ever donate their stuff to native missionaries, even though it was originally "given to God" as an offering.

4. <u>Food, Water and Health Problems.</u> Some foreign missionaries spend half their time buying and preparing food, boiling all their drinking water, and wrestling with sanitation problems in less developed areas where public water is not safe to drink and there are no sewers. Almost all want to take along refrigerators, but electric power is usually unavailable in pioneer areas, or frequently fails even in cities. So they must also take generators or have excessive food spoilage. Such problems have forced many missionaries to congregate in the larger cities where they can hope to control their food, water and sanitation needs. In such locations they find themselves in competition with local churches which have been there for

years. And in spite of being careful, most missionary families have continual problems with sickness because of microbes to which their bodies have no immunity. I have known of many cases where a mission board has spent $200,000 getting a missionary family through all the necessary steps toward foreign service, often including language study in Belgium or Costa Rica, only to have them return to America because of illness after less than a year of actual participation in some kind of "missionary work."

5. <u>Language Barriers.</u> Once at a meeting I attended in China an American missionary was trying to deliver a message. He had been in China for 20 years and thought he knew the language. But the leaders of the meeting had to interrupt him because no one could understand what he was trying to say. They requested that he speak in English with a Chinese interpreter. New languages must be learned in childhood. Only about one American in ten can learn to speak a new language well after he is 20 years old. And the older we are the less likely it is that we will ever become fluent, especially if the language is a different family from our own. Native missionaries of the Philippines who have learned three or four languages in childhood can quickly pick up another on a different island after they are grown because they have an aptitude from experience and the new language is similar to their own. But the average foreign missionary from America whose only language has been English is almost never successful in adequately learning to speak something else. While in China I tried to learn Mandarin, but to properly pronounce the four tones was beyond my capability. Later in Korea, and also Japan, I discovered that there were polite and impolite ways of saying things, and I would make a fool of myself if I even tried.

6. <u>Cultural Differences.</u> I remember reading once how President Lyndon Johnson almost started a riot when he offended the King of Thailand by crossing his legs while seated with His Majesty. The sole of Johnson's shoe was directed toward the King – an ultimate insult. I saw a missionary to India almost get killed when he kicked a cow that had laid down across his driveway and didn't want to move. Another had his house burned down by Hindus when his son shot a monkey that raided his vegetable

garden. Many Hindus worship cows and monkeys as gods. Very few if any foreign missionaries can successfully learn the customs of a diverse ethnic group without first causing irreparable harm by innocent blunders. That's why it's better never to send a missionary to work "cross culturally." A native missionary from an adjacent society is much less likely to offend, and his message will thus be more readily received.

At that conference held by Prairie Bible Institute, most of the time was spent listening to returned missionaries share all their problems. Life for them was one unending struggle, and funds were collected in abundance to help cover the exorbitant costs involved with perpetuation of the process. The cause seemed so noble and the objectives so high that no price was deemed too great to be paid. But one faithful brother there was not so sure. That was the railroad worker named Ben Coleman.

All the emphasis of the conference had been on sending white missionaries to black Africa (and other foreboding places) as valiant soldiers of the cross, regardless of the consequences. Nicholas Benghu was asked to give his personal testimony, and in appreciation they gave him a small honorarium plus travel expenses. Otherwise, he was casually ignored. Except by Ben Coleman.

"What about Bhengu?" Ben asked. "Couldn't he be a missionary?"

But no one else at the PBI conference seemed particularly interested in that possibility. All were focused on the more romantic objectives of sending their darling young people out to the regions beyond.

But that railroad worker didn't give up easily. He went to have a talk with the young African who had so stirred his imagination.

"When you go back, will you have all these same problems that American and Canadian missionaries have?" Coleman asked. "Like the language barrier. Will you have to go to language school before you begin your work?"

"Well, I learned seven languages in childhood," the Zulu replied in perfect English. "I guess that will be enough."

"Do you think you might have any serious health problems

when you go out on the mission field?"

"When you speak of the mission field you are talking about my home. I have been eating our food and drinking our water all my life and I've hardly ever been sick since childhood. I expect to continue living as I have always lived in Africa for the rest of my life."

"What about visas?" Coleman continued. "Will that be a problem?"

"My grandfather was a Zulu chief," Bhengu replied. "As a Zulu I can go anywhere in Africa with no questions asked. We aren't likely to be excluded by our own people. I can visit a hundred tribes without even a passport" [remember, this was 1951].

"So, of course, that means you won't have to worry about cultural barriers," Ben reasoned. "It looks to me like you are better fitted to be a missionary in Africa than any of these other young people here. Will you need to take along supplies and equipment the way they do?"

"No, I don't need to take back anything from America," Bhengu explained. "But if I carry out the ministry I believe God has for me, I will need to rent a large tent, some chairs, loud speakers and night lights. I will also need money to pay for printing announcements of our meetings, and to pay for gospels and literature for those who are newly saved."

"How much will you need?"

"I don't want to say, because I have never asked any man for any thing. I make my specific requests unto the Lord, and accept whatever He provides."

Then these two brothers, the older Canadian and the younger African, got on their knees and prayed to see a mighty work of God in Africa.

As Ben Coleman continued to pray in the weeks that followed, he became convinced that God wanted him to have a major part in the work of this native missionary in Africa. So after Bhengu returned to his homeland, this humble railroad worker of modest means dug down into his life savings and came up with $1000 which he quietly sent on to Africa. The equivalent in 2004 Canadian funds would be about $30,000.

Had any colonial missionaries known what Brother Coleman

had done they probably would have, as politely as possible, called him an utter fool. It is likely that they would have tried to convince him that he had thrown away a major portion of his life savings on an unknown character who would probably squander it on personal indulgence. The prejudice of Canadian and American missionaries toward Africans at that time, based on the sad experiences they had suffered within their religious colonies, was really pathetic.

Needless to say, young Bhengu was astounded to receive so large a gift from his newfound friend. Any Zulu man at that time would have to work in the mines for half his lifetime to earn that much money, if he could find a job. The gift was received with thanksgiving as a sacred trust from the Lord, and every cent was carefully guarded in its use.

The first thing Nicholas did was form a team that included other fellows about his age who had a zeal to serve the Lord. Then they printed posters and handbills announcing some big meetings. This was new. Heretofore, no native Africans had money for such printing. Only white people could advertise big meetings, and if any natives (other than those from the religious colonies of the foreigners) did attend the white man's meetings it was likely for the purpose of throwing overripe tomatoes at the white preachers (remember, this was 50 years ago – things have changed since then). Also new was the appearance of black faces on posters advertising the meetings. They generated a lot of curiosity among the native people.

One thing Bhengu did was thought to have been a mistake at first, but later proved to be a tremendous blessing. He rented the largest tent in South Africa, capable of holding 5000 people. But over 10,000 came the first night and not even half of them could get inside the tent.

Hastily, the whole team joined in stringing lights across the vacant hillside beside the tent, and relocated the public address system they had rented. There was no time to move the chairs. The entire 10,000 sat on the ground as they sang some lively songs which the team leaders taught them. Then Bhengu preached with power. At the end of his message, he gave an invitation for sinners to make peace with God through faith in the finished work of Christ upon the cross. Those making decisions were asked to come forward, and 5000 surged to the front of the crowd.

Bhengu sent them all back. He thought they had misunderstood. He told them they must count the cost and give their lives completely to Him who gave His life for us. Then he gave the invitation again for all who were ready to repent of their sins and live for Christ alone. About 5000 came forward again.

Then the team knew why God had led them to rent that big tent. It was just the right size to serve as a place of prayer where those 5000 penitents could kneel in the sawdust and get right with God. Folding chairs served as prayer alters, and as places for counselors to sit and explain the gospel to new converts.

Word of this big meeting, the first of its kind in that part of Africa, spread quickly, and over 15,000 came to sit on the hillside the second night, with another 5000 seekers filling the prayer tent at the end. There were about 20,000 the third night and by the second week attendance had grown to 50,000. The prayer tent was packed to capacity after every meeting.

New believers were encouraged to demonstrate their faith in public baptism, but so many were converted that the team couldn't baptize them all. One Sunday afternoon Brother Bhengu personally baptized 1400 converts in the Buffalo river, and although physically exhausted preached again that night.

Word of these meetings spread far and wide from tribe to tribe among native Africans, and seekers started coming from Swaziland, Lesotho, Botswana, Mozambique and Zimbabwe. Many would sleep on the sawdust in the tent from midnight till daybreak prayer time. With so many pilgrims staying over, it followed naturally that morning meetings should be held also. Attendance swelled to 40,000 every morning and 50,000 every night – 90,000 daily – for six months. Total attendance was over ten million. This was probably the largest series of evangelistic meetings ever held anywhere until that time.

Significantly, no white faces were to be seen in those tremendous crowds at the beginning, although some few white Christians did attend to observe later on. But they had no part in the leadership of the meetings.

These were not pentecostal-type meetings, and there were no "healers" on hand praying for the sick. But the Spirit of God came down into the meetings frequently and let people know He was there by visiting those who were maimed, diseased or afflicted. With no human hand touching them, no one praying for them individually, many who were considered to be "incurables" would rise up with shouts of praise, "I've been healed!" Those whom God chose to touch with His mighty power were probably more surprised than those who were well. Had any "not for today" heretics been on hand, I'm sure they would have insisted these miracles must be some kind of trick.

The miracles served to draw thousands of unbelievers from many tribes to the meetings, and the preaching of the Word brought them from eternal death to eternal life. Then in due time they returned to their respective tribes and villages as witnesses for the Lord. Bhengu told me that at least 1000 new churches were planted among perhaps 100 different tribes all over the southern part of the African continent by those who were touched by the Spirit during those six months of meetings.

So for every single dollar which Ben Coleman gave to get this new work started, a new church was planted somewhere in southern Africa. That's why I said that Ben's comparatively small gift probably had a bigger impact for the kingdom of God than the combined gifts of all the other saints who attended that PBI conference in 1951.

In one African city a large group of Bhengu's converts began to meet together as one body in Christ. With their own hands and limited means they put up the largest church building on the African continent. They planned it to seat 10,000 but about 13,000 jammed into it for several hours every Sunday (and many nights in between) for many years. Some who had regular jobs and couldn't help with the labor gave half their wages every week until the building was finished. They demonstrated that churches will be self supporting from the beginning if they are truly indigenous and no rich foreigners are around to cast a shadow of inhibition or discouragement. When the Spirit of God is truly working among any people group their local congregations will, in most cases, flourish with self-support, even in the poorest places on earth. It's the para-church ministries like Bhengu's missionary team that need support from affluent Christians in developed countries.

That original series of meetings which Bhengu conducted was only the beginning of a movement that would bring forth multiplied thousands of new churches, many in towns where there had never been churches before. Bhengu and his team fanned out from city to city, country to country, preaching Christ and winning souls. They conducted many large meetings, but even more smaller ones. With financial assistance from Christian Aid and other sources, the team purchased several flatbed trucks on which gospel tents seating about 300 persons could be transported. These would be sent out with two native missionaries in each truck. They would erect their tents in areas surrounded by numerous villages with no local church nearby. Crowds would gather, curious as to what might be on display within the colorful stripes of the tents. And as the sound of drums reverberated through the stillness of hills and valleys, every tent would overflow with rural villagers. Most would soon be singing Christian songs for the first time in their lives.

The two (and sometimes three) young men who served as pioneer missionaries with each tent would sleep in the tent or on the truck. Food and water would inevitably be brought to them by hospitable villagers. And within a few weeks a new church would be born in that community. One of the missionaries, or another sent out from team headquarters, would remain to build up the new congregation spiritually, and the truck would move the tent to a new location. At the peak of Bhengu's ministry, he and his team were planting an average of one new church every day – about 400 every year. *Time* magazine ran a full-page story on his work, calling him the "Black Billy Graham." When some African Christians saw the article they commented that it should say rather that Billy Graham was "the Nicholas Bhengu of America."

Three major differences were evident between these two giants of Christian ministry. Graham was essentially an evangelist whom God greatly used to bring church members into an experience of salvation, and also to build up existing churches numerically by winning men and women to Christ through his meetings. Bhengu was likewise an evangelist, but he was also a pioneer apostle. God used him and his team to plant a Christian witness among hundreds of nations and in thousands of towns and villages where previously our Lord had no people for His name.

Another difference was that God came down and demonstrated His presence in Bhengu's meetings through miraculous healings of the sick. True, His presence was also evident in many of Billy's meetings as sinners came under conviction and would often break down in repentance with tears. But spontaneous, miraculous healing miracles did not occur in Graham's meetings as they did in Bhengu's.

A third contrast was in the attention which these two ministries received from the general public. Media moguls hyped Billy Graham as a super celebrity. Bhengu's meetings, which were much larger than Graham's in their earlier years, were all but ignored by the general public. The article in *Time* was a notable exception. Though not publicized in the media, news of God's working spread like wildfire from person to person in southern Africa. Some have suggested that the reason these great meetings attracted so little media attention was that they were 100% African, with no white people involved. Events among Africans didn't attract much attention in the rest of the world at that time.

My purpose in relating them now is to provide some guidance for stewardship to God's people in industrialized countries. As I said earlier, out of their sad experiences in missionary colonialism, mission board executives have spread the saying, "You can't trust Africans with handling money; you had better send it all to us instead." So millions of dollars are still being poured into the coffers of colonial missions which consume it perpetuating their tradition of sending Americans, Canadians, Australians and Koreans to misrepresent our Lord in lands of poverty. We should redirect our missionary giving by ceasing the support of high overhead colonial missions and diverting those funds to indigenous missions instead.

Hundreds of former overseas American missionaries are now supporters of indigenous missionary ministries all over the world. Many of them have said or written to me that the chief value of their being sent "to the field" by their respective mission boards was to open their eyes to the actual situation, which can be summarized as follows:

At least 90% of the effective pioneer missionary work being done in the world today is carried out by indigenous missionaries who are native to lands where they serve, or who work among nearby ethnic groups whose culture is similar to their own. Less than 10% is being done by foreigners from industrialized countries. But that 10% consumes 90% of the total funds contributed by God's people for missionary work. Only 10% of missionary contributions are made available to the servants of our Saviour who do 90% of the work. And any one of those native missionaries is likely to be ten times more effective for the cause of Christ within the context of his own culture than any foreigner could ever be. So, judging by results, 99% of the truly fruitful work is accomplished with one percent of all funds given to advance the kingdom of God in unevangelized areas. The other 99% is consumed by continuation of the costly practice of sending out mission board representatives from affluent countries and financing their various operations in poorer countries of the two-thirds world.

We should not allow this imbalance to continue. A complete reformation of the entire foreign missions agenda is essential if we are to conform to the will of God and advance His kingdom to the uttermost part of the earth. But how will such change affect our churches? Foreign missionary emphasis has been a major source of motivation and inspiration for leading our people forward in their commitment to Christ. Is there a better alternative? In the next chapter you will read that there is.

CHAPTER SIXTEEN

HOW THEN SHALL WE MOTIVATE OUR YOUNG PEOPLE?

✦

Soon after I had returned from service in Asia I was invited to be one of the speakers at a large summer Bible conference. About two hundred high school and college age young people were among those in total attendance. Since other speakers were urging young people to volunteer to be foreign missionaries, I avoided the subject in public meetings lest I cause dissension within the ranks. But I did speak freely in private.

One 18 year old girl seemed stirred by my messages and wanted to tell me that God had "called" her to be a missionary to Korea. So I asked her to sit down and tell me all about it. Her zeal to serve her Saviour was a joy to behold, but it soon became obvious that her "call" was really an emotional response to the persuasive appeals of some speakers she had heard. She knew nothing about what had been happening in Korea since before she was born. All she knew was that she had been "called to the mission field" and something she had heard or learned caused her to believe that Korea was the place she should go.

So I told her a few things about South Korea. I had been to her home town, so I could tell her that evangelical churches were more active in most of Korea than they were in her home community. Then

I quoted a church leader in Korea who said to me: "We cannot understand why these Americans keep coming to our country with their cars and all their dollars. They don't know our language and our people can't understand what they are trying to tell us. All that money any one of them spends for their big houses and servants and private schools for their children would support 50 Korean missionaries, many of whom are out in the villages spreading the gospel with no income at all except the food offered them by the people they are evangelizing" (remember it was in 1950 that he spoke to me).

"The same applies to you," I told this young lady whose idealistic dream of "going to the mission field" was in conflict with reality. I urged her to continue her vision of fulfilling the great commission by getting a job and making all the money she could, but to live simply and sacrificially so she could use that money to support 15 or 20 native missionaries who were already on the field.

She responded positively and shared the concept with her friends at the conference, who shared it with their friends and parents, who shared it with the leaders of the conference and some of the speakers. The result was an uproar of confusion. An emergency meeting was called to deal with the "heresy" which I was spreading. I felt like Martin Luther at the Diet of Worms. Most vitriolic in their condemnation were representatives of Bible institutes and Christian colleges who were there to recruit students to attend their institutions for the express purpose of preparing them to "go to the mission field."

Conference leaders all but threatened me, and slapped me with the injunction that I was not to say one further word publicly or privately at that conference which might deter any young person from "going to the mission field."

Over the past 47 years I have received literally hundreds of similar admonitions from pastors, church missions committees, college presidents, Bible institute faculty, Bible conference directors and other men and women in positions of leadership within the evangelical community, whenever and wherever I may have been invited to speak or teach. The colonial pattern for missionary enterprise is set in stone by tradition, and one dare not suggest an alternative.

In 1946 I conducted a workshop at a big student conference

conducted by InterVarsity Fellowship at the University of Toronto. With passionate zeal I insisted that every born again Christian should "go to the mission field" unless he or she could come up with a really good excuse for not going. Other leaders and speakers did likewise, and hundreds went forward on the final night to declare themselves as volunteers for missionary service. Every three years since then the scenario has been repeated at the University of Illinois in Urbana, with attendance swelling to about 20,000. I attended the 1994 session and found that little had changed. Leaders and speakers were all urging young people to "go to the foreign field." With one exception. In the workshop which I conducted the students were told the truth about colonial missionary operations and urged to seek alternatives such as reaching foreign students from closed lands who are now in the USA, or sending financial support to indigenous missions based in "mission field" countries.

Needless to say this more Biblical perspective was not appreciated by IVF sponsors of the convention. Since I represented Christian Aid there, we were forbidden to exhibit at the next Urbana conference. However, a more charitable attitude was exhibited later, and Christian Aid was again included at Urbana in 2000. In fact, the support of indigenous missions was publicized as one of the goals of the conference.

But how can we motivate our young people if we don't challenge them to join the ranks of semi-martyrs who have forsaken home, family, friends and country to go out to strange lands overseas as soldiers of the cross?

Simple! Give them something even more challenging.

American kids go through billions of dollars every year, indulging themselves in junk food, music, athletic shoes, videos, movies, clothing fads, computer games, and hundreds of other costly items of dubious value. What some Christian kids spend on recorded music, videos, computer games and related hardware is probably equal to the entire foreign missionary enterprise of their respective churches. What's the point of talking about being a missionary "someday" if there is no sacrifice or discipline in the present? Young people should be challenged to begin service in the kingdom of God NOW, not "someday" after they finish several more years of school and are tied down with spouses and children. They should be taught to see the total picture as God sees it, not some sectarian niche into which they are programmed like robots. So here are some steps for challenging our young people.

1. Be reconciled to God. *Just joining a church means nothing unless we first recognize that God is holy and all humans are unworthy sinners deserving of His righteous judgement. We will remain in the outer darkness until we accept by faith the fact that God's only Son loved us and gave Himself for us, bearing our sins in His own body upon the cross. Only by claiming in faith His substitutionary death on our behalf, and the fact that it was confirmed by His resurrection, can we make peace with God and be accepted into His heavenly family.*

2. Recognize that when we accept Christ, He accepts us and puts His Spirit within us to make us new creatures. *Being thus born again we should be continually growing in God's grace and in the knowledge of His Word. And developing special relationships with other true believers who are members of God's family.*

3. Be crucified and risen again with Christ. *If He died for us, we should die for Him, not "someday" but the moment we believe. Old things should pass away so that from now on we live not for ourselves but for Christ. We are not our own but are bought with a price (I Corinthians 6:19-20), which means all that we are and all that we have, including our money, belongs to Christ.*

4. Recognize that the most important thing on this planet is that our Lord might have a witness for Himself, a people for His name, among every people, tongue, tribe and nation. *Diversity of nations began at the tower of Babel when God confounded the one language of mankind and scattered people all over the world in ethnic groupings according to their new languages. He "gave them up" (Romans 1:24,26,28) temporarily and limited His witness on earth to one nation descended from Abraham, Isaac and Jacob. But all along it was His purpose to regather the nations, as He indicated when He promised that through one of Abraham's descendents (the Messiah) all nations would be blessed, and "the children of the desolate (other nations) would be more than the children of the married wife (Israel)" (Isaiah 54:1, Galatians 4:27). Also in*

Isaiah 54 God indicated that "for a small moment" He had forsaken the nations, but that with great mercies He would regather them. Thus would the Messiah "inherit the nations . . . and the God of the whole earth shall He be called." So when the Messiah came He repeated over and over that His primary purpose on this earth was to have a witness for His name among all nations. When that objective has been reached, He said, He would come back again (Mark 13:10, Matthew 24:14). Of the more than 6000 nations on this planet, our Lord thus far has placed His temple (spiritual house) among about 4500 of them. So the supreme task that lies before every local church and individual Christian is to have a part in planting God's temple within the remaining unreached nations, as was foreshadowed by Solomon's temple within the one nation where He had His major witness for 1000 years.

In accordance with these four (and there are also others) basic pillars of Christian faith, young people can best be motivated by having their focus turned away from themselves and toward the kingdom of God. They need to learn that God's eternal purpose is not man centered but Christ centered. It is not essentially "the salvation of lost souls" (although that is important), but that our Lord, looking down from the heavens, might see His temple, His house, His witness planted among all the nations that inhabit the globe.

The kingdom of God is not about Christianizing cultures, or populations, or countries or nations. The majority in every society are going down the broad way that leads to eternal death. The kingdom of God consists of those few within every society who recognize that their citizenship is in the heavens and that they are strangers and pilgrims on the earth, serving as ambassadors for Christ among those who do not know Him. The greatest possible challenge for young people is that they shine as lights for Christ within their homes, churches, schools, neighborhoods and places of employment.

But what about the regions beyond? Shouldn't Christian youth be challenged to pray about someday "going to the mission field?"

Definitely not. Most young people are easily influenced, and any suggestion about them going off to foreign countries is likely to distract them from learning about how our Lord is building His church in every nation without the involvement of foreign crusaders. There are distinct similarities between the Student Volunteer Movement of a century ago and the Children's Crusade of 1212 that saw thousands of children from France and Germany follow a pied piper to their deaths in the naïve belief that God was calling them to liberate the "holy land."

It is of far greater value to the cause of Christ that children be given a vision of how the gospel of Christ is spreading among unreached peoples, and how we are one body in Christ with those whom He is using to accomplish His purpose. And every Christian, regardless of age, can have a part in advancing the kingdom of God NOW in pioneer areas throughout the world. While serving with Christian Aid during the past 50 years, I have taken the names and photos of thousands of pioneer missionaries with me when speaking in churches throughout the U.S. and Canada. At every opportunity I have invited Christians to accept responsibility for supporting one such missionary. Among those who responded was a high school girl in Tennessee who made a faith promise to provide full support for a missionary on the India field with what she earned baby sitting. Two boys attending junior high school in suburban Baltimore took on the full support of a missionary in Nepal with what they earned, working together, shoveling snow for their neighbors in winter, washing cars in the spring, mowing lawns in the summer and raking leaves in the fall. What greater challenge can young people have than to know that they are serving NOW as the supply line for a pioneer missionary who is advancing the kingdom of God in places where Christ was never known before? And to know that many of those natives serve in places where American missionaries are not allowed to go.

I have communicated with many Christian parents who have inspired their children to give half or more of their weekly cash allowances to help our fellow believers in lands of poverty and persecution. Many also have taught their children to share what they might have received at Christmas time with native missionaries overseas whose children have never owned a toy. Instead of being lavished with gifts they don't really need these American children receive money to be used for the support of native missionaries.

Hundreds of Sunday school teachers have encouraged their classes to take on the support of a local missionary in a poorer country, and thus vicariously to become active in completing our Lord's great commission NOW.

Granted, many of these same types of things have been done by Christians who were encouraging their children to support colonial missions, but the kids soon become disillusioned when they discover the comparative wealth of the ones they are supporting. A good friend of mine in suburban Washington, the father of ten children, was very successful in business. Though living in a spacious, comfortable home, he taught his children to live simply and sacrificially so they could support traditional missionaries. Among their friends at school these children were considered to be somewhat poor because they didn't have money for hamburgers and ice cream, or the latest fad in clothing, or electronic gadgets, or fancy athletic shoes. But in due time those Christian kids met others about the same age from the families of missionaries they were supporting (on average at $60,000 per year) and discovered that most of the MKs had the very things their supporter's children were being denied.

When young people realize that they are supporting native missionaries who live in one room houses with no furniture, sleep on the floor, have no phones or electricity (which means no television) and whose only clothing is what they are wearing, then the support those children give will not seem to be a painful sacrifice. Even more so when they learn that many of the children of those missionaries have never owned a toy or slept in a bed or seen a TV program.

The traditional appeal for missionary service is counterproductive. High school and college students are asked to give up earning a living and become dependent on others in order to "go to the mission field." What a waste! There may have been a need for it 100 years ago but not now, because some 300,000 indigenous missionaries are serving Christ on all the world's mission fields, and at least half of them have inadequate support, if they have any at all. How much more effective it would be for the kingdom of God if American youths were challenged to pursue productive careers, yet live simply and sacrificially in order to support native missionaries who have nothing. The common sense of this approach is magnified by the fact that indigenous missionaries are likely to be ten times more effective than foreigners, and also that in most cases the presence of the foreigner often hinders more than helps because he or she identifies the gospel with foreign political influence. If they only knew these facts, most Christian young people would be eager to have a share in the total picture.

Of all people who should discern the dynamics of traditional missions, it should be evangelicals. Ever since Martin Luther liberated monks and nuns from lives of segregated dependency in the monasteries of Germany, most evangelicals have dismissed the concept of an elite class of cloistered Christians who are supposed to give up working and be dependent upon others. Most Protestant churches in our culture look upon their ministers as paid professionals who serve as church administrators as well as preachers, and should be compensated accordingly. But not so our missionaries. As the foreign missionary movement developed in the late 19th century a special class of clergy began to be segregated from the mainstream. These were the ones who were expected to sacrifice the comforts of home and family relationships in order to devote their lives to foreign service. And it did indeed entail that kind of sacrifice 100 years ago, before airplanes, telephones and email. But not any more.

The "missionary class" within evangelical churches is made up of people who are not productive economically. Rather, billions of dollars annually are drained out of God's treasury to support them. If they all gave up the idea of going abroad as economic dependents and became income producers instead, think of what an impact that would make for the kingdom of God. Those billions of dollars now being consumed by the costly practice of sending 50,000 Americans abroad would be enough to support more than 500,000 indigenous missionaries. And the fruit of each one's labor would likely be ten times greater than that of any foreigner. And all those American missionaries now dependent on the contributions of others would become income producers instead, potentially providing other billions of dollars to further God's work in unevangelized lands of poverty and persecution.

So what should be the role of evangelical Christians living in industrialized countries for advancing the kingdom of God in the rest of the world? And how will it appeal to our young people? Let's take a lesson from a military strategy that helped to bring allied victory in World War II.

CHAPTER SEVENTEEN

THE RED BALL EXPRESS

W hile naïve do-gooders in Britain and America were clamor-
ing for disarmament between 1920 and 1939, Germany,
Italy and Japan were building war machines. Their industrial
production was geared toward the manufacture of military materials. So when war began the German forces overran the European
continent within a few months, and Japanese troops just as quickly
took over all of eastern Asia.

What turned the tide was the industrial might of the USA.
Britain and the Soviet Union survived, to a large extent, because
under a "lend-lease" arrangement massive quantities of arms, vehicles and military supplies were shipped to them from America. As
industrial plants in the USA shifted into the production of war
materials, and were not disrupted by air raids, the balance of power
was tipped in favor of the allies.

So what's my point? Just this. I'm leading up to a strategy for
missionary conquest. In my lifetime I have never seen anything to
compare with the all out commitment made by whole populations
to a single cause as was demonstrated during World War II. First it
was by citizens of Germany and Japan, including millions of teen
age youths. Every individual wanted to contribute toward victory
for their forces, regardless of the cost or sacrifice involved. Then
after hostilities erupted, the same devotion became evident within
the entire populations of Britain, Australia, Canada, USA and other

allied countries. Home and family concerns were laid aside. Millions of mothers went to work in war plants, as their sons and husbands went off to fight.

Those who were engaged in actual combat made by far the greatest sacrifice and justly deserve the highest honor. But in the U.S. army as a whole, probably no more than one soldier in five ever fired a gun in combat. Serving to back up the infantry and artillery was the signal corps, the ordinance corps, the transportation corps, the quartermaster corps, the medical corps, and a host of other supporting services. And none of those in uniform, whether army, air force, navy or marines could serve at all were it not for the civilians back at home producing materials and weapons: planes, tanks, vehicles, guns, ammunition, textiles, food, fuel, and other supplies that enabled the troops to advance. Everyone was a soldier. All were committed to winning the war.

So it should be in Christian missions. Two hundred years ago the emphasis was on sending Europeans and Americans overseas as soldiers of the cross, while civilians back at home "held the ropes" by serving as their channel of supply. But that phase is finished. Now the soldiers on the front are local citizens of the countries where they serve. The role of Christian "civilians" in industrialized countries is to supply the needs of destitute soldiers on the front. The greatest hindrance to this process during the past 50 years has been the tragic consumption of available resources by colonial missions that budget $60,000 or more annually to send one American missionary family overseas. But let's suppose that some of the traditional missions should shift their policies and begin to support indigenous missions instead. How should it be done?

Let's go to France in 1944. Allied forces have landed at Normandy and are advancing eastward. Ships are arriving at liberated areas along the coast, bearing precious supplies from civilians at home for the troops at the front. Each group has done, and continues to do, its respective part. But how do we bridge the gap between ships at anchor and troops on the move?

Enter the Red Ball Express, beginning August 26, 1944.

No more important soldiers served in France than the truck drivers of the Red Ball Express. These were vehicles that transported food, water, fuel, ammunition and other supplies from ships along the coast to forces on the front. Each truck had a highly visible big red disk mounted on the front of it for identification. Whenever one approached going eastward, all else was sidetracked to let it through. These indispensable supply line vehicles were given precedence over all other traffic along the way. Even a general in his command car would have to move aside. Whether any battle would be won or lost could be contingent upon the timely arrival of trucks in the Red Ball Express.

As Allied troops moved steadily eastward, the German strategy was to gradually fall back, waiting for the invaders to run out of food, water, fuel and ammunition. Then the Nazis could counterattack and drive them back. In every previous war troops which advanced too quickly had exhausted their supplies and been easily repulsed, if not destroyed. So the Germans waited for their opportunity. And waited. And waited. But it never came.

The reason? It was the Red Ball Express. Never before had such a strategy been employed in warfare. The Allied troops continued to advance, mile after mile, day after day. And they seldom ran out of fuel or ammunition because the Red Ball Express kept them continually supplied with all their basic needs.

Now let's apply the parable. The front line troops today are native missionaries serving Christ with indigenous mission boards in every country (almost), particularly those in lands of poverty and persecution where local support is not available. The supply ships are individual Christians and evangelical churches in industrialized countries. The Red Ball Express represents agencies that convey support from the ships at home to the troops on the fields.

If this strategy were implemented by traditional missions and their supporting churches, the cause of Christ would be advanced a hundred fold around the world. Instead, most mission leaders pursue a strategy that when compared to actual warfare seems hopelessly inefficient and out of date.

"Don't trust those tanks out there on the front," they say. "Give all those supplies to our boys with BB guns (air rifles) and we will send them out to win the war."

"Don't give your supplies to the Red Ball Express," say others.

"The troops at the front may become dependent on them."

"Shame on those truck drivers. All they do is supply others. They should park their trucks and go into battle themselves to do some real fighting."

If all this sounds silly, I wish you could have heard a prominent mission leader who spoke in a meeting I attended recently. He admitted that it was okay for U.S. missions to raise money wherever they wish, but insisted that missions based in Myanmar, Nigeria, Kenya or India should limit their support raising to their own communities. And I could barely believe it when he recommended that a man with an income of a million dollars a year should give up his productive career and go off to some foreign country so he himself could serve as a so-called missionary. He would have to give up his ability to supply the needs of a thousand soldiers of Christ on the front lines, and become dependent on others instead.

On the battlefields of France no one ever suggested that the Red Ball Express drivers were any less soldiers than Dwight Eisenhower or George Patton. The brilliant strategy of this operation shortened the war and made a tremendous contribution to ultimate victory. But, sadly, in the battle for world evangelization the troops at the front have been, to a large extent, left without supplies. Ample resources are available, but the colonial missions establishment has often tried to block the transfer of necessary supplies to the front lines.

Until very recently only two major agencies are known to me to have served as Red Ball Express types. These two missions have been sending financial help to indigenous missions for the past 50 years. All other foreign mission boards, as far as I know, have tended to carry on their own work in foreign countries. Some say they "use nationals," which is what they do. They hire away workers from indigenous missions and use them to propagate the work of their U.S. or other foreign agency in a given country. Other than the two ministries just mentioned, I know of no other major mission board or denomination willing to serve as a supply line for indigenous missionary ministries without trying to colonize, claim, control or affiliate with them. However, there are numerous small mom and pop organizations which send limited financial help to overseas missions. Many individual churches do it also by direct communication with our overseas brethren.

I should mention, too, that certain organizations have sent help to indigenous missions overseas in the early years of their operation, but then later switched over to doing their own thing. One of them began by sending financial assistance to several indigenous ministries based in India, but over the years there was a gradual shift in emphasis until it's projects were taken over and became just another foreign denomination operating in India. This group then ceased to help ministries that were not affiliated with it. Several others have followed the same general pattern, and ended up with their own representatives and employees within India and other countries. Historically, the tendency of all missionary organizations has been toward institutional colonialism. That tendency is so strong that I live in fear lest the ministry to which I have devoted most of my life will eventually become just another colonial operation.

And it's not limited to Europeans, Canadians and Americans. I have already mentioned the Koreans. Several missions based in South Africa have branches in neighboring countries. So do some in Singapore. And Taiwan. Australia. And elsewhere. The colonial mentality of 19th century evangelicals has spread throughout the world. That's another reason why a reformation is long overdue.

In summary, I wish to throw out a challenge to leaders of traditional mission boards. Let me do it by way of illustration.

In 1940, at age 18, I came to Christ while attending Shenandoah Presbyterian Church in Miami. I had gone to Florida alone the year before (after graduation from high school) seeking work in building construction. Many years later I was invited to return as a main speaker for the 50th Anniversary of Shenandoah Church.

Around that time new developments were taking place within Presbyterian denominations. The Presbyterian Church, U.S., in southern states was merging with The Presbyterian Church, USA, a larger body found throughout the rest of the country. Some who did not like the union withdrew and formed a separate body. Several leaders associated with Shenandoah Church were active in the setting up of the new branch of Presbyterianism, which was taking place around the time of the 50th Anniversary. So I gave them a challenge. Why set up another colonial type foreign mission board? Many thousands of evangelical missionaries are already on the fields of the world with no support. Why not have this new Presbyterian group be the first denomination to recognize all true believers as being one body in Christ? Why go through the elaborate, costly process of setting up another colonial mission board to expand this new denomination into other countries? Wouldn't God be much more honored if it should be the first denomination to help God's servants in other countries without colonizing them?

Some good Presbyterians who attended that Anniversary celebration promised me that they would present my proposal to leaders of the new body, but if they did, nothing ever came of it. The new Presbyterian denomination established another traditional foreign mission board and repeated the 19th century colonial pattern as had other denominations before them. In fact it became one of the most colonial operations now in existence among evangelical Christians.

Nevertheless, I continue to throw out the challenge. What mission board in America is willing to phase out the traditional way of sending Americans abroad, and instead use the donor base of their mission to support indigenous missions instead? What mission will cease to be a colonial outreach and instead become a Red Ball Express supply line for some of the thousands of missionary ministries which our Lord has raised up in "mission field" countries, especially those where American missionaries are not allowed to evangelize?

That's my challenge to the leaders of traditional foreign mission boards and organizations. Now read on for a challenge to our churches.

CHAPTER EIGHTEEN

A CHALLENGE TO THE CHURCHES

W hile teaching the adult Sunday school class at a church where I was scheduled to preach in suburban Toronto about 30 years go, I raised a question: "What would it take for you to become a Pentecostal church?"

"Didn't you know?" came the answer. "We belong to the Pentecostal Assemblies of Canada."

"But you aren't truly Pentecostal," I replied, "because you are all Anglos. The church at Pentecost was composed of 120 native Palestinians and 3000 foreign visitors. Where are the foreign disciples in your assembly?"

Therein lies the key to a Biblical missionary strategy for local churches. The original apostles (missionaries) did all their pioneer work among unreached people who were visiting Jerusalem. The text of Acts 2:1-47 and 8:1-4 seems to imply that all their converts on the day of Pentecost were pilgrims from many nations.

That church in Toronto had missed the true significance of Pentecost. At that time Canada had been flooded with millions of recent immigrants. Hundreds of thousands of Hindus, Buddhists and Muslims from the closed lands of Asia and North Africa. But the so called "Pentecostal" church people, with a few exceptions, kept to themselves and by and large ignored the fabulous foreign missionary opportunity that surrounded them.

Another church in the Toronto area where I was invited to preach from time to time, as I have mentioned previously, was People's Church located originally on Bloor Street where the pastor, Dr. Oswald J. Smith, devoted the entire month of April to missionary emphasis. As they raised a million dollars each year for the support of foreign missionaries, the willingness of their members to give was an inspiration to other churches all over North America. But the total thrust at Peoples appeared to me to be focused on sending North Americans overseas. Foreign students in the universities and millions of immigrants from "mission field" countries were generally ignored. If anything, they were looked upon as an annoyance as they poured into the inner city around Bloor Street. More affluent members of Peoples Church retreated to the suburbs where they could get away from the Hindus and Buddhists and Muslims plus multiplied thousands of Chinese who seemed to have no religion at all. The Bloor Street property was sold and Peoples Church relocated to a new facility in suburban Willowdale where Dr. Smith (and his son Paul) could hold even greater meetings to raise yet more funds to send ever more Anglos out to "the mission field." I don't want to appear critical of their actions because I admired them greatly. Also, I well know that our Lord used and blessed many of the missionaries they supported. Rather, I say these things as a way to move toward a missionary challenge for our churches.

This scenario has been repeated thousands of times since Hudson Taylor started sending English missionaries to China in the 1860s. All seem to have missed the New Testament strategy of reaching foreign visitors who are away from home and sending them back to plant a witness for Christ among their own people. The faithful volunteers who zealously went out with CIM were so preoccupied with "going" that they apparently had no time for recruiting Chinese missionaries from among the thousands of Chinese working in restaurants, laundries and factories in London and other English cities. Those who went from America likewise ignored the thousands of Chinese immigrants in California and other states. Why was there not a traveling missionary among the Chinese laborers who built the first transcontinental railroad in the 1860s?

Who was the most influential missionary to China? Was it not John Sung who found Christ after earning his Ph.D. at Ohio State University in 1926? Who has had the greatest influence for Christ of any Canadian missionary to India? Was it not Edith Hayward who won and discipled Bakht Singh in Winnipeg and through him planted thousands of assemblies in India and the first witness in Nepal. If only our churches could realize that winning one Bakht Singh and sending him back would be more valuable to the cause of Christ than sending five thousand foreigners to India. And one John Sung might be worth ten thousand Anglos in China.

When anyone advocates phasing out colonial type foreign missionary operations, pastors and church missions committee members tend to recoil in opposition. "How then will we motivate our people toward fulfillment of the great commission?" they ask.

I have already mentioned the need to redirect our church finances towards the support of indigenous missions. But there is also the challenge of the local church becoming a foreign mission station. Reach the foreign visitors in our midst and send them back as missionaries among their own people, as the original apostles did.

At the time I am writing this no less than 30 million foreign born people are residing in the U.S. and Canada. A majority of them are from "mission field" countries. Go to almost any fine restaurant in a major city like Washington or Chicago and you will find that 90% of the waiters and waitresses do not speak English as their first language. It was more likely Arabic or Turkish or Hindi or any one of a hundred others. The same is often true of hotel employees, taxi drivers and shop keepers. Physicians, nurses and other personnel in our hospitals include tens of thousands of foreign born men and women. Over a million foreign students and scholars (including some wives and children) may be found in our high schools, colleges, universities, medical schools and research facilities. Another million are here as trainees in finance, communications, industrial production and the military. The largest segment of all are the foreign businessmen (and women) who are here to sell their products or represent their companies. Many of them have their family members here also.

Due to social pressures of the culture, an educated professional would hardly ever enter a church meeting in Japan. But thousands of those assigned to represent their firms (Honda, Toyota, Sony, Canon, etc.) in the USA would gladly accept an invitation to visit church meetings while they are here. Over the past 50 years I have taken hundreds of Japanese visitors to churches where I have been speaking, and virtually all of them have been open to learning about the Christian faith. Hardly any of them would be so open back in Japan. And many of those who accepted Christ while here have been His most effective apostles when they returned to Japan. The same has been true of foreign visitors from many other countries.

The presence of 30 million foreign born in our midst is a situation parallel to the day of Pentecost when, according to Josephus, a million pilgrims were visiting in Jerusalem.

Many years ago I gave a message based on this fact at the annual convention of the Full Gospel Businessmen's Fellowship. It was transcribed by editors of *FGBMF Voice* and published in that magazine under the title *A Parallel to Pentecost*. Reprints were then published by International Students, Inc. and widely distributed as a brochure. At the FGBMF International convention the following year I was again one of the speakers. Upon my arrival there I was greeted by Demos Shakarian, who (at that time) was president of FGBMF. To my surprise he pulled out of his coat pocket a copy of the brochure, *A Parallel to Pentecost*, and waved it before me. "This is the way we need to go," he said.

But the idea of this Biblical concept never really caught on with many leaders of FGBMF or the churches they represented. It is my personal conviction that our churches are not likely to seize this opportunity until there is a paradigm shift away from the 19th century "colonial crusades" concept of "sending and going." Preoccupation with "our missionaries out there on the foreign field" is a distraction that keeps us from the two major activities we should have been doing in the first place. These are:

1. *Every individual Christian and every church congregation should be sending financial help to our fellow believes in poorer countries, thus providing support for evangelistic mission boards that are planting new churches among unreached peoples, as well*

as to Bible institutes and other parachurch ministries engaged in education, Bible translation, medical work, broadcasting, child care, refugee relief, feeding famine victims and the publication and distribution of Christian literature.

2. Those in our churches who have special graces for apostleship and evangelism should concentrate on winning immigrants and visitors from "mission field" countries who are now in the USA. Not just leading them to the Lord but bringing them to maturity in the faith and sending them back as pioneer missionaries among their own people.

If we followed these two guidelines, the funds now being expended to support 50,000 language inhibited colonial-type missionaries would provide full support for more than 500,000 native missionaries, all of whom are proficient in their respective languages.

And from among foreign visitors gifted apostles would be recruited to take the gospel back to all the closed countries on earth where foreign missionaries are not allowed.

When I was serving as CEO of International Students Inc. from 1953 to 1970, our missionary staff shared an intense concern to plant a witness for our Lord among the people of Afghanistan. Islamic rulers there had never allowed foreign missionaries to enter the country, although some, including one of our staff, had worked along the borders in neighboring countries. For Afghan students who came to the Lord in the USA we held two conferences to encourage new believers. Two of those who attended were later killed by Muslim Afghans, and others were severely persecuted after they returned to their homeland.

Numerous Afghans have come to Christ through the ministries of International Students, Inc., Overseas Students Mission and Christian Aid, but none of them were successful in planting viable churches after they returned to Afghanistan. The primary reason is, of course, the hostile attitude of Suni Muslims who dominate the population. But a contributory factor has been that those who have returned did so one by one, and had to stand alone against the opposition. Their attempts at Christian witness were doomed from the start because they were so totally isolated from their former friends, families, and the population in general. There was no community of believers to stand with them and lend encouragement – to sustain them in their times of trial.

This situation might have been different if evangelical Christians in North America had caught the vision of "foreign missions at home" and had made concerted efforts to bring to Christ some of the thousands of Afghans living in our midst. Most of the Afghans I have known have been very open to the gospel, and many have begged me to visit in their homes, pray with them, and share the Word of God with them. I could do very little as one person, but if enough other evangelical Christians had become involved we might have seen hundreds, even thousands, of Afghans coming to Christ

Regular conferences could have been held for baptized believers at which strategy could have been worked out for groups of them returning to Afghanistan all at once and meeting together there as living churches within that closed land. In fact, it's not too late to do it now. Where are the churches and parachurch organizations that are willing to concentrate on this large country which until recently had never allowed an active congregation of native believers within its borders?

As the number of Afghans residing in the USA increased into the thousands, I became more and more burdened to see U.S. missionaries working among them full time. But there were none until very recently. Many evangelicals were praying that our Lord might have a witness in Afghanistan, but the only way they could conceive of doing it was to send Americans there as "tent makers." All who went signed an affidavit saying they would not "propagate their religion" in Afghanistan, yet their supporting churches called them "missionaries."

Once I tried to talk to Dr. Oswald Smith about trying to get his members at Peoples Church interested in reaching Afghans in Toronto. My approach to him was that Afghanistan was a closed land which could be penetrated only by evangelization of Afghans in Toronto and other places outside their homeland.

"Closed land, you say?" Dr. Smith responded. Whereupon he pulled out a list of the 100 or more "missionaries" being partially (if not fully) supported by Peoples Church. The countries where they served were in alphabetical order, and at the head of the list were two families in Afghanistan.

End of discussion. Peoples Church had fulfilled its obligation by partially supporting two "missionary" families to Afghanistan, and therefore would not be interested in supporting a second class "stay at home" missionary to work among Afghans in Canada. Which aptly illustrates what I said about the need for our churches to experience a paradigm shift away from our present preoccupation of going and sending.

At ISI we gained the confidence of Afghans and other foreign students by an approach of "friendship first." Since we had cars and they didn't we would drive them to bus and railroad stations as needed, help them to find rooms to rent, and invite them to Christian social gatherings. One who responded favorably was Hafinzullah Amin, a graduate student at Columbia University in New York whom I entertained when he visited Washington. He told me he no longer believed in Islam and "was going to be either a Christian or a Communist." Had there been a "missionary" on the job in New York to concentrate on Afghans, I believe he could have been won to Christ during his time at Columbia. But Communist "missionaries" won him instead.

Some years after his return Hafinzullah became prime minister of Afghanistan and, like Tito of Yugoslavia, led his country toward becoming a Communist state independent of the USSR. The Russians didn't like that, so they killed him and partially occupied the country for eight years, with their own puppet acting as prime minister.

My point is that our churches should support missionaries who are reaching foreign students and other overseas visitors who are here from closed lands, rather than perpetuating the traditional "tent maker" approach of sending out lay missionaries for clandestine activities where open evangelism is not allowed.

An Afghan prime minister who preceded Hafinzullah Amin was stricken with a serious illness and flew to Washington, D.C. for surgery. His attending physician, whom I will call "Dr. Habibi," came with him and stayed in D.C. for about two months. Returning students had previously told him of my kindness to them, so he knew my name as a possible friendly contact in D.C. Not knowing where to find me, but understanding that I was an active Christian, he went to the (Episcopal) Washington Cathedral on Sunday morning and asked for me.

I had never been there except while taking foreign students (including Afghans) on sight seeing tours, but miraculously Dr. Habibi happened to inquire of a friend who knew me. After church services were over he telephoned and I went to pick up Dr. Habibi.

This Afghan physician was very inquisitive as to why so many Americans had been helpful friends to Afghan students in the U.S., so I explained to him how the love of Christ constrained us to love our neighbor (including the stranger) as our self. He became increasingly interested in the Christian faith until I took him with me to a church where I was speaking. On a big bulletin board map inside were photos of numerous missionaries partially supported by the church, including two in Afghanistan. He didn't understand how this could be because his country had never admitted Christian missionaries.

When he returned to Afghanistan Dr. Habibi looked up each of those two "tent makers" whose names he had copied from the church's missionary map. When confronted, each one denied he was a missionary. Dr. Habibi's response: "Oh yes, but you are. I saw your name and photo in a church in America, and information about your missionary work in Afghanistan." Dr. Habibi was really turned off by their duplicity, and called them liars. But he was very receptive to the testimonies of Christians he met in Washington.

Why is it that so many of our churches fail to follow Biblical principles in foreign missions? Hundreds of them have been eager to provide support for Americans to go to Afghanistan where they were not allowed to communicate the gospel, but during the 17 years I worked with ISI we could never find one church that was willing to support a missionary to work among the tens of thousands of Afghans in the USA.

After ISI moved its headquarters from D.C. to Colorado Springs, one tentmaker named Dwight Richie saw the opportunity while home "on furlough." He worked as a missionary to Afghan visitors with ISI for a short while, but for whatever reason (peer pressure? lack of support? traditional influences?) he gave it up and went back to Afghanistan again. Soon after his return he was driving along a blacktop road one night when his car collided with a heavy piece of road grading equipment that had been left with no lights or barriers in the middle of the road. He was killed instantly. Thus we lost our one and only (at that time) missionary working openly among Afghans (while in the USA).

During the many years of war in Afghanistan, hundreds of thousands of Afghan refugees have spilled over into the neighboring countries of Uzbekistan, Tajikistan, China, Iran, Pakistan and India from whence they have spread to every continent. Open evangelism has been carried on among them in some places, and small evangelical Afghan congregations have come together in Pakistan, Europe, Australia and other places. Also, finally, a few full time missionaries now work among the tens of thousands of Afghans in the USA. But it took almost half a century before missionary minded churches would be willing to support them.

The availability of foreign visitors in the USA is astounding. Recently I stopped in a Seven Eleven store and discovered that the cashier was from Afghanistan. Likewise the attendant at a nearby Exxon station was an Afghan. As was the gatekeeper at a parking lot. And a carpet cleaner engaged by one of our Board members to clean his office. And all are eager to "talk about religion" with anyone who is interested. But few evangelicals seem interested. They tend to focus only on the foreign (colonial) missionary programs of their churches while native Afghans are everywhere in America these days, as are Iranians, and Vietnamese, and Tibetans, and Cubans, and Indians, and Pakistanis, and Nepalese, and natives of every other country on the face of the earth.

While checking out of a super market in Charlottesville, I was in front of a taller than average Asian fellow who looked Chinese. I tried a Mandarin greeting on him and he sparkled like a diamond. He was from Shanghai, a graduate scholar at the University of Virginia. I gave him a ride to the rooming house where he occupied a tiny apartment with three other Chinese scholars. They invited me to share a bowl of rice and noodles, with chopsticks.

My new found friend soon began to attend a Chinese Bible

study fellowship conducted by staff missionaries of Christian Aid Mission, and in due time I baptized him. After his baptism he confided, "I was a member of the Communist Party until tonight." Later he returned to Shanghai and led his fiancée to Christ. They were married there and he then brought her back to be with him while he completed work toward his Ph.D. I joyfully baptized her also. Then his parents came for a visit and also accepted the Lord. All are back in Communist China now as ambassadors for Christ.

My point here is that opportunities to be "foreign missionaries at home" are all around us. Altogether in Charlottesville alone over 100 scientists and scholars from Communist China have accepted Christ and been baptized in the past ten years through the part time work of missionaries serving with Christian Aid and members of local churches. The same sort of thing can happen in every college town in America if our churches catch the vision and become foreign mission stations.

Think of a country like Saudi Arabia. Never had a missionary. Never had a church. Never had a witness for Christ. But thousands of Saudis are in the USA as students, businessmen and trainees with the oil companies. Many years ago while ministering in southeastern Florida I was free one evening so decided to visit the University of Miami. I went into an open dormitory where the first student I saw was obviously from the eastern Mediterranean area. When I tried an Arabic greeting he responded enthusiastically. He was from Saudi Arabia, and right away we began talking about Islam (I asked him if he was faithful in praying five times a day, as all true Muslims are supposed to do).

This young man invited me into his spacious room and called in five other Saudi scholars to join us. We talked fervently about Christ, Muhammad, the Quran and the Bible until after midnight. These fellows were so excited to find an American eager to "discuss religion." They said the others they had met showed no interest. In Saudi Arabia, everything is done in the name of God and with prayers. Children begin to recite the Quran and study theology as soon as they can talk. They are very different from materialistic Americans.

Here again my point is to illustrate how the foreign fields have come to us. And how people are open to the gospel while away from home. A few years ago a Christian from the Philippines was caught having Bible study and prayer with a few other Filipinos working as domestic servants in Saudi Arabia. The authorities condemned him to be hanged and only the weight of world opinion caused his sentence to be commuted to expulsion instead. Yet outside the borders of their oppressive country, multiplied thousands of Saudis are eager to meet Christians who will talk about their faith, and to attend Christian meetings. What a tragedy that so few of our churches have seized this amazing opportunity. Most are still, as if by rote, blindly preoccupied with perpetuating the 19th century tradition of "going and sending."

As the guest speaker at a church in suburban Washington a few years ago I was invited to dinner by a member of the missions committee. He was somewhat disturbed by my thesis about the need for our churches to do their foreign missionary work at home instead of perpetuating the more expensive process of sending Americans overseas. He questioned whether I might not have exaggerated statements about the number of foreign nationals living in the USA. So I asked him who his neighbors were and he admitted that he had met only the two on either side adjacent to his house. Then I invited him to go with me that Sunday afternoon to ring some doorbells and see who lived on either side of the street within the block where his house was located. We found neighbors from China, Japan, Pakistan, Russia, India, Brazil and El Salvador, and all could speak English. Every other house was occupied by foreign-born persons from "mission field" countries. Eventually this brother got a neighborhood Bible study started among them.

Of course that was the D.C. area where the percentage of visitors and immigrants is higher than it would be in Omaha or Memphis. Nevertheless, foreign-born persons can be found in every community if we would only look for them. They are here today, and every local church can become a foreign mission station by reaching out to them.

If only we could forget about heroes of the past and start over, our churches would be transformed. Every congregation would have its own missionary heroes who are daily meeting foreign visitors in stores or restaurants or hospitals or universities or research facilities or places of business. And as increasing numbers come to Christ and begin to share their concern for Christian witness in their homelands, every church meeting could be a miniature missionary conference. And a highlight of Christian experience for the church's members would be the day they send a new believer back to his homeland to share Christ with his own people.

The focus would shift from concerns about "our missionaries" who have gone "over there" to the true body of Christ being formed and located among every people, tongue, tribe and nation.

So I repeat: the best way for American churches to advance the kingdom of God is to share our vast wealth with our fellow believers who struggle to bear witness for Christ in the midst of extreme poverty in "mission field" countries overseas. And the second best way to plant a witness for our Lord where as yet He has no people for His name is to reach foreign born people in our midst who have come to us from closed lands all over the world. As they grow to maturity in Christ, He will lead many of them to return to their homelands as His ambassadors among all nations.

But aren't there some exceptions to these two types of foreign missions ministry? After I had grown in grace and knowledge to the point where I realized we should phase out the "going and sending" tradition, I was challenged by Carl Hart, the Baptist pastor who baptized me in 1943. "Are you saying we shouldn't send out our missionaries any more?" he asked. For my answer, keep reading.

CHAPTER NINETEEN

AREN'T THERE SOME EXCEPTIONS?

In previous chapters I have pointed out how our physical presence in cultures that contrast with our own can be offensive to local residents, and thus be a hindrance to their acceptance of the gospel. During the past 50 years I have shared this message in hundreds of places including church services, missionary conferences, Bible conferences, Bible institutes, colleges, seminaries and other gatherings of Christians throughout the world. Usually I have presented some of the experiences and conclusions discussed in this book. Invariably a number of persons have come to me afterwards to ask, "But what about this work, or that, or the other? Aren't they exceptions? Surely the conclusions you have reached don't apply to them."

In most such incidents I believe I have tried to be gracious, but also honest before God. I have tried to make it clear that many good things have come out of traditional missions, even though the good is sometimes a hindrance to the best. Some who are especially persistent about the need to continue traditional missions are those who support some specialized form of missionary activity. When asked for my evaluation of some particular ministry I have usually refused comment lest I appear to be critical of some really wonderful Christians who are sincerely seeking to serve the Lord. Even now I am reluctant to mention any specific work lest I appear to be putting down another point of view in order to support my own.

Missionaries are so dear to evangelical Christians in general that all of us are reluctant to give frank evaluations of what they do. If we dare to be honest and objective, it's very difficult not to appear critical. Nevertheless, in a book like this we have to speak forth regarding the pros and cons of specific operations. Otherwise, the book is incomplete and evasive regarding information that needs to be made known within the churches.

When I worked with Youth for Christ, I continually heard criticism of what we were doing. Usually we received it in good humor and tried to profit from it. The same was true during my years with InterVarsity fellowship. And the Billy Graham Evangelistic Association. And International Students, Inc. of which I was founder and CEO for 17 years. And also Christian Aid, where I have served for the past 50 years. All these ministries have been criticized continually, and in most cases we have profited from it. So now let me dare to say a few words pro and con about some specialized forms of missionary activity.

Take Wycliffe for instance. Perhaps more than any other, this linguistic ministry has been held up to me as an example where Americans, Canadians and Europeans are needed among nations that have no system of writing for their language. The Wycliffe goal is to reduce to writing every unpublished language on the planet. And it is, no doubt, a noble objective. And I would be one of the first to praise God that some of the Wycliffe translators have planted assemblies of believers among the people whose languages they have put in written form for the first time. Most have used a portion of the Bible as the first material to be written in the new language, and in hundreds of cases have advanced the kingdom of God where Christ was not named before.

But is there still a place for this sort of thing in today's world? I asked that question of my dear friend Cameron Townsend almost 40 years ago. Wycliffe had its birth when Cam started out selling Spanish Bibles in Guatemala in 1917. He found that few of the "Indian" tribespeople knew Spanish well enough to even speak it, much less to read it. So he lived within the Cakchiquel nation for 12 years, learned their language, devised an alphabet, and wrote the New Testament in the Cakchiquel language. In 1934 Townsend convened a small training program in Arkansas to teach others how they might duplicate what he had done, and from that simple beginning came the technical side of Wycliffe, the Summer Institute of Linguistics. And the two combined organizations grew to be (at one time but not now) the largest evangelical mission in the world.

"So is there still a need for Wycliffe in 1967?" I asked Cam Townsend when he visited the Washington headquarters of International Students, Inc. I found my answer when he and I went for lunch at the U.S. Civil Service cafeteria two blocks from the ISI office on E Street. Two long parallel serving lines had formed by the time we arrived, and it took us 20 minutes to reach the food. In the line beside us two well tanned fellows were talking away in a language I did not understand. I asked Cam if he recognized it, and when he said he didn't I proceeded to find out who these men were. It turned out they were native Americans from the Yakima Valley in the state of Washington. When I asked how many different languages were spoken by indigenous nations in the Pacific Northwest, the answer was, "Twenty-six." And how many had been reduced to writing? "Only two."

So I asked my dear brother Cam whether or not Wycliffe might be interested in sending linguistic experts to Oregon, Washington and British Columbia to reduce those remaining 24 languages to writing so they could read the New Testament in their own native tongue. Of course not. Children from all of those tribes were now going to English language schools. And many of them were now reading the Bible in English. They would have little interest in reading it in their tribal languages, even if it were available. And there would be nothing else for them to read in their own languages, either, should their tribal languages be reduced to writing. Besides, Wycliffe would have a hard time raising support for missionaries working in Yakima. It wouldn't be nearly as easy as it was to find support for those working in Brazil or Guatemala.

But things have changed greatly in Latin America since 1917. Most governments now have schools among the indigenous tribes, and all are learning Spanish (Portuguese in Brazil). So what's the point of putting tribal languages in writing if there is nothing to read? Coming generations are going to be reading everything in their national languages.

I gently suggested to "Uncle Cam" (he was 26 years my senior) that perhaps the time had come (in 1967, no less) for Wycliffe's leaders to shift some of their vast resources to helping indigenous missions. If churches are planted first among isolated tribes, I told him, they will soon be operating schools where new generations will all learn their national languages which already have the Bible and other Christian literature in abundance. He smiled pleasantly, but I knew that inwardly he was laughing at me. No way could the thousands of committed linguists in SIL change their focus now (in 1967) to helping indigenous missions plant churches in every tribe and nation. A few years later my suggestion would be underscored in boldface reality by Wycliffe's clandestine operations in the Hindu kingdom of Nepal.

I was somewhat involved, but indirectly, in the failed venture. To restrict and control Buddhist and Muslim minorities, Hindu rulers of Nepal had a law that no one could change his religion. Even to try getting someone to change would bring a three-year jail term. Prem Pradhan and other Nepali apostles who found Christ through indigenous churches of India spent many years in dreary dungeons for daring to win souls and plant churches when they returned to their homeland as Christ's ambassadors. From the earliest years Christian Aid sent financial help to Nepali Christians who were going through great tribulation. We helped them set up and operate schools in dozens of places throughout the country. All teaching was in the Nepali national language, even though children came from a score of tribes with different languages.

My source of information about Wycliffe's linguistic operations in Nepal was a Nepali citizen who was employed by Wycliffe as a member of their staff in Nepal. I had led him to Christ and baptized him in 1972 when he was sent to the USA as a foreign scholar by the Nepalese government. After his return I visited his home in Kathmandu, and invited him and his wife to spend some time at the Christian Aid training base in Washington. He was there for six months, during which time his wife also accepted Christ and I baptized her at Temple Baptist Church in D.C. Then they attended a Bible college in Michigan for a year, and while there my disciple was recruited by Wycliffe.

Negotiations with the Nepalese government had been done, not as Wycliffe Bible Translators but as the Summer Institute of Linguistics. A task force was assembled and the country invaded with equipment worthy of a small army. The contract called for linguistic work only, reducing some of Nepal's 60-plus languages to written form. All foreigners were required to sign an affidavit saying that they would not propagate their religion within the country. But many Wycliffe translators had missionary motivation, and in one place they introduced some tribespeople to faith in Christ. The government found out about it and the entire Wycliffe operation was expelled from the country.

My point here is to suggest that it might be far wiser to change the way we work than to perpetuate traditional ways of doing things. Think of what Cam Townsend and his teammates at Wycliffe could have accomplished for the kingdom of God if they had been willing to use some of their abundant financial resources to help our fellow believers in Nepal. Growing, spreading churches could have been provided the necessary finances to set up and operate schools among all the different tribes throughout the Himalaya mountains in that beautiful but poverty stricken country. Through such schools thousands of children could have learned the national language and read God's Word. Believers there at that time were in desperate need of help for setting up schools and supporting teachers. Much more could have been accomplished in shorter time if U.S. Christians had sent more financial help. Nevertheless, there are now over 600,000 professing Christians in the country and more than half of them can read their national language. Churches have been planted and believers educated in every one of the 60 or more (some say 70+) tribes and languages within the country.

Wycliffe might have had a tremendous share in this development if they could have changed focus to helping indigenous churches to enable the younger generation from illiterate tribes learn to read their national language rather than trying to give the older generations a chance to read a few Bible verses in their tribal languages. In Nepal today, educated Christian young people are making free translations of the Scriptures for their illiterate parents, who then commit them to memory in their native languages. Hundreds from many tribes are now in Bible schools, all of which use the national language. Over 300,000 Nepalis are enrolled in Bible correspondence courses, all in the national language, conducted by an indigenous mission supported by Christian Aid.

Few Americans can comprehend these things because most of us know only one language. Many of the Christian leaders within a score of native missions supported by Christian Aid in Nepal speak four or five languages. Earlier I mentioned how the great Zulu apostle, Nicholas Bhengu, spoke seven. Almost all educated Christians in multi-language societies want to do their Bible reading in the same language as their other reading materials. And that's not likely to be their original native tribal language. Ask some of our brothers in Yakima.

If Cameron Townsend were with us today, I would urge him stronger than ever, "Shift gears, dear Brother. Change direction. Use your God-given resources where they will count most in the kingdom of God."

Wycliffe is just one of many ministries that could, I believe, accomplish far more for the cause of Christ with a change of direction toward helping indigenous ministries. But I'm not sure that the leaders of such organizations are likely to appreciate my suggestions. I wouldn't be a bit surprised if they told me to mind my own business. Also, I am well aware that some have changed already, or are in the process of making changes. These are more likely to appreciate the things I am saying.

We all know that there are many ways to communicate the gospel message without having a physical presence in a strange culture. One of the most effective of these has been Christian radio and the extent of this outreach is well known. There is no need for me to comment on it further except to say that when a particular ethnic group is targeted it is essential that the communicator be a native of that language and culture. Alien music and speakers with foreign accents are likely to be suspect in the minds of those who listen. And the actual broadcast facilities should not be situated within countries that are hostile to the gospel.

Many American broadcasters put their personal radio and TV shows on foreign stations with direct translations or subtitles. These are more likely to be offensive rather than helpful because material aimed at American audiences (such as pro-Zionist opinions) can be irrelevant or undesirable in another culture. They are also unwise because they identify Christian witness with foreigners, or even foreign governments.

Some missions put ads in local newspapers overseas and offer free Bibles. Others obtain address lists and mail Bibles in various languages to areas where those languages are spoken. Still others offer Bible correspondence courses to ethnic areas. In this way many individual seekers have obtained information about the Word of God without bringing themselves under suspicion by being identified with (supposedly) subversive foreigners who are often considered to be enemies of their state or culture. It is essential in all literature ministries that none of the material contain a U.S. name or address because it may cause the recipients to think it is political propaganda. The most recent really fabulous opportunity to communicate the gospel without intruding our physical presence into a strange culture is via the internet. I will leave it to others to describe more fully how this open door may be entered by Christians who are impelled by the Holy Spirit to communicate His Word to those who have not yet received it.

In this book I am dealing mainly with the need to phase out the traditional method of seeking to represent our Saviour by going in person to foreign countries. But when we talk about terminating the colonial approach to foreign missions, we must deal with the wave of nostalgia that makes us want to perpetuate the deeds of our fathers. Frequently I am asked, "Aren't there exceptions? Can't we still send Americans somewhere overseas where they may help more than hinder the cause of Christ?" My response is: "Of course there are exceptions, not only in foreign missions but in every aspect of spiritual life among God's people." David ate the show bread which was intended for priests only. Apparently Moses, adopted son of Pharaoh's daughter, was never circumcised (Exodus 6:30), yet God gave instructions for it through him. And God threatened to kill the oldest son of Moses until Zipporah circumcised him (Exodus 4:24-26). Exceptions do not change general rules, and those who base their conduct on exceptions are likely to get out of God's will.

I am reluctant to discuss exceptions regarding things I have said in this book lest someone use them as a basis for perpetuating colonialism. Many exceptions are once for all examples of God's grace. The Jordan River parted for Joshua, but not for anyone else except Elijah and Elisha. Daniel survived the lion's den but many other faithful believers were killed by lions in Roman coliseums. So in listing exceptions to the general situation in foreign missions, I would urge all readers to be very cautious about proceeding without careful study as to whether it is wise to do so.

Take relief organizations and emergency assistance programs, for example. No doubt they do a lot of good in helping to relieve the misery of suffering humanity. But these activities need to be carefully monitored. I have seen some sad examples in cases involving earthquakes and typhoons. Most relief agencies rush in, distribute food and water, possibly even blankets or tents, take lots of photos and videos, then pull out within two weeks. But there are some exceptions, because victims may still be buried under the rubble. Relief efforts need to go on for several months or even years to rehabilitate hundreds if not thousands of homeless people who have lost everything in the disaster. Local Christian citizens are usually left to do what they can to help, alone and without resources. Very few foreign relief organizations are willing to leave behind some financial help for the local Christians when they pull out of a disaster situation. But some of them do and these are the exceptions. Again I will say it: "Change is needed in the way most wealthy organizations operate."

Having said these things, I will reluctantly admit, "Yes, there are special times and special situations when Christians from affluent countries may have a temporary or even permanent place in poorer countries and strange cultures." Here are some guidelines we might want to follow when we do.

1. Go as visitors to observe, but for no longer than a week or two.

Generally speaking, Christians from industrialized countries can be greatly enlightened by traveling as tourists to poorer countries. Those of us who have never been really poor can gain a whole new perspective by seeing how people live in places where there are no industries, hence no jobs. No regular rain and not enough land for sizable farms; so not enough food to support the population. It is impossible for comparatively rich people to fathom what life is like where families live in one room hovels, sleep on dirt floors with no furniture, and have no electricity, running water, telephones, automobiles, refrigerators, change of clothing or sanitary facilities. By observing such conditions in poorer countries, American Christians can more readily understand why it is better to support indigenous missions than to send comparatively rich foreign missionaries to live among the poor. On some short term trips it is possible to visit indigenous Christian ministries in free countries such as India, the Philippines, those in Latin America, and many in Africa. But it is not wise to do so (at present) in countries like Vietnam, Cuba, Communist China, or Islamic nations where such visits may bring suspicion and persecution upon the local believers.

When visiting indigenous ministries it is important to observe certain rules:

a. Communicate only with leaders. Don't single out individuals for favors, or offer them gifts or money. Remember how in the early church all offerings were laid at the feet of the apostles, who then took care of distributions as needed. Give all love offerings to God-appointed leaders of the ministry.

b. Be careful of your conduct and appearance. Don't flaunt your wealth or gadgets. Don't wear shorts or other inappropriate dress. Never touch a person of the opposite sex unless he or she first extends his or her hand for a handshake, and nothing further. Never touch members of your own party of the opposite sex in public, not even your spouse. Avoid touching any person or food with your left hand in a country like India. We should not visit strange cultures without adequate orientation concerning how to avoid offending the people there.

c. Do not accept invitations to speak in public meetings (many cultures require that you be invited to do so, but good manners require that you decline other than to offer a brief greeting for two or three minutes). Rather, say you have come to learn and to receive from them. Then listen to what they have to say. If you and your party require private translation, request to be seated in the rear or other out of the way place where the interpreter's voice will not cause a disturbance.

d. Carefully compute what funds are expended by your hosts to entertain you, including all transportation (a car and driver will likely have been rented); food (they may starve themselves for a week in order to feed you) including that served in homes, rented facilities, phone calls, and gifts which their culture requires to be given to guests and visitors. Your last act upon departure must be to privately present each of your hosts (both in a home and in groups) with a plain white envelope containing more in local currency than your hosts have spent on your behalf during your visit. Remember how King Solomon lavishly entertained the Queen of Sheba, but the gifts she left with him undoubtedly exceeded the cost of her entertainment. Such exchanges are still customary among two thirds of the world's population.

e. Unless you are making substantial financial contributions to their work, do not take pictures, videos, recordings or other media images of the ministries you visit. Thousands of Christian tourists have caused irreparable harm by so doing. It gives the impression that you intend to publicize their ministry at home, in which case you must either send them thousands of dollars or else you may be considered (by them) to be a fraudulent crook who has come to exploit them for your own financial benefit.

f. Eat and drink such things as are set before you without wincing, but with pleasant smiles and words of appreciation. Never find fault or complain about any sight or experience, but be truly appreciative for everything that takes place. Likewise, never say one uncomplimentary word about their country, its government, its economic or other conditions, or about its people or their customs and religions.

2. Certain well known, highly gifted individuals may go to minister.

If Billy Graham had gone to India and tried to start a branch of the Billy Graham denomination, he would have seriously hurt the churches there. But many of them were much encouraged when he went at their invitation for a series of evangelistic meetings. The same is true of Richard Bonke in Africa, who had over a million people in attendance at one single meeting he conducted in Nigeria in October 2000.

To the best of my knowledge, I think Billy Graham's organization always paid all expenses of his ministry in poorer countries so that money would not be collected in the meetings. But others have been less wise. Asking non-Christians to contribute money at large public evangelistic meetings aimed at their salvation has driven millions of would be seekers away from Christ.

Certain other high profile preachers have hurt their testimony by not paying their own expenses. While visiting in an impoverished country of Latin America I had fellowship with local believers who were struggling to raise funds within their ranks to pay an outstanding bill. A prominent English speaking preacher had been there for meetings, and was now demanding that they pay all of his expenses. He wanted two thousand dollars from them. I knew this man personally and was aware that he had amassed a considerable fortune from his books and speaking engagements. Yet here he was trying to extort even more money from fellow believers who were pitifully poor. And he is not an isolated example. There are many like him.

Outside of inner circles within the evangelical community, very few preachers from industrialized countries are well known in the two thirds world. In 1992 I was invited to participate in the orientation of about 60 foreign scholars newly arrived from China. As part of my presentation I mentioned some well known people in America, and asked how many had ever heard of them. Not one person in the entire group, mostly graduate students and doctoral candidates, had ever heard of Billy Graham. Not one knew the name of the Vice President of the USA or other prominent persons I named. But even though no one ever heard of them where they go, many American preachers have found that it's easy to draw a crowd in major cities of Asia, Africa and Latin America. Some have done more harm than good by spending large sums of money to promote meetings in public stadiums when their main objective has been to assemble large audiences to provide exotic footage for their television programs in America. They publicize these events to motivate the faithful back at home to contribute ever more funds for their "missionary" endeavors. The expenses incurred are a business investment that will hopefully pay off with increased contributions. Sometimes these self-promoting individuals do great harm to the cause of Christ with their insensitive activities.

Certain organizations raise their funds, not with big meetings since they don't have a high profile TV personality to promote, but by sending small groups overseas on what they call "short term missions." These are different from those who go to observe and learn. The Christians, young and older, who go on these trips are told that they are going to "have a ministry on the mission field," even though they may spend only two or three weeks in the "mission field" country. Astronomical sums are collected for these tours, but the concept is dubious. If those who go seldom if ever participate in missionary evangelism among strangers while at home, how do they expect to suddenly blossom into pioneer apostles when they go to a foreign country? And in most cases they won't know the local language, so their evangelistic attempts will generally be an exercise in futility. Several U.S. groups send busloads into Mexico to distribute tracts and put on mime or drama shows that purport to be "evangelistic." Many Christian leaders in poorer countries have told me that these missionary tourists convey a carnival atmosphere wherever they go, and are likely to discredit the Christian faith in the eyes of local citizens.

Well planned learning trips to observe the work of Christ in other cultures can be productive in the lives of those who go if they are honestly seeking to learn. But those who claim to be going for "short term mission ministry" would do well to stay at home.

3. **Physicians, especially qualified surgeons, and dentists can be effective on short term visits if invited by indigenous ministries.**

Our God designed the DNA of the human body in such a marvelous way that all the people in the world (except the few who are genetically deformed) have the same organs, same average temperature and same internal systems regardless of outward appearances. So a skilled ophthalmologist can remove a cataract from the eye of an Asian or African with equal dexterity. As a surgeon might remove a tumor from inside a patient whose language he cannot understand.

Thousands of makeshift medical clinics are operated by Christian missions in poorer countries all over the world. A short visit by a qualified physician from an industrialized country could be a great boost to their ministry. As would a visit from an otolarangolist with surgical instruments and hearing aids. Or a dentist, if he takes along some basic equipment. Such agents of mercy are seldom looked upon with suspicion or resentment, as are those who go simply to spread their beliefs.

Short term visits by medical professionals? Yes. But should medical personnel go permanently? Generally, no. For many reasons.

Medical facilities in poorer countries are likely to be primitive and poorly equipped. Highly trained professionals usually find it exasperating to work in them. So if the foreigner wants to work there long term his only alternative may be to set up his own clinic or hospital. This puts him in competition with the locals, and is likely to be looked upon as a form of institutional colonialism. So it's better to go short term as the guest of local Christians and contribute his or her expertise to perform a few much needed procedures. This gives a tremendous boost to the indigenous ministry without causing conflicts.

Most important of all is the economic factor. Doctors and dentists in America have an opportunity to earn huge sums of money. If contributed for indigenous missions in poorer countries (through tax deductible agencies at home) these earnings would enable the overseas ministries to upgrade their facilities, employ local physicians, and enlarge their outreach. In most cases a generous financial contribution by a medical professional will go 50 times further in advancing the kingdom of God in a poorer country than he or she would by going there personally on a long term basis.

Granted, many primitive areas do not have physicians or dentists available when churches are first started there, but get behind those native believers financially and in one generation they will have their own schools, hospitals and other institutions which we take for granted in industrialized countries. I have followed such developments closely for 40 years in one of the poorest countries on earth, the isolated Himalayan kingdom of Nepal. The churches were there first, started by Nepalis who found Christ while away from home in neighboring India, and other countries also, including the USA. As they increased in number they soon had their own schools, and within 15 years were sending young people abroad for higher education. In 1973 I was a guest in the home of a Christian physician who had completed medical training in Calcutta and returned to Nepal to practice. His long one story house had mud walls, a thatch roof and dirt floors. His family was pleased to have five cobras living within the walls and roofs to feed on troublesome insects, rats and mice that also infest such dwellings. One of those snakes woke me up as it crawled over my legs while I slept. I had been advised to remain perfectly still if so approached, which I did, and it moved on through the darkness. It was hard to believe that this was the home of a medical doctor. But then I realized that 90% of his patients had nothing to pay.

4. Go as immigrants.

One of the most vibrant Christian communities in Africa came about as a result of a group of German men going as immigrants to a German colony there around 1900. They didn't go as colonial missionaries supported with funds from home. They got jobs or started businesses to support themselves and after winning favor among local residents they were able to persuade village elders to give each one an African wife. As children were born to them, they quickly developed a community of Christian families.

That's the only way immigration will succeed. Those who emigrate as husband and wife will hardly ever integrate successfully into the local culture. The first house churches in Tibet came about as some Christian men in China patriotically offered themselves to go there as immigrants after that Buddhist nation was taken over by the Chinese Communists. The most successful in their Christian witness were single men who married Tibetan wives and integrated into their Tibetan families.

Our Saviour said, "As my Father hath sent me, even so send I you" (John 20:21). He came into this world as an immigrant, and was so fully integrated into the local culture that hardly anyone suspected Him of having come down from the heavens. If we believe God has called us to serve in another country and culture, we should give up home, family and citizenship in our native land to begin anew as our Saviour did when He came to this earth. I know many who have done so, and have been greatly used of God to begin a witness for Him where none existed before.

To emigrate successfully and become an ambassador for Christ within another country and culture involves several necessary procedures:

a. Apply to the government (through their embassy) of that country for an immigrant's visa. Sometimes these are hard to obtain, but one way is to marry a citizen of that country who is away from home. I know several consecrated Christian ladies who married foreign students in the USA and went with them when they returned to their homelands as ambassadors for Christ. These women have been greatly used of God in their adopted countries.

b. Do not go as a "missionary" supported by contributions from your original homeland. If you do the word will soon spread that you are a spy sent by the CIA. You must determine in advance how you will support yourself once you have arrived at your destination, whether in business, a profession, or secular employment.

c. Unless you have already married a citizen of the country where you are going, you should go as a single person with the intention of marrying a local citizen after you have arrived there. If you go as an English-speaking married couple you will never be able to completely learn the local language or integrate into the culture.

d. Unless you are going to an industrialized country like Japan, you must be prepared to live simply and sacrificially in your new location. Remember our Saviour, "Who though He was rich yet for our sakes became poor, that we through His poverty might be rich" (II Corinthians 8:9). Unless you are able to live on the same economic level as the average person in the place where you are going, your witness will likely be ineffective and unfruitful.

5. Go as a foreign student.

In 1948 I visited the American University in Beirut where I found students from every Islamic country from Iran to Morocco. Originally it had been a missionary school, but had long since lost its Christian emphasis. The few foreign missionaries I met in Beirut had little or no influence among the Muslim students in the university. Back in the USA a few years later I would meet Maurice Hanna of Shreveport who was of Lebanese ancestry. God had called him to spread the gospel so I suggested he go as a foreign student to AUB. He did so, and found the Islamic students eager to talk with him about his faith and Christian experience. Within a year he would have about 100 of them in attendance at evangelistic meetings which he conducted on campus. His fellow students received him much more freely than they would a professional foreign missionary. He had an acceptable reason for being there, which the missionaries did not have in the eyes of local residents.

In the 1970s Mongolia was without a Christian witness. The Lama Buddhists who originally controlled the country never admitted Christian missionaries. Then atheistic Communists dropped an iron curtain around the country and totally closed it off to Christian influence. The only exception I know of was a group of Japanese believers from Emmanuel Church in Tokyo (John Tsatuda, pastor) who went there as immigrants in the 1930s and started a few small fellowships. But I fear they may have been eliminated by the Communists. Then came John Gibbens, a foreign student from England, in 1972.

Though the country was still under Communist rule, John was able to start a Bible study at the university he attended and soon had won some disciples. Wisely, he married one of them and stayed on in Mongolia as a permanent resident. From that beginning the number of believers grew to more than 2000 by 1990. Then foreign missionaries were allowed into Mongolia, and to John's dismay they promptly colonized the local churches and split them up into numerous foreign denominations. Nevertheless, through John Gibbens our Lord demonstrated how one may go to a closed land as a foreign student and be used to start the first Christian witness there. Similar opportunities await mature Christians in many other places. One of the greatest is the *Cite Universitaire* in Paris where may be found hundreds of open minded foreign students from almost every "mission field" country in the world.

6. Go as Bruce Olson went to the Motilone Tribe in Colombia.

Our Lord used Bruce to demonstrate one sent as His Father sent Him. The story can be read in his biography, **Bruchko**, published by Creation House in Carol Stream, Illinois. As a 19 year old boy he went from his home in Minnesota into the jungles along the borders of Colombia and Venezuela to contact the Motilone nation. They were very protective of their territory and were likely to kill intruders who came too near. Olson was almost killed by defenders of another tribe on his way to contact the Motilones. Between arrow wounds, sickness and hunger, he barely survived. When he finally did make contact, instead of killing him the Motilones kept him alive (just barely). He ended up living with them for several years, learned their language and culture, and eventually brought many into a knowledge of Christ and understanding of the kingdom of God. 'Bruchko" was the way they pronounced his name.

Many other examples could be cited of apostles who have gone as single individuals, owning no property, to live among peoples who otherwise had no knowledge of the Christian faith. Sadhu Sundar Singh of India, for example, was in and out of Tibet on foot, without baggage, 13 times during two decades ending in 1929. He would make friends with Tibetan traders who came to northern India during their winter months, then return back with them over the high passes of the Himalayas for the summer. By developing personal relationships with these Tibetans, and learning their language, Sundar Singh became the first man ever to enter the forbidden territory of the (then) murderous Dalai Lama as an ambassador for Christ. The Buddhists apparently killed Sundar during his last journey, because though only 40 years of age he was never heard from again in the world outside Tibet.

Sophie Muller left New York to travel up and down the rivers of Colombia and Brazil, alone and unafraid, staying in the huts of various tribespeople and sharing Christ with them. God used her to plant numerous churches in almost miraculous ways. Had a foreign family with all their gear approached these villages, they would likely have been looked upon as a threat and been greeted with spears and arrows. But if a single woman goes all alone, many tribal villagers may be eager to take her in as a curiosity.

The way not to go was demonstrated by five fellows who invaded the territory of the Huaorani (Auca) nation in Ecuador on January 2, 1956 by landing their plane on a river sandbar. Not for one moment would I question their love for our Lord or their zeal to bear witness for Him to unreached people. They were men of God and their hearts were right. I can even believe the reports that heavenly angels were heard singing above them as their spirits were released from their mutilated bodies and carried into the presence of the Saviour they loved and served. I am confident that He was pleased with their willingness, if not with their wisdom. My purpose is simply to advise how we should proceed in such cases.

As I have said earlier, the way to plant a witness among unreached people, particularly those that are vigilant in protecting their territory from outsiders, is to reach one (or more) of their number who is away from home, and send them back with the message. So it was that an Auca woman named Dayuma was befriended by Christians and won to Christ while away from the tribe. When she returned she took along Elizabeth Elliot, widow of Jim (one of the five martyrs), and Rachel Saint, sister of Nate Saint who had piloted the plane. Those two brave women were received with kindness and hospitality by a tribe known for murderous cruelty because one of their own had brought them along as guests. And by living among these primitive people those two dear ladies were able to gradually introduce them to the Christian faith. The resulting transformation of the Huaorani nation has been an inspiration to evangelical Christians all over the world.

So if you insist that God is calling you to advance His kingdom in a foreign country by going there yourself, you have six choices.

1. Go for a short visit to meet with our fellow believers and observe their work. Then come home and help to find support for them.
2. If invited by local citizens, specially gifted Christian leaders may go briefly to minister, paying all their own expenses.
3. Go short term as a physician or dentist to carry out specialized procedures for an indigenous medical ministry.
4. Give up your U.S. (or other) citizenship and go permanently as a single immigrant, leaving homeland and family, to begin life anew in another country among some unreached people group. If God so leads, be married to someone of that nation.
5. Go as a foreign student in a major university.
6. Go alone, without baggage, preferably as the guest of someone from the group, to live among the people you wish to reach. Don't expect to survive more than a few months, although through God's providence you may possibly last for a few years.

These are exceptions to the suggestions I have made earlier, that Christians from industrialized countries should not go to do missionary work in poorer countries. Doubtless there are others, but each should be given careful study before being implemented by any Christian who is sincerely seeking to advance the kingdom of God.

CHAPTER TWENTY

WORDS OF CAUTION, SUGGESTIONS FOR ACTION

━┿━━┿━

As every reformation has unfolded throughout church history, mistakes have been made and tragedies have occurred. It is of utmost importance therefore that we be vigilant in monitoring the paths we follow, the procedures we adopt and policies we pursue. So I want to list a few guidelines which I believe should be followed as we proceed.

1. Avoid the "both/and" pitfall of compromise.

Luther reformed theology in Germany but retained the dead form of the state church. A century of wars was an inevitable result. Moravians, Mennonites and other anabaptists called Luther a "half reformer." It took 300 years for the problem to be only partially corrected. A major hindrance to the reformation of foreign missionary programs among evangelicals will be the desire to please both sides. Already, hundreds (if not thousands) of church and mission leaders are saying, "We must pursue both: continue sending Americans overseas but also help indigenous missions." Such a policy is fatal to the reformation and will drastically hinder the cause of Christ throughout the world. A complete about face reversal is the only satisfactory solution to residual missionary colonialism, and to bring about the rebirth of a Biblical expression of

Christian faith and practice among evangelical churches in every country.

2. Also avoid the "fraternal worker" mistake.

As many countries gained independence in the past century, branch churches of foreign missions also tried to achieve independence from their foreign parents. Mission executives in industrialized countries did not give up easily. They continually tried to work out ways to keep the apron strings tied to their progeny. One means was the "fraternal worker" concept. The idea was that representatives of the foreign body would no longer lord it over the branch churches as rulers, but would rather serve "alongside" their denominational brothers in other countries.

To understand how such an approach is perceived in contrasting cultures, imagine a Baptist or Presbyterian church in a small town of Georgia or Alabama whose members are all of European ancestry (so called "white" people). Denominational headquarters insists that each have a wealthy fraternal worker from Nigeria come and live among them (in the finest house available) to work along side the elders and deacons, participate in all their meetings, and generally advise the ministers and congregations concerning how their church affairs and activities should be conducted. I've never seen such an arrangement yet within the USA, and don't expect that I ever will. But a similar procedure has been followed in many other countries by colonial missions. The presence of any man of European ancestry in Asia or Africa is just as much a cultural misfit. As would be a Japanese man in the Philippines or a Chinese man in Japan. Fraternal workers have usually been an embarrassment to local churches wherever they have been sent.

Colonial influence is so strong that few American churches are willing to send financial help to indigenous missions without some further involvement. One such was a church that had a speaker from Christian Aid share at their missions conference. They began to send support for a ministry in the Philippines as a result of learning about the effectiveness of that work. But after three years of sending help they decided that "just sending money" was not enough. The church notified Christian Aid that they wanted to "give themselves" in addition. One of their young men who had completed Bible school was eager to "go to the mission field," so the church commissioned him to go as their missionary to work along side the Philippine group. Since he was not married they considered him to be a "low budget" missionary – only $35,000 a year. Apparently they never paused to consider that what they deemed to be a low figure was almost equivalent to the entire cash income of the indigenous mission where he was going, including support of 50 missionaries and a Bible institute with 50 more future missionaries in training.

From the day that fellow arrived at the headquarters of the mission in a mountainous area of the Philippines, he was nothing but trouble. He intruded into all their staff meetings where he had a misguided opinion on everything they were doing. His obvious wealth was a stumbling block to young men in the Bible school, and his presence a curiosity at every church meeting he attended. If he could have understood their language he would have known that they really resented his intrusion into some of their activities and decisions, because they didn't hesitate to say so when talking among themselves. But local customs required them to be polite when speaking to him in English, so it took two years for him to realize that throwing his weight around among them was a disgusting problem that they did not know how to resolve.

What a tragedy that the well meaning deacon board of that fellow's home church in America had such poor insight into the actual situation in other countries. But most of our churches here have been programmed with a colonial mentality by 100 years of the "send out your missionaries" philosophy. The head of that ministry in the Philippines had been a foreign student in America before he went home and began the Bible school. He and his co-workers endured horrendous financial struggles as they trained and sent out pioneer missionaries to plant churches in places where none had existed before. This particular American church that had helped them in a small way could have lifted the burden and doubled the effectiveness of their ministry. Instead they squandered their resources by sending "one of their own" over there to cast a shadow and hinder the work.

3. Work with existing indigenous mission agencies.

Most churches that want to do their own thing in foreign countries end up doing more harm than good. Almost 25 years ago two pastors in a Midwestern state decided to visit India and asked me for contacts. I gave them the address of All India Prayer Fellowship in Delhi. On the strength of my introduction, Dr. P.N. Kurian sent them to visit numerous churches in his fellowship. At two of these churches the visiting Americans made this approach: "We want to adopt you as our sister churches. We will provide your pastors with ample salaries, help you construct new buildings, educate your young people and provide for your widows, elderly and diseased."

How could such an offer be refused? Those two Indian churches gained the world but lost their souls (lost out spiritually). They broke off from AIPF which, through much travail and sacrifice, had given them birth. Their "pastors" trended more and more toward seeking material gain and no longer continued in fellowship with other workers and churches in the AIPF family. Members ceased to give because church needs were being met from abroad. Knowledge of the foreign subsidy spread among the Hindus and thereafter no additional Hindus were brought to Christ through their ministry.

Individuals and churches in America should avoid direct involvement with specific churches or individual workers in poorer countries. Help should be sent rather to established indigenous mission agencies which are engaged in planting new churches in pioneer areas. Local churches should be self supporting, not subsidized. All missionary ministries being helped should provide financial accountability to make sure that individual workers are serving under the oversight and discipline of apostles and elders.

4. Send support to a group rather than to an individual.

No person is above temptation. Almost anyone can be corrupted by money. So when funds are sent overseas, more than one person must be made aware of it. Ideally, distributions should be made to the treasurer with the ministry leader being notified separately. A mission board in Nigeria has about 500 missionaries on the field, reaching more than 50 tribes and nations with the gospel. Once each month the 24 presbyters who head this mission gather for a day of prayer. One of their monthly prayer concerns is the application and distribution of all funds, foreign and domestic, received by the mission that month. As they pray, remembering particularly the needs of their 500 missionaries, God leads them regarding distributions to be made. Christian Aid has sent many thousands of dollars to this mission, and staff personnel who visited Nigeria found excellent records of financial accountability as well as the spiritual fruits of faithful stewardship. But if funds are sent directly to a single individual overseas, he may suddenly appear rich among his fellows and may cease to have an effective witness for Christ. He will no longer have the respect of his neighbors or rapport with other Christians. Funds sent directly to a single local church may cause similar problems. Distributions should be made to the headquarters of indigenous mission boards, or to an association of churches.

5. Don't believe every report you hear.

Many years ago Christian Aid reprinted and distributed an article titled *"Caution: Evangelical Swindlers at Work."* It was written by Dr. Clyde Taylor, then head of the Evangelical Foreign Missions Association. He gave several examples of persons from poorer countries who itinerated in the USA collecting money for ministries and projects that didn't exist. Such swindlers are still making the rounds, and many of them can be very persuasive, even when lying. Some carry around photographs of genuine works of God with which they have no affiliation, and use these photos to raise money for themselves. This is another reason to have an agency such as Christian Aid or Partners International evaluate a ministry before sending funds to it. This goes for American swindlers too. Many of our fellow evangelicals, fundamentalists and Pentecostals in the USA raise money by making false claims and use it for their personal benefit.

6. Try to discern neo-colonialism.

Many mission agencies promote their ministries in fund raising materials by saying, "We use nationals." Some go on and on about how "their nationals" are so much more effective than foreigners and therefore should be supported. But does the U.S. agency work for our brothers overseas, or do they employ those whom they call "nationals" to work for them? There is a big difference. We should support only those mission agencies which share their largess with indigenous ministries without colonizing them. Those who carry on their own work in other countries, even though they employ local citizens to do it for them, will be looked upon overseas as religious colonialism and ultimately hinder the cause of Christ. We should support only those agencies which send financial help to indigenous missions with no strings attached, other than determination of financial accountability, purity of faith and effectiveness in ministry.

7. Don't create local church dependency.

Even in the poorest countries on earth, I have seen local congregations of believers live within their means. If rich foreigners come along with grandiose ideas of pastors, buildings, social welfare and other foreign programs they will interfere with the spiritual life of the churches. It's like giving a 12 year old his own car. He's not ready for it yet. As members of a congregation grow in grace and knowledge, as well as numerically, they may in due time be ready for a meeting hall or Bible school, and a one time gift can be a great encouragement to them then. But initiative for growth must not come from outside the group. It can be harmful if a visitor comes along and says, "You should have this, or that, or the other." Let them make their own decisions and get the project started. Once they are well on their way, doing it themselves, a financial boost from outside their fellowship can help greatly without hurting.

Earlier I mentioned how Rachel Saint went to live with the Huaoani (Auca) people in Ecuador and helped to introduce them to faith in Christ. When she passed away in 1994 her nephew, Steve, went there to join them at her burial. I have also mentioned earlier how Steve's father, Nate Saint, had been killed by these people after he landed a missionary plane on a river sandbar in their territory. Steve wrote an excellent article on his observations during this visit which was published by Bill Berry in the 2001 issue of his handbook titled *Into All the World.* Steve observed how "this small tribe has been lavished with missionary attention for 40 years." Yet the foreign missionaries who were still around complained that the Huao lacked initiative. They wouldn't even fix the rotting floor of the nice church building the foreigners had constructed for them.

But Steve gained a different perspective from the Huaorani. "We don't have permission to work on the foreigner's church," they told him. "If we fix it they may get angry." Steve had this observation: "From their perspective, this church building funded, designed and built by 'outsiders' belonged to the outsiders who had built it."

Let's stay away from making decisions for our fellow believers in poorer countries. But when they are moving ahead on their own initiative, a financial boost from believers in wealthier nations can be of tremendous benefit. Steve Saint learned this when he got a chainsaw for the Huaorani. Once they had a tool like that in their hands they proved what they could do on their own. With no prompting from the foreigners they cut boards freehand from logs and built themselves a clinic. Then several of them joined together and built a rustic house in the jungle for Steve and his wife to live in while they sojourned among the people who had killed his father.

8. Avoid personal financial involvement with individuals.

While traveling overseas you may meet a missionary who walks 12 miles barefoot from his tiny home to a village where he is planting a new church. You feel sorry for him and give him a bicycle. By so doing you may cause division within the fellowship with which he serves. It would be far wiser to speak privately with the leaders (apostles) of that ministry, give your offering to them anonymously, and let them choose which worker should receive a bicycle after you are gone.

A good example of this principle appeared in the December 2000 issue of Ralph Winter's magazine, *Mission Frontiers* (published by the U.S. Center for World Mission in Pasadena). Christopher Little had gone to teach at a Bible school in Mozambique for the Africa Inland Mission beginning in 1993. "As I began to get to know the students and the other professors [Africans] in the school," he writes, "I quickly recognized the disparity between their lives and mine. I traveled to school in a car. With further to travel, they had only their feet. I felt it was appropriate to purchase bicycles for two professors in the school.

They were thrilled with the thought. I managed to get the bicycles [and] felt very pleased when they showed up to class riding their bikes. But I had no idea . . . I had made a grave mistake. I did not go through the proper channels before giving the bikes." Little goes on to explain how his well intentioned interference eventually split the church there. When we as rich foreigners come along and take it upon ourselves to make decisions regarding distributions of money or goods within a local community of believers, we are likely to end up doing what Christopher Little said he did: "Out of my desire to be compassionate and unselfish, I had done more harm than good."

It will be presumed that you are rich if you show up in a poor country. Immature believers may approach you for benefits, just as staff personnel of U.S. missions often submit applications to churches and foundations for grants or support. Even though your heart bleeds with compassion, you must discipline yourself to say no while you are there. Here are some examples of things not to do. DO NOT; repeat, DO NOT:

    a. Offer money as a loan.
    b. Offer to help anyone visit the USA (or any other country).
    c. Help anyone obtain a visa for another country.
    d. Get directly involved helping someone's children to gain admittance to U.S. colleges or study abroad anywhere.
    e. Participate in any way with importing foreign products into the USA.
    f. Carry parcels to be mailed or delivered to someone in the USA.
    g. Offer to be a guarantor for the expenses of a foreign student or other visitor to the USA as required by the U.S. Department of State before a visa is issued.
    h. Become involved with the conduct of any type of business in a foreign country if you intend it to be a form of ministry.
    i. Make suggestions as to how a Christian ministry should be carried on in another country, or how what is being done could be done better (in your opinion). As a guest in someone's home in America, you would not tell your hostess her floor is dirty or that her furniture should be rearranged.

Remember you are always a guest wherever you go over-seas. Never find fault or make suggestions as to how things should be different.

Having said these things as precautions, let me at the same time urge you to action regarding things you should do once you begin to learn something of indigenous evangelical ministries which are doing 90% of the effective pioneer missionary work that is being done in the world today.

1. Link up with a non-colonial agency.

After your return to your home (industrialized) country you should establish a relationship with a non-colonial missions agency such as Christian Aid or Partners International and offer to contribute through that organization to provide financial assistance to ministries you have visited, or to similar works in poorer countries. In this way you can make a far greater impact for the kingdom of God than you ever could if you went overseas yourself as "a missionary on the foreign field."

2. Become an advocate in your home church.

Every evangelical, fundamental or Pentecostal church in America should have an advocate for the support of indigenous missions within its membership. Many who have done so eventually were able to persuade others to catch the vision and send support for God's servants in poorer countries. Some have succeeded in having such support included within the foreign missions budgets of their respective churches. Others have faced criticism and opposition from fellow members who wish to perpetuate colonial traditions, just as our Lord and His disciples were opposed by the orthodox religious establishment of their day.

3. Start a prayer group for indigenous missions in your home.

Many individual Christians in America have an effective ministry for the support of overseas missions by bringing together a group of friends to hear news from the fields and pray for God's servants in poorer countries. Kay Colville, formerly the owner of a

Christian book store in northern Virginia, conducted such gatherings in her home every Thursday morning for many years. When leaders of indigenous missions visited the Washington area she tried to schedule them to visit her group and share about their work. From voluntary contributions received over many years, she was able to send tens of thousands of dollars through Christian Aid for the various overseas missions with which she was familiar. Several individuals who attended her meetings sent still more directly to Christian Aid for the support of indigenous missions. If a few hundred other Christians conducted similar meetings in their homes, they could, potentially, provide support for 100,000 native missionaries who are out on the fields of the world right now with no regular income.

4. Arrange speaking engagements for visiting leaders.

When Prem Pradhan of Nepal was sponsored by International Students, Inc. for a visit to the USA in 1970, a Christian businessman in Seattle arranged for him to share at some type of evangelical meeting every day for three weeks. Some of these engagements were in churches, others in homes, and several were regularly scheduled meetings of men's groups or women's groups. As a result of offerings Prem received in Seattle, fledgling churches of Nepal were rescued from the deprivation brought on by persecution, and the number of believers doubled within the following year. And Prem was able to set up the first Christian day school in that closed country.

For several years while he was serving on the Board of Directors of Christian Aid, Dave Caperton accepted responsibility for arranging an itinerary for every indigenous mission leader who visited his home city of Columbus, Ohio. Their accommodations were provided by John Rothaker, a Christian dentist who maintained a suite of guest rooms on the upper floor of his dental clinic. Offerings received at these engagements eventually provided tens of thousands of dollars for indigenous missions on four continents.

Hundreds of native mission leaders from countries where Christians are oppressed visit the USA every year, and volunteers who arrange for them to be heard in churches can make a tremendous contribution to the cause of Christ in the lands from which they come.

5. Serve as area representative for a non-colonial mission agency.

The average Christian in America, Canada and other industrialized countries knows next to nothing about indigenous missions. If they care about foreign missions at all, the extent of their involvement is usually to contribute to the perpetuation of the frightfully expensive colonial programs of their respective churches. There is an urgent need for education and the dissemination of information about the dramatic changes that have taken place in "mission field" countries during the past 50 years. This situation provides an excellent opportunity for missions minded Christians who want to make a meaningful impact for the cause of Christ around the world. Why not become a volunteer area representative for an agency that supports indigenous missions without claiming or colonizing them? Most such agencies want to send everything possible to those who really need it in poorer countries, so they probably can't pay you a salary. You will need to be self-supporting. An ideal area-rep is a retired person who has enough income to provide for his or her personal needs, or a married woman without young children whose husband's income is adequate for both. Here are some things you can do as a volunteer or area rep for a non-colonial mission:

a. Help arrange itineraries for visiting native mission leaders and provide for their transportation and accommodations while they are in your area.

b. Visit missionary conferences in area churches to put up displays and distribute literature about indigenous missions, and to show videos when possible.

c. Contact pastors and missions committees of churches in your area and persuade them to include indigenous missions in their church budget.

d. Convince local churches to have an "Indigenous Missions Sunday" at which they use a special bulletin provided by your missions partner organization and distribute a brochure or the mission's magazine to all in attendance.

e. Develop relationships with individuals to whom you can provide stewardship counseling regarding their personal sponsorship of a native missionary, Bible institute or other mission project.

Earlier I mentioned how Edith Hayward of Winnipeg became the most influential and effective of all Canadian missionaries to India by doing things like these for Bakht Singh after he returned to India following his student days in Canada. You, too, can be similarly effective as a foreign missionary serving at home by opening up supply lines for some of those thousands of missionaries who are out on foreign fields today with no other source for their material needs.

CHAPTER TWENTY-ONE

A SUMMARY OF REFORMATION CONCLUSIONS

As we read in Hebrews 8:1, "Of the things which we have spoken, this is the sum." Present day foreign missionary operations of evangelical Christians are in dire need of reformation. We should phase out the colonial approach and stop sending missionaries from industrialized countries to lands of great poverty and deprivation. Instead, we should mobilize our vast resources to gather funds and send them to indigenous ministries of like precious faith in the poorer countries of the world. I believe that the reasons why such change is essential have been made clear in the foregoing chapters of this book. Let me review them once again.

1. With a few notable exceptions, the presence of foreign missionaries from industrialized countries like the USA, Canada and South Korea in poorer countries such as India and Uganda or Bolivia and Nepal hinders the cause of Christ far more than helping it. In the eyes of local citizens, it is "cultural colonialism."

2. The chief excuse for perpetuating missionary colonialism is the traditional belief that God commands it. But no such instructions are given in Scripture. There is no record anywhere in the New Testament that God ever sent an apostle (missionary) where he did not know the major language of the area or would be looked upon as a foreign invader.

3. The Biblical pattern for spreading the gospel is to reach visitors who are away from home and send them back to reach their own people. God gave us 3000 examples of this strategy on the day of Pentecost. Other examples are Saul of Tarsus, Barnabas, Andronicus, Junius, John Mark and the Treasurer of Ethiopia.

4. God showed His displeasure with the colonial approach by allowing all foreign missionaries to be excluded from China, the largest of all "mission field" countries. And most were removed from India, the second largest. At about the same time an American missionary wrote home from what was then the Belgian Congo, "Even the Christians here are asking us to leave." Tens of thousands of evangelical Christians the world over have said to the foreigners, as they said to me in China, "It would be better for us and for the cause of Christ if you would please go home now; you being here makes things more difficult for us."

5. Most foreign missionary work during the past 50 years has been carried on as denominational and mission board expansionism, patterned after the free enterprise business model. It ignores the New Testament principle that all true believers are one body in Christ and every one members one of another. Although many idealistic young people are moved by the Holy Spirit in the beginning, once they go overseas they invariably become entwined in a web of carnal competition that is of the flesh rather than of the Spirit.

6. Missionaries from industrialized countries appear fabulously rich when they go to the poorer countries of the world. No way can they represent our Lord who though He was rich yet for our sakes became poor. They misrepresent Him. A Christian leader in Nepal told me that in the early years (beginning in 1954), when foreign missionaries were not allowed entrance, Nepalese who professed faith in Christ paid a price and made a great sacrifice. Often they were put out of their homes and villages, and lost everything of material value. But beginning in the late 1980s a large contingent of foreigners, each supported on average at above $40,000 a year, manipulated their way into the country as "social workers." When their obvious wealth and apparent materialism was observed by the younger generation of Nepalese believers, it had a devastating effect on their spiritual lives. Instead of counting the cost and

paying the price of living as Christians in a hostile Hindu environment, as did their parents, they became much more interested in the materialistic values which they observed in the foreign "missionaries." For this reason a group of Nepalese apostles, elders and pastors got together and adopted a formal resolution asking all foreign Christians to please leave their country.

7. The form of Christianity exported by most traditional mission boards involves social institution churches dependent upon buildings where formal "worship services" are conducted by ordained ministers. This particular expression of Christian faith, indigenous to industrialized countries, may work well where members have cars to drive over paved roads to central meeting places. And where they are able to contribute money to pay for buildings and salaries for church staff. But it is alien to the cultures of poorer countries. When these kinds of churches have been established in "mission field" countries they have often become financially dependent upon their parent bodies and have failed to grow spontaneously.

8. The more Biblical pattern is for local churches to function as does the human body (called "the body of Christ" in the New Testament), with each member exercising the particular grace which God has given him. Such churches will take root, grow and spread much more effectively if no rich foreigners are around to inhibit the spiritual life of native believers.

9. As a new generation arose in China after all foreign missionaries were removed, the number of Christians and local churches exploded beyond all expectations. It could never have happened if the foreigners were still there. The same thing happened in Taiwan during World War II, and in Ethiopia from 1937 to 1945. Also in Nepal, India and many other places when no foreigners were on hand to suppress the life and growth of the churches. These examples demonstrate emphatically how it would be better for the cause of Christ if all missionaries from industrialized countries withdrew from their chosen fields and used their fabulous resources to assist indigenous works instead.

10. The sheer folly of many colonial missionary operations is clearly evident from the fiasco of hundreds of wealthy Americans rushing into the USSR after the collapse of Communist rule.

Although hardly any of them could speak the Russian language, most were supported at upwards of $50,000 a year while thousands of Russian, Ukrainian and other Soviet missionaries were seeking to evangelize their people with support of less than $30 per month per worker. To ignore the needs of native missionaries and consume our resources by sending hordes of rich foreigners into their midst was a crass demonstration of spirituality gone bankrupt.

11. Strong, mature evangelical churches and missions ministries have been active in all countries of Latin America for half a century. More than a full century in many areas. When North Americans intrude into those countries bent on starting their own branch operations they are likely to hinder the cause of Christ more than help. The same is true of missionaries from South Korea or any other countries outside the Hispanic world. Exceptions would be Christians whose mother tongue was Spanish or Portuguese. Occasionally there may also be an exception where someone is invited to go alone without baggage to live with one of the smaller tribes in mountains and forests. The most effective missionary work that North Americans can do in Latin America is to send financial assistance to some of the excellent missionary ministries and Bible schools which are indigenous to those countries.

12. African Christians are deeply grateful for the part which foreign missionaries had a century ago in putting the Word of God into their languages and introducing the Christian faith into the various tribes of their respective countries. But most are agreed that when the independence movements gained momentum it would have been better if all Christian workers of European ancestry had left Africa entirely. The continued presence of so called "white people" casts a shadow that inhibits the full expression of African leadership within the churches. Some will welcome outstanding preachers as their guests for special meetings, but not as long term residents. It is sad that American and Canadian mission boards failed to recognize this situation 50 years ago. If we want to further the cause of Christ in Africa, we should send financial help to some of the thousands of indigenous evangelistic ministries which are being so greatly used of God in all of Africa.

13. Most traditional foreign missionary work today is carried on

by immature Christians who lack faith in our Lord's promise that He would endue His disciples with power from on high. We do not really believe that He will be with us always, unto the end of this age. That He will guide us into all truth. That He would be present in our midst when we gather in His name. Traditional evangelical missionaries generally treat new believers in other cultures as children, and are intent on keeping them in a state of spiritual dependency. A good friend of mine from long ago spent 20 years with the China Inland Mission, then left to start another work which became a major colonial mission. He told me that one reason he left the CIM was because after a church had been established for 50 years in a Chinese town the Mission insisted on keeping two English ladies there to look after it. With a few exceptions, the Holy Spirit usually waits until the paternalistic foreigners are removed from the scene to demonstrate His presence and power. Pentecostal missionaries are seldom different. The faith of their missionaries in the Holy Spirit's working is often limited to ecstatic experiences. Rarely do we see a Pentecostal missionary turn loose of a work they have started in a foreign country and let the Holy Spirit shepherd its life and growth. While preaching in a Pentecostal church in California I told how many of their branch churches in Africa had abandoned their foreign denominational affiliation and associated themselves with indigenous churches in fellowship with those started by the great Zulu apostle, Nicholas Bhengu. A returned missionary of that denomination came to me afterwards and said, "Bhengu *stole* our churches." He certainly didn't steal the church buildings. After gaining independence from the American denomination, many congregations had to purchase their own meeting places from the U.S. headquarters. At least that's the way I heard it: that title to property of each of its branch church properties in Africa was held by the U.S. parent, even if the congregations had constructed the buildings with their own hands. We Americans tend to follow a business model, and can seldom visualize the Holy Spirit working supernaturally apart from us. Indigenous works, on the other hand, are frequently like that of a Yuroba brother I met in Nigeria. Having learned the Fulani language from neighbors in childhood, he went to a Fulani town in the eastern part of the country as a missionary. No church existed within that community until he arrived, but within two years he had a thriving congregation of 900 new believers. When I asked how he did it he said simply that it was not him but God. "I believe in the power of the Holy Spirit," he said. Foreign missionary operations may be structured like businesses now, but when we have a reformation and the resources of agencies are redirected to the whole body of Christ, we will see the Spirit of God working among unreached peoples in ways we never dreamed possible.

14. If we go as foreign invaders to closed lands our presence will likely cause barriers of prejudice to be raised against the gospel of Christ. It is far better to reach people from those lands while they are away from home, and then send them back as ambassadors for Christ. Such strategy has resulted in 600,000 Hindus and Buddhists being brought to Christ in Nepal, a closed land which has never legally admitted Christian missionaries who were honest enough to admit their purpose for going there. But churches planted by Bakht Singh of India won Nepalese such as Prem Pradhan (who came to India for military service) to the Lord and sent them back to plant indigenous churches among their own people. When no foreigners are involved, such churches often mature and multiply beyond our wildest imaginations.

15. Indigenous missionary ministries based in "mission field" countries are doing more than 90% of the effective pioneer missionary work being carried on among unreached peoples in the world today. But they have only 10% of the resources available among evangelical Christians worldwide to do it with. Traditional (colonial) missions based in industrialized countries, however, do less than 10% of the effective work among unreached peoples, but they consume 90% of the finances given for evangelical missionary outreach throughout the world in carrying on that 10% of the work. To be right with God, Bible believing Christians, and their churches, who live in the more developed countries must redirect their missionary giving. We must stop using God's money to finance a continued expansion of our own denominations and organizations to poorer countries. Instead, we must recognize the headship of our Lord Jesus Christ over all of His people. Whatever we do for the furtherance of His purpose in other countries must be in

consideration of his headship. He is not pleased when we ignore His body, or divide it, or decimate it with competition. Whatever we do in His name and for His cause in poorer countries should be to supply the needs and strengthen the work of our fellow believers who are already there.

16. We must no longer misdirect the young people of our churches by trying to motivate them to go live and work in foreign cultures. Rather, we must challenge them to take up the cause of our Saviour NOW by living simply and sacrificially, and using their awesome power to earn money as a means to supply the needs of some of the thousands of God's servants who are out on all the mission fields of the world with little or no support. We must also inspire our young people to reach out in friendship to some of the millions of foreign visitors now in our midst, with the goal of winning them to Christ and sending them home as missionaries among their own people.

17. The effective missionary of the future who lives in an industrialized country will not feel guilty if he or she does not go to live and work in a foreign country. Rather, we will recognize the strategic position which God has given to us as stewards of His treasury. The front lines of God's army today are indigenous ministries which have over 300,000 missionaries on the fields of the world. But many of them have little or no support. The most important thing we can do is to be their supply line. Our position parallels that of the Red Ball Express, a contingent of truck drivers who in 1944 transported fuel, ammunition and supplies from ships along the French coast to allied forces which were advancing eastward toward Germany. They made a far greater contribution toward ultimate victory by driving those trucks than they would have trying to fight on the front without fuel or ammunition. The future missionary who earns money and gives it to support indigenous missionary ministries will feel good about what he is doing. There should be no more guilt trips brought on by rejecting the colonial conception of "going to the mission field."

18. After the reformation our churches will no longer feel that we have to send someone overseas to fulfill our missionary responsibility. Our overseas focus will be on our Savior's witness through

indigenous churches in the most difficult places on earth. We will back up our support of indigenous missions by following news of their progress, and of the tribulations they endure. But that alone will not be enough. We will lift up our eyes and look on the fields to see the millions of foreign born persons from every country who are living in our midst. We will reach out to them one by one and bring them into God's household. Then every local church will become a foreign mission station. And also be a sending church when those we have won and discipled go back as Christ's ambassadors to their respective nations.

19. Neither will future missionaries be judgmental toward those few exceptions exemplified by devout Christians who give up their American citizenship and go as immigrants to unevangelized countries in order to share the gospel. Or those who go as foreign students. Or even those who go without baggage to live among isolated tribes. We will recognize these as valid exceptions to the basic strategy of the reformation, because God in His sovereign will may choose to use someone whose way is different from the mainstream.

20. Inherent in every reformation is the danger of excess. Of arrogance and pride. Of divisions. Of poor judgement, or lack of caution. Even of fraud and deception. As changes occur in the way we carry on our foreign missionary activities in the 21st century, we must be ever vigilant lest false disciples take advantage of our new directions and capitalize on them for personal gain. God's Word continually reminds us that all men are sinners by nature. We all know that one of our Lord's 12 disciples turned out to be a thief and a traitor. Almost all the denominations and para-church ministries in America have seen cases of embezzlement and self-gratification within their ranks. Those in poorer countries can likewise be tempted. So we must have safeguards in place in the administration of the Lord's treasury. We must be careful also to see that those who become champions of the reformation do not adopt an attitude of intolerance toward our fellow believers who are slow to change. We must pray for the virtue of patience, and continue to love all the saints regardless of their rate of growth in understanding how best to carry out the commission our Lord and Saviour has given to us.

CHAPTER TWENTY-TWO

A FINAL WORD

━━━

Two main attributes are ascribed to Christians in the New Testament. The first is our "faith in the Lord Jesus" and the second is our "love for all the saints." It has been my goal in life to embrace these two attributes, and to give expression to them both in all I do. I have not always succeeded in doing so, but I hope I have exemplified them in this book.

One thing I have emphasized is that born again Christians should relate to one another as members of God's heavenly family. We tend to divide ourselves up into sectarian groups and ignore, or even oppose, those who are not part of our company. I believe such attitudes are dishonoring to God, and pray that those who have read this epistle will be moved to accept more fully the Biblical concept that we are one in Christ with our fellow believers all over the world.

I am not talking about an ecumenical union of ecclesiastical bodies. Just the opposite. Family members don't incorporate into legal entities in order to relate to one another. Brothers and sisters are taken for granted as having a special relationship with one another even though they may live miles apart. One may be a brick layer, another a bus driver and the third a school teacher. Each has his or her particular vocation, yet all are one family. So it should be in the family of God.

In the First Epistle of John (original Greek) four kinds of believers are addressed: infants, little children, young men and fathers. In a loving family the older brothers don't bawl out or reject the little children because they can't comprehend algebra. Give them time and they may master calculus. At the annual missionary conference of an independent Baptist church I recommended that they support some indigenous missions in countries where American missionaries are not allowed. The pastor then took me aside and in fatherly fashion let me know they had no intention of supporting any mission unless "it" believed exactly as they did ("they" meaning the members he had successfully brainwashed). But as I got to know him better I came to realize that he was just a little child in the faith. He wasn't even a young man yet. So his idea of missions was to send little children overseas to beget more little children and hold them back from ever reaching maturity in the faith. That attitude is one of the chief causes of competition and carnality in missionary work. We put what we believe to be all the truth in a bottle and put a cap on it. We then want to work only with those who fit inside our bottle.

As I have come to know the family of God in various countries of the world, I have found that many members in Asia are more mature in the faith than any I know here in the U.S. or Canada. They are the fathers. Others are strong young men, while many more are like little children (as are most Christians I know in America). But if we are redeemed by the blood of the Lamb of God and quickened by His Spirit we are all part of His family.

So, please, Fellow Christians, don't rush off to foreign countries and ignore our brothers and sisters in Christ who already bear witness for Him in almost every country. Let's recognize them as members of our family. Let's not compete with them. Let's not divide them. Let's not hire them. Nor use them. They are our equals, the body of Christ in their locality. Whenever God moves us to further His cause and kingdom in a foreign country, let's make contact with our fellow believers there, then get behind them financially to help them carry on their work for the Lord. Without claiming them. Or colonizing them. Or affiliating them with our groups. Or ordering them around. Or trying to manipulate their beliefs and practices.

Let's recognize that our Lord is the Head of His whole church. That He alone is the Shepherd and His Holy Spirit the guide into all truth. The source of power and wisdom for all of His servants. And His Word is the lamp unto their feet and a light unto their path. He will never leave them nor forsake them. He will be with them unto the end of the age.

CHAPTER TWENTY-THREE

A GLOSSARY OF SPECIALIZED TERMS

Throughout church history certain words have been given specialized meanings to the extent that when church people use them they do so with unique definitions. Some examples include the Trinity, the Eucharist, the Inquisition, the Renaissance, the Reformation, the Enlightenment, the Rapture, the Tribulation, the Millennium, etc. Specialized meanings have likewise been given to certain terms by persons involved in the evangelical foreign missionary movement during the past 200 years. They have specific meanings for those who are involved in foreign missionary activities.

The purpose of this glossary is to prepare the reader for change. Traditional meanings attributed to some of these terms often lack validity, or may now be obsolete. In some cases they are offensive to our fellow Christians in "mission field" countries. Others may be contrary to Biblical principles, or simply erroneous.

My definitions are twofold. In some cases I have given the meaning commonly perceived by the evangelical community within the USA. Others may be the way a term is perceived by our fellow believers in "mission field" countries overseas. Sometimes I may use a definition that appears objectionable to traditional missionaries who have gone from industrialized countries to poorer countries. My reason for so doing is that I have tried to present the way the term is viewed by our fellow believers in what we call "mission field" countries.

Africans. Usually this term signifies the native peoples who live south of the Sahara Desert. Residents of North Africa are more likely to be called Egyptians, Tunisians, Algerians, etc. after their country of origin. Some residents of South Africa who are of European ancestry also call themselves Africans, but leaders of original African tribes may question their claim.

Apostle. A transliteration of the Greek word, "apostolos," which in turn is a combination of "apo" away, and "stello" to send. One Latin equivalent is "missio" which, when transliterated into English is "missionary." In the epistles of Paul the word is used in a specialized way to indicate those who have received a distinct grace (Greek, *charisma*) from God to plant churches where none existed previously. Apostles plant new churches in pioneer areas, then usually move on. Evangelists and teachers build up these churches numerically and spiritually.

Assembly of Believers. Many thousands of Christians substitute this term for "church" because it more accurately denotes what they are. Among the first to use it were the "Brethren Assemblies" which are said to have originated in Plymouth, England. In the USA it was used as a name by the Pentecostal denomination now called the Assemblies of God. However, many other groups use it as well, signifying that when they gather together in the name of the Lord Jesus, He is present in their midst, as He promised.

Body of Christ. Used in the New Testament to signify a group of Christians meeting together in a given locality. In Romans 12, First Corinthians 12 and Ephesians 4 it is presented as God living on earth in a body of humans, corresponding to when God lived on earth in a single human body, the Christ. Twice in the New Testament (Colossians 1:24, Ephesians 1:22-23) it is used to refer to all true believers everywhere. Evangelicals, fundamentalists and Pentecostals tend to use it only in this universal sense and seldom to indicate a gathering of believers in a given locality, as in the sense of First Corinthians 12:27.

Born Again. A Biblical term (John 3:1-7, I Peter 1:23) equivalent to the theological concept, "regeneration." It is used by Christians to signify conversion from one's former life, being dead to God, to a new life in which the Spirit of God indwells the believer and makes him alive to God. It signifies a transition from the former self to becoming an entirely new person. For most evangelicals it includes the whole procession of conversion, including confession of one's sinfulness, repentance, faith in Christ's atonement and reconciliation to God. Born again Christians are most likely to be identified as those who are called evangelicals, fundamentalists or Pentecostals.

The Call, the Called. This term is used in the New Testament in several ways.

First, in a specific Biblical sense (Romans 8:28), to denote God's choice of a remnant of Hebrews (144,000 total) chosen between A.D. 30 and A.D. 70 to be included among His people as believers in the Messiah. This remnant, 12,000 from each of the 12 Hebrew tribes, is called "The Israel of God" in Galatians 6:16 and is also said to include "all Israel" in Romans 9:6-8 and Romans 11:26. As foretold by the prophet Isaiah, God called a remnant to Himself, and the rest, because of their rebellion, were "broken off the olive tree" (Romans 11:17,19-20), as were Ishmael and Esau, and not counted as the descendants of Abraham any longer. The remnant (144,000) whom God foreknew, are spoken of as being predestinated and called, after which they are identified as God's "elect."

Secondly, the word is used in a general sense to refer to all believers who respond to the Word of God in which He "calls upon all men to repent" (Acts 17:30). Not willing that any should perish (II Peter 3:9), God, who would have all men to be saved, has been calling humanity to Himself through His apostles and evangelists for 20 centuries. Those who respond to His call and accept Christ as Saviour are admitted to the heavenly family of the redeemed.

Thirdly, the word "call" or "called" is used to refer to a believer having received some specific direction in his or her life. An example is found in Acts 16:9-10 where the apostle Paul was forbidden by the Holy Spirit when he planned to go to Asia and Bythinia, but "called" to go to Macedonia through a vision. This is the only example of such a "call" anywhere in the New Testament.

During the past 200 years evangelical Christians have developed many specialized uses for the word "call" or "called." For example, there is the term, "called to the ministry." But the equivalent word for "minister" or "ministry" in the New Testament is *"diakoni,"* (English: deacon), meaning those who distribute food to the poor. The first "deacons" were appointed by the apostles (Acts 6:3-6), and most "deacons" in contemporary Protestant churches are either elected or appointed. The "minister" concept in Protestant churches developed during the Reformation when Roman Catholic priests were said to be unbiblical, but institutional churches were not. In order to continue those churches, Protestant leaders developed the concept of "ordained ministers" to replace the priests. In evangelical churches today most "ministers" serve as a combination church administrator, pastor, preacher, teacher, evangelist, personal counselor, meeting leader and conductor of ceremonies such as baptisms, weddings and funerals. One of them, a Methodist, wrote an interesting book entitled, *How to Become Bishop Without Being Religious.* The position of ordained minister is no doubt a noble profession within our society, and I have the highest regard for hundreds of them whom it has been my privilege to know. In fact, I have been one myself for almost 50 years. But since there is no Biblical precedent for the position, how can one say he has been "called to the ministry?" If we are going to use that term it would be more accurate to say that one has been "called to be a deacon."

The same is true of the "call to the mission field." It also is a modern tradition that has no Biblical precedent. Are these not rather just personal convictions which we develop within our own minds and hearts in response to many influences: emotional, intellectual and spiritual? Calls to specific places are similar. I was a guest in the home of a man in California who was chairman of the "pulpit committee" in a large church where I was preaching. Their pastor of many years had to give up his responsibilities because of failing health, and a search was on for his replacement. My host told me that the committee responsible had received dozens of letters and resumes from ministers across the country requesting that they be considered for the open position. And almost every one of them was quite sure that "God had called him to it." Most of the 6000 foreign missionaries who were put out of China in the 1950's (including me) were sure that God had called them there. Did He then suddenly change His mind and "call" us to leave, never to return?

There can be no doubt that God calls consecrated Christians into His service, and leads us into specific areas of service, but where and how we do it is more likely to be the result of earthly influences, rather than the voice of God.

Charismatic. Transliterated from the Greek, *charismata*, an expansion of *charis*, which is usually translated "grace" or "favor." Ephesians 4:7 says that God gives grace by measure to every believer, and the measure of grace we receive determines our function in a local body of believers. One has grace for apostleship, another has grace for teaching, another for evangelism, and so on. An excellent definition of how the word should be used may be found in Thayer's *Greek-English Lexicon*, published in 1887.

Thayer put it this way: *In the Pauline sense,* **charismata** *denote extroadinary powers, distinguishing certain Christians and enabling them to serve the church of Christ, the reception of which is due the power of divine grace operating in their souls by the Holy Spirit.* Beginning around 1950 numerous Christians within traditional denominations began to experience what Pentecostals call "speaking in tongues." But since they were not associated with regular Pentecostal churches, these new Pentecostals were generally referred to as being "charismatic." The term "charisma" has also been used to describe the personalities of outstanding public figures such as Winston Churchill, Franklin D. Roosevelt and John F. Kennedy.

A Church. In the New Testament a church was the sum total of Christian believers in a local community. In American culture it is something quite different. My home town during childhood had a square block at the center and on each of its four corners stood a "church." My parents attended "the Presbyterian Church" on one corner. Opposite it stood the Methodist Church. On one corner between was the First Baptist Church and opposite it the Episcopal Church. These four social institutions were an integral part of our civic community. All had memberships, clergy, staff, choirs, Sunday schools and other things characteristic of a church in American culture. After I became a born again Christian in 1940 I visited three of these "churches" looking for other true believers. I found half a dozen each among the Presbyterians and Baptists, but almost none among the Methodists. I didn't even bother looking for evangelical types among the Episcopalians at that time. These examples show what happens when churches are institutionalized. When the Wesley brothers and Bishop Asbury launched the Methodist movement in the 18th Century, nearly all of their followers were born again believers. But in successive generations Methodist church membership became largely a cultural tradition. Most Baptists and Presbyterians have followed suit, with a few notable exceptions. During the latter half of the 20th century, however, there was a revival of evangelical influence and many more born again Christians could be found in Protestant churches. The word "church" is derived from the Greek *ekklesia,* a combination of *ek* (from out) and *kletos* (called), hence those whom God has called out of the world system and unto Himself. In the New Testament it refers primarily to a group of Christians in a given locality. It is also used two times to indicate all "born again" Christians collectively. Roman Catholics tend to use "the Church" to denote all Catholic priests, nuns and communicants within a given city, or state, or country, or the whole world. Anglicans often use it the same way to indicate the Church of England. State churches in other countries may do likewise. Evangelicals often say "the church" to mean all true (born again) believers in a given place, or in the world. More liberal Protestants may use it to mean all Christians everywhere, including Roman Catholic and Greek Orthodox.

The Churches. Used in the New Testament to indicate numerous assemblies of believers in a given area, such as "the seven churches of Asia" (Revelation 1:4, 20).

Church Denomination. Some social institution churches are linked together in such a way that all of them together are considered to be one church. The largest in the USA is the Roman Catholic. Then there is the United Methodist Church, the United Presbyterian Church, the Presbyterian Church in America and so on. Baptists supposedly recognize the autonomy of each local group, so their largest affiliation is the Southern Baptist Convention (as opposed to *Baptist Church*). But sometimes a state Baptist

Convention may wield power as though it were actually one church organization like the others.

Church Service. Little is said in the New Testament about what Christians did when they met together. There is no mention of a formal "church service" as such, although many aspects of such gatherings, as we know them, are mentioned. There was "teaching and fellowship and breaking of bread and prayers" (Acts 2:42). Also singing and preaching (Acts 16:25,20:7). During what we call "the Middle Ages" Roman Catholic and Greek Orthodox priests developed a liturgy by which they could control the participation of their communicants. Reformers such as Luther and Calvin sought to restore some of the activities mentioned in Scripture, but did so in a formalized manner controlled by "ministers." Any participation by non-clergy was strictly controlled.

When I have taken foreign students to church services in America, their most frequent comment has been that it's like attending a theater. There is usually an impressive auditorium, a master of ceremonies, musicians and a program. Things start and stop on schedule but instead of buying a ticket before entering we are not asked to pay until some time after the show has started. Of course, many church services are more theatrical than others. I have attended some that were outright religious show business and others that were as dull as evening devotions in a retirement home.

Few churches would allow believers to prophesy until the 20th Century, and then it was mainly among the Pentecostals. And prophets exposing secret sins of members or traitors within the congregation have been rare except among the young churches of Asia. The European model of a church "service" is not compatible with a culture such as that based on joint family relationships which we find in China. As a result foreign missionaries have generally failed in their efforts to impose it. Indigenous leaders who bring new believers into a family type fellowship, and conduct meetings like family gatherings, have begotten far more children for the kingdom of God than have foreigners with their formalized church "services."

Colony, Colonialism. This term appears in the New Testament (Acts 16:12) in reference to Philippi, a Roman colony. Roman conquerors colonized much of Europe, North Africa and Western

Asia. Since that time a colony has been defined as a territory under the rule or influence of a foreign power. When church denominations or independent mission boards establish and perpetuate branches in countries outside the one where they are based, it is called "institutional colonialism" or "missionary colonialism."

Country. A political entity having distinct borders and its own government, such as the country of Switzerland. Very few countries are populated by only one nationality, e.g., Switzerland is divided mainly among French and German populations but has other ethnic groups as well. India is made up of probably 1600 nations. Politicians often try to unify a country by declaring it to be one nation. In his Gettysburg address President Lincoln spoke of the United States as having been brought forth by the founding fathers as "a new nation," and said that the civil war was testing "whether that nation, or any nation so conceived and so dedicated, can long endure." A country that allows for political diversity and protects minority nations or religious sects within its borders is more likely to be at peace than one which tries to force all groups into a single mold.

Cross Cultural. As this term has developed it has become a dogmatic concept by which certain groups define what they think a "missionary" is. It is used by colonial missions to identify a Christian who leaves his homeland and goes to a diverse culture to spread the gospel. Conversely, they would say that any Christian worker who remains within his own culture would not qualify for the title of "missionary" by those who use colonial terminology. There is no mention of cross cultural missionary work in the colonial sense anywhere in the New Testament.

Developing Country. The politically correct term for a country that is not industrialized. Following World War II, the term was "underdeveloped," but to make it sound more positive, the term "developing" came into favor a few years later. It is more technically correct to say "poorer country."

Ecumenical. Generally used to indicate cooperation or close association by various church bodies. Those who take it seriously want all denominations to merge into one super church, thus eliminating denominational divisions altogether. Most evangelicals oppose the idea because it would merge Bible believers with those who deny the truth of God.

Evangelicals. See fundamentalists.

Evangelist. In the New Testament this term is used to identify a Christian to whom God has given special grace for communicating the gospel in a persuasive manner. Among churches in America the term came to be used to designate an itinerant preacher who conducted evangelistic campaigns in numerous places, as contrasted with a pastor who served one church for an extended period. Foreign missionaries from industrialized countries have tended to apply the word "evangelist" to native missionaries (apostles) who plant new churches among their own people. That way they can reserve the term "missionary" exclusively for themselves.

Evangelistic. This term identifies a Christian ministry which seeks to make converts of unbelievers, including those who may already be members of churches. Very few traditional Protestant churches are really evangelistic. Most rely on a gradual process of teaching, education and association to Christianize their followers. Truly evangelistic churches, on the other hand, tend to assume that all men, including those raised in church families, are sinners in need of salvation. Members of the church family may not be regarded as Christians until they are born again through a personal acceptance of Christ as Saviour.

Fundamentalists. During the first half of the 20th century liberal clergy among Protestants came to be called modernists, while more conservative ministers were known as fundamentalists. The latter held to the traditional Protestant beliefs that the Bible is the divinely inspired, infallible Word of God while modernists did not. Fundamentalists affirmed the deity of Christ, His virgin birth, sinless life, substitutionary death for our sins, bodily resurrection, ascension and second coming, while modernists generally did not. Around mid-century some fundamentalists began to be dogmatic, sectarian or legalistic and to identify their doctrines with patriotism, demanding that the whole country accept their beliefs and practices. So a more moderate form of fundamentalist emerged, still holding to traditional beliefs but in a less rigid manner. They preferred to be called **evangelicals**. But that term has become so broad that it now includes all Christian fundamentalists, some liberals and most

Pentecostals. It excludes Roman Catholics and Greek Orthodox, as well as most liberal Protestants who deny the inspiration and authority of the Bible.

Furlough. Borrowed from military terminology, it is equivalent to "annual leave" or an extended period of absence from duty. In the early days of missionary colonialism persons who went from industrialized countries to live among the poor soon found themselves physically and emotionally drained, ill or exhausted. So after five, four or (recently) three years "on the field" they would return to their homelands for a year of recuperation. Native missionaries who serve with ministries based in poorer countries never take a year off for an extended vacation called "furlough."

Heathen. Though not used often today, this derogatory term was repeated frequently in missionary circles a century ago to designate any group of people who were not integrated into a nominally Christian culture. The equivalent term used by Muslims (especially in reference to Christians) is "infidel."

Identify with the people. A concept used by missionaries from industrialized countries who are concerned about the cultural divide between themselves and the people among whom they have gone to work. Their goal is usually to integrate themselves more fully into the local communities where they are living in foreign countries in an attempt to minimize the cultural divide. But all such attempts are doomed to failure because of economic disparity and other differences.

Imperialism. The term used when an empire expands by subjugating other nations or territories and making them colonies. When a church denomination or other missionary organization expands to a country diverse from its home base, and forms branches there, the process is called "cultural imperialism."

Indigenous. Essentially this term means "native to the land." The kangaroo is native to Australia but not to Hawaii. If any were to be found in Honolulu they would have been taken there by people and kept in a zoo. So it is with churches. If they are imported into a culture by foreigners they can not be considered indigenous. But if a resident of any given country travels abroad and becomes a Christian, then returns and introduces the Christian faith to his people and starts a church or ministry with no foreigners involved, it would be indigenous. Many colonial missionaries have started branches of their organizations or denominations in foreign countries, then tried to "make them indigenous." But they can never be truly indigenous if the works were begun by foreign invaders.

When leaders of colonial missions speak of making their branches indigenous, they usually say they are trying to get them to be self-supporting, self-governing and self-propagating. But it is very difficult for the rich foreigners to bring this about as long as they are there. In China the Communist government launched a "three self" campaign to bring it about after the foreign missionaries were all put out, but it ended up with government bureaucrats assuming the role of the foreign missionaries in exercising control over the churches.

Middle East. Countries lying between Western Europe and the "far east" (meaning the original British India and China). Today the term is generally used to indicate countries that lie between the eastern shores of the Mediterranean and the western borders of Pakistan.

The Mission Field. A collective term used by U.S. church people to mean any foreign country; hence to Americans it refers to almost anywhere "out there," meaning outside the USA.

Missionary. This term is used in industrialized countries to denote an American, Canadian, European, Australian or Korean who goes abroad to carry on religious activity in a foreign country. But in "mission field" countries it is used by native Christians to identify any local resident who takes the gospel to unreached people.

Nation. English equivalent of Greek *ethnos,* used frequently in the New Testament. The English word *ethnic* is a transliteration of the Greek. It denotes a particular people group, usually distinguished by a common language and culture. Native Americans usually identify themselves as distinct "nations," such as the "Six Nations of the Iroquois Federation." More than 6000 different nations have been identified throughout the world. Unfortunately, the Greek word *ethnos* is frequently mistranslated as "gentile" in almost all English versions of the New Testament. It is also unfortunate that the word "nation" is often misused to denote a given country made up of many nations. Before Europeans occupied the Americas over a thousand nations were already here, such as the Seneca nation, the Cherokee nation, the Navajo nation, etc. Today America is a conglomerate of people whose ancestors were an integral part of two or three thousand different nations in Europe, Africa, Asia, North America, Central America and South America. Likewise the populations of many other countries, such as Indonesia, India or Nigeria are made up of many different nations.

Nationalism. Used as a derogatory term by some Americans to deprecate patriotism, national pride or the desire for independence and self reliance by Christian leaders in poorer countries.

Nationals. A derogatory term used by colonial missionaries to designate Christian workers who are citizens of other countries. For most Americans it is not acceptable to give the title of "missionary" to a "national."

Offering (church). During most church "services" money is collected in one form or another to finance the church budget. To make it sound religious rather than financial, it is usually called an "offering" of gifts to God. Most churches have found that an effective way to raise money is to make the collection of it an act of worship, and giving toward the church budget is presented as a duty to God.

Offering (love). When churches have special speakers the congregation may be invited to contribute money for the personal use of the speaker. This is more likely to occur if the visiting evangelist or teacher speaks at a series of meetings lasting several days. Some American evangelists have been accused of using this custom to pad their pockets and finance a lavish lifestyle.

Offering (missionary). When churches have speakers who are representatives of mission organizations, it is usually expected that a "missionary offering" will be received. Those in attendance are invited to contribute whatever they wish for the missionary and the work he represents.

Pentecostal. This term came into general usage at the beginning of the 20th Century. It was assigned to church meetings or groups where individual Christians, during moments of intense prayer or devotion, would give expression to some form of ecstatic speaking. These experiences were generally believed to be identical with those recorded in Acts 2:4 when, on the day of Pentecost, the original apostles "began to speak with other tongues, as the Spirit gave them utterance." From these beginnings came numerous Pentecostal churches and denominations, some characterized by a new doctrine that "speaking in tongues is the initial evidence of the baptism of/in/with/by the Holy Spirit."

Rich Foreigner. A comparative term. When they go abroad, most American missionaries live on a lower economic level than they did at home. Nevertheless, they often appear to be fabulously wealthy to the poverty stricken people among whom they work in poorer countries. So they are called "the rich foreigners."

Sanctuary. A term applied to the main auditorium of a church building to give it a sanctimonious connotation.

Sunday. The day you are supposed to "go to church" (usually about an hour before noon). Never mind that it's a workday for half the people of the world. In Islamic countries Friday is the holy day (Sabbath), while in Hindu and Buddhist lands it's on Saturday, as it is also for orthodox Jews and some Christians. A majority of professing Christians recognize Sunday as "the day for church." After church and dinner in America it is also a special time for millions of professing Christians to enjoy athletic events.

Third World. Following World War II and the end of European colonialism, the former colonies were often referred to as being underdeveloped, while their former rulers were developed countries. Those in between were semi-developed. Less polite persons in the more industrialized countries began to speak of former colonies as being backward, while more considerate persons began to call them developing countries. Then there emerged the term "third world" as a polite way of categorizing all the poorest, or least industrialized, countries in the world.

Two-Thirds World. Another expression to denote the third world, based on the fact that two-thirds of the world's population live in the poorest, or third world, countries.

Tithe. In Old Testament times God required the Hebrews to contribute a tenth of their income for support of their priests and related purposes. Under the New Covenant the early Christians gave everything to God, and were more likely to keep only a tithe for their own use. In more recent times some social institution churches have found that a tithe requirement works well as a means of getting members to finance the church budget. Some apply the Old Testament concept of bringing all tithes "into the storehouse" (Malachi 3:10) as a way to get their church members to give a tenth of their income to support the church budget. Many teach that offerings should be contributions over and above the tithe.

The West, Western. These are obsolete, though still frequently used, terms carried over from the days of European colonialism prior to World War II. Colonial rulers in Europe generally regarded themselves as being superior in culture and development, while their colonies eastward in Asia were usually regarded as being inferior, or just "different." Conquests by the Japanese, and their technological achievements after the war, put an end to the myth of "western" industrial superiority. Former colonies in Africa and Latin America were never east of Europe anyway, so the term "western" was somewhat irrelevant to them. So during the past 50 years it has made no sense to divide the world by east and west, or to use the term "western" to designate European culture, technology or achievement.. To the average American a "western" is a cowboy movie, and "the west" (to those on the Eastern seaboard) is what lies beyond the Mississippi River. However, the terms (the west, western) persist in general usage to denote ideologies, cultures and customs that had their origins in Western Europe, or in Canada and the USA which are extensions of West European culture, commerce and industry.